Ancient Maya Civilization

NORMAN HAMMOND

Ancient Maya Civilization

RUTGERS UNIVERSITY PRESS, NEW BRUNSWICK, NEW JERSEY

Third printing, updated edition, 1988
Copyright © 1982, 1988 by Rutgers, The State University of New Jersey
All rights reserved
Manufactured in the United States of America

LIBRARY OF CONGRESS CATALOGING IN PUBLICATION DATA

Hammond, Norman.
    Ancient Maya civilization.
    Bibliography: p.
    Includes index.
    1. Mayas.   2. Mayas—Antiquities.   3. Mexico—
Antiquities.   4. Central America—Antiquities.
I. Title.
F1435.H35   972'.01   80-39819
ISBN 0-8135-0904-1
ISBN 0-8135-0906-8 (pbk.)

*The cover illustration is a lintel from Yaxchilan depicting a blood sacrifice.
Photograph courtesy of the Trustees of the British Museum.*

FOR JEAN

Contents

Preface

THIS book is an attempt to survey what is currently known about the civilization of the ancient Maya of southern Mexico and Central America for a nonacademic audience. It does not pretend to be original, although some results of original research are reported in it, nor does it claim to be a work of scholarship, though it builds on the work of many scholars. I have tried to make it accurate and to keep the information up-to-date in a changing field during the process of writing it. The basic structure of the book was decided and most of it drafted in 1977, and material and ideas have been modified from then onward in the light of new discoveries. Some material not yet formally published has been mentioned with the kind permission of those whose work it is; some has been omitted for lack of such permission.

The book is neither infallible nor comprehensive: it has not been written with the decades of experience of the Maya and their past that illuminated Eric Thompson's *The Rise and Fall of Maya Civilization* and Sylvanus G. Morley's *The Ancient Maya*, nor with the educated appreciation of Maya art that informs Michael D. Coe's *The Maya*. It sees Maya civilization from a lowland perspective and places some emphasis on the eastern lowlands in what is now Belize, which were almost ignored by earlier authors and where much important research has taken place in the last decade. In contrast the highland zone, peripheral both to the development of Classic Maya civilization after the initial Early Classic and also to my personal experience of Maya archaeology, is downplayed. The intricate meshing of documentary and archaeological sources that is needed, and that began with the work of Robert Carmack and John Fox, would take up more space than a short book such as this can afford. At the end of the book, under *Further Reading*, I have listed a number of books to balance some of my sins of omission.

Sins of commission are, by definition, present in the book and are my fault, not that of any of the friends and colleagues who have helped with information and illustrations and who are acknowledged. A pedant is one whose accuracy is slightly greater than one's own: pedantry in reviewers will, I hope, benefit any subsequent edition of this book. Skeptical inquiry by my wife, Jean Wilson, has improved the text, and her impatience with my snail's progress has helped in its completion; she deserves the dedication.

Acknowledgments

A GENERAL book such as this one necessarily utilizes the discoveries and ideas of many people: archaeology is a collaborative enterprise, and few of its advances come from isolated work. The notions put forward in this book have occurred to me as the result of talking and listening to my colleagues and friends; some have been included after a reading of the first draft by R. E. W. Adams, Wendy Ashmore, Warwick Bray, Karen Bruhns, T. Patrick Culbert and Robert J. Sharer; and others derive, with my grateful acknowledgment, from the work of E. Wyllys Andrews V, Joseph W. Ball, Ignacio Bernal, Michael D. Coe, William R. Coe, Clemency Coggins, David M. Pendergast, Ian Graham, John Graham, William A. Haviland, Christopher Jones, David H. Kelley, Gareth W. Lowe, Alfred P. Maudslay, Dennis E. Puleston, Payson D. Sheets, Linda Schele, J. Eric S. Thompson, and Gordon R. Willey. The useful work of several other scholars has been noted in the text or in the further readings, but any palpable omissions will be rectified with pleasure should this book be reprinted.

Illustrations have been provided by a number of my colleagues and their institutions, and, in addition, line drawings have been done by Arthur Shelley, Paul Stempen, and Michael Davenport, and photographs printed by Don Naunton and Vic Calderola. All five of them have tolerated my vagaries with more patience than I deserved.

I am grateful to William R. Coe and the Tikal Project of the University Museum, University of Pennsylvania, for providing or allowing the use of Figures 2.7, 4.14, 4.16, 4.17, 5.10, 5.13, 6.7, 6.8, 7.7, 7.8, 7.9, 7.10, 9.6, 9.25, and 10.5; to the Peabody Museum, Harvard University, for similarly providing or permitting the use of Figures 3.11, 5.8, 6.5, 6.6, 7.3, 7.4, 7.14, 8.7, 9.3, 9.5, 9.22, 9.23, and 10.9, including some from the Carnegie files held at the Peabody. The illustrations derived from my own work in Belize result from research supported by the British Museum, National Geographic Society, British Academy, Wenner-Gren Foundation, Peabody Museum, Cambridge University, and Rutgers University. The British Museum has, in addition, permitted the use of Figures 5.3, 6.2, 6.4, 6.10, 10.7, and 10.8. Individual scholars associated with these institutions who have kindly allowed me to use their illustrations include Tatiana Proskouriakoff, Figures 9.5, 9.22; Gordon R. Willey, Figures 5.8, 6.5, 6.6; Richard M. Leventhal, Figures 6.5, 6.6; Peter D. Harrison, Figure 5.9; William A. Haviland, Figures 5.10, 6.1; Ian Graham, Figure 7.14; Evon Z. Vogt, Figure 3.11; Charles H. Miksicek, Figure 4.9; Sheena Howarth, Figure 4.12.

Other providers gratefully acknowledged include Chip Morris and the Science Museum of Minnesota, Figure 3.12; Gary Gossen and Alexander Marshack, Figure 3.14; Martha Cooper, Figure 3.15; Susanna Ekholm and the New World Archaeological Foundation, Figures 4.10, 8.3; Eric Taladoire and the Mission Archéologique Française en Mexique, Figure 4.18; David M. Pendergast and the Royal Ontario Museum, Figures 4.23 (by Duncan Pring), 9.4 (by H. Stanley Loten) and 9.29. Merle Greene Robertson provided the rubbing in Figure 2.8 and permitted the use of Figure 7.13; Lady Thompson lent the original print for Figure 2.5; Payson D. Sheets provided Figure 5.9; Richard E. W. Adams, Figure 5.7; B. L. Turner II, Figure 5.4; Jay Johnson, Figure 4.20; John A. Graham, Figures 4.13 and 4.15; Jorge Guillemin, Figure 4.22; Figure 9.28 rollout photograph, copyright © Justin Kerr, 1982. Figure 5.6 was taken by permission of Dennis E. Puleston, and Figures 9.24 and 10.4 are used with acknowledgment to the Society of Antiquaries of London and the Archaeology Department of the Government of Belize, respectively. Figure 10.4 was drawn by Susan Bird; Figure 8.5 is taken from data established at the Lawrence Berkeley Laboratory by Fred Stross, Frank Asaro, and Helen Michel. To all of you, my thanks.

Ancient Maya Civilization

Introduction

THE ancient Maya created one of the most surprising civilizations of pre-Columbian America: it arose, flourished, and vanished in a little under a thousand years in the unprepossessing environment of the tropical rain forest, leaving behind hundreds of massive ruins to excite the wonder and the attention of European travelers. Just how, why, and when these cities buried in the jungle were built has been the subject of speculation ever since the Spanish conquest of the Americas and of scholarly investigation for the past century and a half. In this book, I have tried to summarize those investigations, and what we now know of Maya civilization as a result.

Believing that the historical growth of a discipline is vital to understanding it, I have used the travels of John Lloyd Stephens and Frederick Catherwood in 1839–1842 to introduce some basic information and ideas about the ancient Maya and to give some idea of the excitement of Maya archaeology; in Chapter 2, I have then placed their work in perspective. There follow two chapters outlining, respectively, the geographical and chronological backgrounds to Maya civilization, and I have then proceeded to examine a series of topics, working successively from the economic foundations of Maya culture to the superstructure of artistic and intellectual achievements. Each chapter has a discussion of possible further reading from the professional literature in English.

The Maya themselves are an American Indian group related to the other aboriginal inhabitants of Mexico and Central America and, more distantly, to the populations of North and South America. For at least the past four thousand years, and perhaps for twice that length of time, they have occupied the lands known to archaeologists and anthropologists as the Maya Area (see Figure 1.2): the Yucatan Peninsula of Mexico, Belize, Guatemala, and the western parts of Honduras and El Salvador. Within this area, the Mayan language group is still the predominant native speech, and the two million Maya of Yucatan, Chiapas, and the highlands of Guatemala, the largest ethnic bloc. The distribution of archaeological sites with characteristically Maya architecture, pottery, monuments, and inscriptions occupies almost exactly the same overall area, although many major sites are in areas now devoid of almost any human occupation.

The Maya Area lies between two other major cultural regions, that of central Mexico to the west and that of isthmian Central America to the east. The westward ties were always the stronger, so that the Mexican and Maya areas together share a set of ancient cultural characteristics that include a calendar, deities, items of clothing, and ritual activities, such as the rubber-ball game, which bring both regions within the major cultural entity called Mesoamerica. Defined by Paul Kirchoff in 1943, Mesoamerica reaches from northern Mexico to Costa Rica and its influence beyond, to the southern United States and, perhaps, into northern South America.

Maya civilization flourished several centuries earlier than the best-known societies of pre-Hispanic America, the Aztec and Inca empires. The Aztec (or, as they called themselves, Mexica) ruled much of southern Mexico from the fourteenth to the sixteenth centuries, their influence just reaching to the western borders of the Maya Area. The Inca empire emerged far to the south in Peru, and even though its eventual span covered more than two thousand miles, from Chile north to the borders of Colombia, evidence of contact during its floruit, which paralleled that of the Aztec in time, reached no further than Panama. By the time these two states, technically entering the bronze age, had established themselves, Maya civilization had been in decline for half a millennium.

The Classic period, during which the Maya reached their apogee, lasted from about A.D. 250 to 900: in Europe, the Roman Empire was split in two, adopted Christianity, and saw the rise of Constantinople as a second capital that rivaled Rome and remained to head the Byzantine empire after Rome itself had fallen to the barbarians. In the Middle East, the Sassanians established a strong state in what is now Iran and were eventually overrun by the wildfire spread of militant Islam. The second part of the Maya Classic period, when the major temples at sites such at Tikal and Uxmal were built, runs parallel to the rise of the Holy Roman Empire under Charlemagne, to the emergence of the Tang Dynasty in China and the growth of their capital Chang-an to more than a million in population. The collapse of Classic Maya civilization in the ninth century occurred at the same time as the Viking raids on western Europe and the reign of Alfred the Great as one of the first English kings, and shortly after the final abandonment of some of the last cities in the jungle, the Viking Leif Ericsson discovered America.

Throughout this period, Maya civilization progressed without any contact with the Old World: the horizons of the Maya reached to the Valley of Mexico in the west and to Panama in the east. The Maya were influenced by events within this sphere: the great city of Teotihuacan, northeast of modern Mexico City, was the metropolis of Mesoamerica from the time of Christ until the seventh century, and its violent fall reverberated throughout the region, cutting trade links and realigning the balance of power. Beyond Mesoamerica, though, apart from possible sporadic contact across the Gulf of Mexico with Florida and the lower Mississippi basin, the Maya had no contacts. The civilization they evolved was their own.

Why do we call ancient Maya culture a civilization? To what extent does it compare with the acknowledged civilizations of Greece, Rome, Mesopotamia, India, and China? Can any people living in a tropical jungle really be regarded as civilized?

The last question is the simplest to answer: Maya civilization is regarded as such on the basis of its cultural achievements, not the environment in which they were made. The fact that the tropical forest is hardly the easiest place to build a civilization adds to the Maya achievement rather than detracting from it, and we should remember that in the Old World, the slightly later Khmer state in Kampuchea (Cambodia), which resulted in the great buildings of Angkor Thom and Angkor Wat, flourished in a similar environment.

With the earlier civilizations of Eurasia, there are parallels in Maya and other Mesoamerican cultures, but there are also some striking differences. Two of the most obvious are the absence in Mesoamerica of domesticated animals and wheeled transport: where the early civilizations of Sumer, the Indus, Shang China, Egypt, and Mycenaean-Minoan Greece shared access to a pool of animal domesticates—sheep, goats, pigs, cattle, and dogs—that had been controlled by man for centuries past and exploited for meat, skins, wool, milk, and traction, the Maya had only the dog (a comestible as well as companion). By the time of the Spanish conquest, the turkey and duck had been added, in Yucatan, at least, and both then and earlier, some taming of larger animals such as deer existed, but meat still came mainly from the hunt, not the farm, and loads were shifted by human- and not animal-muscle power.

The lack of draught animals coupled with the broken nature of Mesoamerican terrain made the wheel an invention of marginal utility. Invented it was, for we know of toy animals on pottery wheels from the Mexican Gulf Coast and Salvador dating to the first millennium A.D. that embody the principle precisely, but there was no potential for its further exploitation.

In spite of these handicaps and a tool technology based on chipped and polished stone that was no more advanced than that available to the builders of Stonehenge, the Maya raised buildings such as Temple I at Tikal, which are as impressive and as beautiful as those of any Old World civilization. Although the Maya never quite achieved the true arch and relied on mass rather than stress to obtain architectural balance, their pyramids (which were high multi-terraced platforms rather than true pyramids of the Egyptian type), palaces, and plazas have a coherence of design that denotes an underlying aesthetic order as well-conceived as that which the classical Greeks used in the creation of the Parthenon.

The Maya have sometimes been called "the Greeks of the New World," in reference to their accomplished vase painting and relief sculpture, which were certainly in their own way the equals of those arts in ancient Athens; the sobriquet might equally be applied to what we have come to know of Classic Maya politics, with the petty dynasties of city-states alternating between warfare and matrimonial alliance across the jungles of Petén and the scrub forests of Yucatan.

One field in which the ancient Maya, lacking metal, wheels, and domestic animals as they did, managed to emulate the Old World civilizations was in the realm of the intellect: a competent mathematical system capable of basic functions, the use of very large numbers, astronomy of a high order without optical apparatus, and the blending of all these into an astrological, numerological, and religious system are among the best claims the Maya have to being called civilized. Such knowledge is, unfortunately, a perishable thing, dying with the minds in which it lives or the books in which it is written: the double collapse of Maya culture, in the ninth century for some still unknown reason and then in the sixteenth in the face of Spanish conquest and European disease, almost wiped out their intellectual achievement. The three surviving codices embody a very restricted range of information, and the recent decipherment of some of the Classic-period historical inscriptions has opened up another narrow vista: they are enticing and frustrating reminders of the world we have lost.

The Maya are still, however, worth studying: our recent gains in the fields of palaeoeconomy, settlement patterns, and chronological development of Maya culture have immensely increased our knowledge of, and our respect for, these talented and durable people. We are now beginning to understand just how the unlikely combination of brilliant culture in a tropical forest was achieved in terms of economic infrastructure. A scholarly fashion of regarding the Maya as secondary beneficiaries of developments made in the valleys of highland Mexico is beginning to be dissipated, and as we come to appreciate the originality of much of Maya culture and the odds against which it was brought to fruition, our understanding of human development in its manifold variety is enhanced. We still have much to learn about the ancient Maya—and they still have much to teach us about ourselves.

1.1 John Lloyd Stephens, a portrait taken from a later edition of *Incidents of Travel*.

PORTRAIT OF MR. STEPHENS.

(From a Daguerreotype.)

I

Discovery of the Maya

EARLY in the morning of October 3, 1839, the British brig *Mary Ann* slipped out of New York harbor, bound for Belize on the Caribbean coast of the Yucatan Peninsula, that long thumb of Mexico that juts northward toward Cuba. One of the two passengers aboard was famous, the other obscure.

John Lloyd Stephens was one of America's most celebrated travel writers, who had won the "hearty respect" of Edgar Allan Poe for his *Incidents of Travel in Egypt, Arabia Petraea and the Holy Land*. The book had romped through six printings in its first year alone, and Stephens had already produced a sequel on his travels in Europe and Anatolia. He was now 34, and had made enough money to do what he pleased (Figure 1.1). What it pleased him to do was to explore the ruined cities in the jungles of Central America, which had been reported by earlier travelers and ascribed to the Lost Tribes of Israel, ancient Egyptians, or seafaring Phoenicians. As a means of getting there Stephens had himself appointed to a "Special Confidential Mission" from President Martin Van Buren; he was accredited to the government, if it still existed, of the warring Central American Federation, and instructed to close down the U.S. legation in Guatemala City and ship its archives back to Washington.

His unfamed companion on the journey was Frederick Catherwood, a British architect already 40 years old with a family to support. Stephens had come across his work in Palestine and then met him in London, and proclaimed himself impressed by the results of Catherwood's decade of "diligently studying the antiquities of the Old World." Catherwood had lately come to work in New York, and had set up a "Panorama of Jerusalem" in a building on Broadway, which Stephens had publicly praised in his recent book.

The catalyst that sent them off to Central America together was the bookseller John Russell Bartlett, who suggested that Stephens follow up his Old World explorations
with some in the New, and whetted his appetite with the
newly published *Voyage pittoresque et archéologique . . .* ,
written and illustrated by Jean-Frédéric Waldeck in an enticing, if not strictly accurate, fashion.

Stephens clearly knew the market value of his adventures: he drew up for Catherwood an exclusive contract
which stated that the latter "agrees to accompany the said
Stephens on his journey to Central America . . . on a tour
through the provinces of Chiapas and Yucatan and . . . will
throughout the said tour exercise his skill as an artist and
make drawings of the ruins of Palenque, Uxmal, Copan
and other such ruined cities, places, scenes and monuments as may be considered desirable by the said Stephens. He will not publish directly or indirectly the said
drawings nor any narration of the incidents of his journey
. . . and he will not in any way interfere with the right of
the said Stephens to the absolute and exclusive use of all
the information, drawings and material collected on the
said journey."

Catherwood was to receive his traveling expenses, together with a fee of $1,500 from which $25 a week would
be paid to his family during the journey; if royalties and
cash were not enough to cover this, Stephens promised to
deliver lectures "for Mr. Catherwood's benefit." An initial
payment of $200 changed hands, and the two travelers set
off on a journey of adventure, with publication very much
in mind, that was to launch Maya archaeology as a serious
study.

On October 30 they landed at Belize (Figure 1.2), where
Stephens was surprised to find, hardly knowing "whether
to be shocked or amused at this condition of society," that
the question of integration between the Negro and white
races—so great a cause of contention in the United States
—had been long resolved and that "colour was considered
mere matter of taste." At an official dinner they met Patrick
Walker, "secretary of the government, and holding, besides, such a list of offices as would make the greatest plu-
ralist among us feel insignificant." As soon as the Americans had left Belize, Walker was given yet another job, that

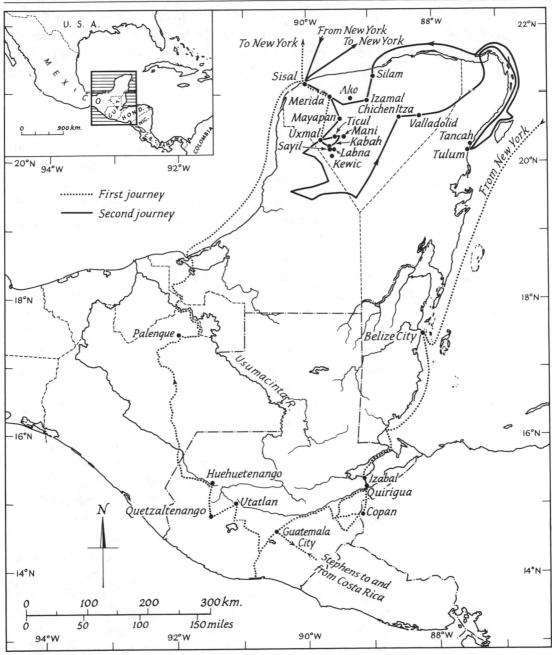

1.2. The travels of Stephens and Catherwood in Yucatan, Chiapas, and Central America, 1839–1842.

of leading an overland expedition to beat them to Palenque.

Stephens and Catherwood sailed south to Izabal, the port of entry for Guatemala City, having now acquired as servant and dragoman "a French Spaniard, St. Domingo born and Omoa bred, bearing the name of Augustin; young, and as we at first thought, not very sharp." He was, however, to prove an intelligent and valuable companion. From Izabal, after visiting the grave of Mr. Shannon, one of Stephens's several recently deceased predecessors as envoy to Central America, they set off on mules. The trail was muddy, all three travelers were thrown off, and the food got covered with gunpowder. They were temporarily arrested in Comotan, and found an unfriendly reception when they did eventually arrive at their first objective, Copan, where impressive ruins in the jungle had been reported.

Copan, however, was rewarding. "Working our way through the thick woods, we came upon a square stone column, about fourteen feet high and three feet on each side, sculptured in very bold relief and on all four of the sides from the base to the top. The front was the figure of a man curiously and richly dressed and the face, evidently a portrait, solemn, stern and well fitted to excite terror (Figure 1.3). The back was of a different design, unlike anything we had ever seen before, and the sides were covered with hieroglyphics. Before it, at a distance of three feet, was a large block of stone also sculptured with figures and emblematical devices. The sight of this unexpected monument put at rest once and for ever, in our minds, all uncertainty in regard to the character of American antiquities, and gave us the assurance that the objects we were in search of were interesting, not only as the remains of an unknown people but as works of art, proving, like newly discovered historical records, that the people who once occupied the Continent of America were not savages."

Stephens had come face to face with not just a ruined city, but a vanished civilization, comparing in sophistication with any he had seen in his Old World travels, "in workmanship equal to the finest monuments of the Egyptians." The anonymity of the ruins fascinated him, as well as their jungle fastness. One monument "standing with its altar before it, in a grove of trees which grew around it, seemingly to shade and shroud it as a sacred thing in the solemn stillness of the woods . . . seemed a divinity mourning over a fallen people.

"Who were the people that built this city? In the ruined cities of Egypt, even in the long-lost Petra, the stranger knows the story of the people whose vestiges are around. The place where we sat, was it a citadel from which an un-

known people had sounded the trumpet of war? Or a temple for the worship of the God of peace? All was mystery,
dark impenetrable mystery, and every circumstance increased it. In Egypt the colossal skeletons of gigantic temples stand in the unwatered sands in all the nakedness of
desolation; here an immense forest shrouded the ruins,
hiding them from sight, heightening the impression and
moral effect and giving an intensity and almost wildness to
the interest."

On meeting the landowner, Stephens decided to buy the
ruins and ship one of the monuments, cut into pieces, and
casts of the others to New York "to be the nucleus of a great
national museum of American antiquities." Purchase was
easy: for fifty dollars Stephens became the owner of the
great Maya site. Meanwhile, Catherwood had begun the
task of recording the sculptures, which were "very complicated . . . perfectly unintelligible . . . in very high relief and
required a strong body of light to bring up the figures; and
the foliage was so thick and the shade so deep that drawing
was impossible." Even after the jungle was cut back to admit light, Catherwood still had to draw standing ankle-deep
in mud and wearing gloves to protect his hands from the
mosquitoes.

While Catherwood drew over his camera lucida, a device
that allowed the monuments to be traced from a screen,
Stephens mapped the ruins of Copan. "The extent along
the river, as ascertained by monuments still found, is more
than two miles. There is one monument on the opposite
side of the river, at the distance of a mile, on the top of a
mountain two thousand feet high. Whether the city ever
crossed the river and extended to that monument it is impossible to say; I believe not, . . ." (correctly, as modern
survey has shown, although the settlement of Copan is
more widespread than Stephens imagined).

"There are no remains of palaces and private buildings,
and the principal part is that which stands on the bank of
the river, and may perhaps with propriety be called the
Temple. This Temple is an oblong enclosure; the front or
river wall extends on a line north and south six hundred
and twenty-four feet and it is from sixty to ninety feet in
height. It is made of cut stones, from three to six feet in
length, and a foot and a half in breadth. The other three

sides consist of ranges of steps and pyramidal structures, rising from thirty to one hundred and forty feet in height on the slope. Though gigantic and extraordinary for a ruined structure of the aborigines I consider it necessary to say it is not so large as the base of the Great Pyramid of Gizeh."

This passage epitomizes Stephens's practical and intellectual approach, both sober and precise, and Catherwood's accompanying plan and drawings complement it in felicity; it is notable that in using the term "aborigines" Stephens explicitly accepted a local and American origin for the ruins, and rejected the notion of transatlantic migration of Egyptians or Israelites. In so doing he followed the trend of Spanish colonial thinking rather than the more exotic views presented by Waldeck and others.

Their time at Copan was short—only two weeks. Catherwood drew only the standing stelae and their recumbent "altars," and the vegetation and buildings were merely limned in as background. Stephens described each monument with considered judgment: "The face of this 'idol' is decidedly that of a man. The beard is of a curious fashion, and joined to the moustache and hair. The ears are large, though not resembling nature; the expression is grand, the mouth partly open, and the eyeballs seem starting from the sockets. The intention of the sculptor seems to have been to excite terror. The feet are ornamented with sandals, probably of the skins of some wild animals, in the fashion of that day.

"The back of this monument contrasts remarkably with the horrible portrait in front. It has nothing grotesque or pertaining to the rude conceits of Indians but is noticeable for its extreme grace and beauty. In our daily walks we often stopped to gaze at it, and the more we gazed the more it grew upon us. We considered [that] in its medallion tablets the people who reared it had published a record of themselves, through which we might one day hold conference with a perished race, and unveil the mystery that hung over the city."

This recognition of Maya hieroglyphic writing, and the interpretation of its portent on the monuments as historical, is a view that has within the last twenty years been strikingly confirmed by the partial decipherment of dynas-

tic inscriptions on the monuments of Tikal, Palenque, Yaxchilan, Piedras Negras, and other sites, including recently
Copan itself (see Chapter 7). Stephens declined to guess at
either the date or the cause of the abandonment of Copan,
"whether it fell by the sword, or famine, or pestilence," but
wrote "that its history is graven on its monuments. . . .
Who shall read them?"

Less than two weeks after their arrival Stephens set off
on his diplomatic mission, in search of the government of
the Central American Federation, to which he added an in-
spection of the proposed route of a canal from the Atlantic
to the Pacific, across Nicaragua. Catherwood spent part of
his time visiting the ruins of Quirigua, deep in the Motagua
valley near Izabal, alone but for a guide. He was unable to
do much exploration or detailed drawings of the magnificent stelae, and the two published engravings show how
poor an artist Catherwood could be without his camera lucida. When Stephens and Catherwood met up again in
Guatemala City the civil war between the factions led by
Carrera and Morazan was in full swing.

At Easter in 1840 they set off at last for their original objective, Palenque, far to the north in the rain forest of the
Gulf Coast and allegedly forbidden to foreigners by the
Mexican government. They passed through the highlands
of Guatemala, visiting on the way the historically documented former capitals of Utatlan and Zaculeu, now heaps
of ruins outside the Spanish towns that replaced them.
Joined by a young American, Henry Pawling, whose use-
fulness lay equally in his enthusiasm and in his armament
of "a pair of pistols and a short double-barrelled gun slung
to his saddle-bow," they crossed surreptitiously into Mexico, and made their way north over the mountains of Chiapas to Palenque.

They were by no means the first visitors to the site,
which had already been written about by Antonio del Rio,
Guillermo Dupaix, and Jean-Frédéric Waldeck; they arrived, indeed, only a few days after the departure of Patrick
Walker's overland expedition from Belize (the report of
which was destined, ironically, to remain unpublished
for over a century). Casual visitors had left their names
scratched on the wall plaster as well, among them Noah O.
Platt, logwood merchant of New York; Palenque was by far

the best known of Maya sites. "What we saw does not need any exaggeration," said Stephens in satisfaction on their arrival; "it awakened admiration and astonishment."

They set up camp in the Palace, the largest building, and proceeded as they had at Copan: Stephens sought out sculptures and had them cleared of bush, and set up scaffolding for the camera lucida with Pawling's help. He then made a plan of the Palace, distinguishing carefully between standing and fallen walls (Figure 1.4). "It stands on an artificial elevation of an oblong form, forty feet high, three hundred and ten feet in front and rear and two hundred and sixty feet on each side. The building stands with its face to the east and measures two hundred and twenty-eight feet front by one hundred and eighty feet deep. Its height is not more than twenty-five feet, and all around it had a broad projecting cornice of stone.

"The front contained fourteen doorways, about nine feet wide each. . . . The building was constructed of stone with a mortar of lime and sand, and the whole front was covered

1.4. Stephens's plan of the Palace at Palenque, as drafted by Catherwood.

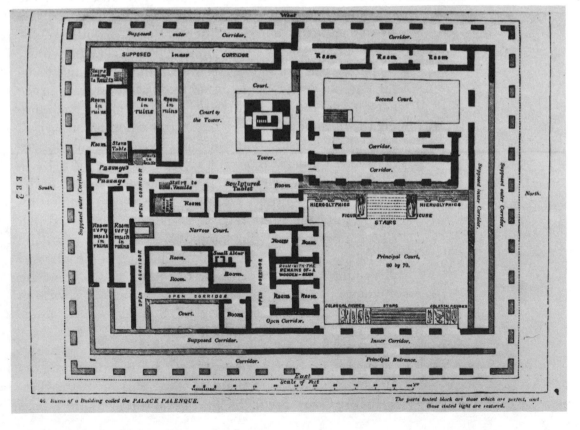

1.5. "Strange figures": one of the stucco panels on the Palace at Palenque (compare Maudslay's photograph of this panel in Figure 9.21).

Page 18, Fig. 1.5 caption, add: First published by the great German traveler Humboldt in 1810, the sculpture was mistakenly said to be in Oaxaca.

with stucco and painted. The piers were ornamented with spirited figures in bas-relief, one of which is enclosed by a richly ornamented border about ten feet high and six wide. The principal personage stands in an upright position and in profile (Figure 1.5); the upper part of the head seems to have been compressed and lengthened—a different species from any now existing in that region of country—and supposing the statues to be images of living personages they indicate a race of people now lost and unknown. The headdress is evidently a plume of feathers. Over the shoulders is a short covering decorated with studs and a breast plate; part of the ornament of the girdle is broken. The tunic is probably a leopard's skin and the whole dress no doubt exhibits the costume of this unknown people.

"He holds in his hand a staff or sceptre, and opposite his hand are the marks of three hieroglyphics, which have decayed or been broken off. At his feet are two naked figures fertile imagination might call strange figures, but no satisfactory interpretation presents itself to my mind. The hieroglyphics doubtless tell its history. The stucco was painted and in different places about it we discovered the remains of red, blue, yellow, black and white." Stephens was correct in assuming the personage to be human, not divine, but he was misled about the race of the person, not knowing of the ancient Maya practice of binding the head of a child to produce this deformation.

Stephens's description continues in this measured manner, with Catherwood's architectural skill being used to provide a plan, elevation, and section of the Temple of the Inscriptions (Figure 1.6). The great hieroglyphic tablets inside the building were recorded, and Stephens noted that "the hieroglyphs are the same as we found at Copan and Quirigua. . . . There is room for the belief that the whole of this country was once occupied by the same race, speaking the same language, or at least having the same written characters." Here, as so often, both Stephens's basic observation and his careful qualification of it were correct.

As the rainy season closed in and made work increasingly difficult, Catherwood struggled to finish two major drawings of the tablets in the Temple of the Sun and in the Temple of the Cross. Stephens used the former (Figure 1.7) as

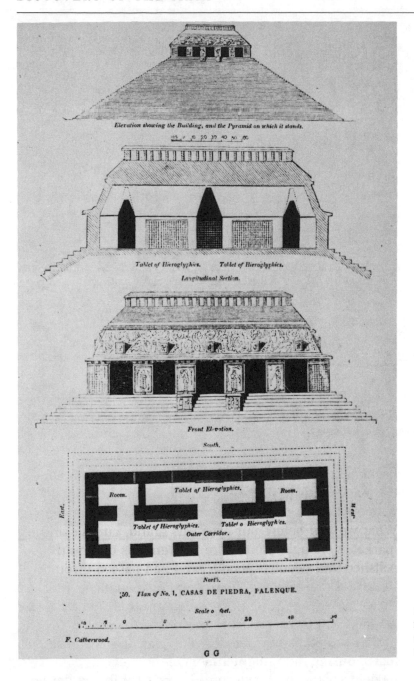

Elevation showing the Building, and the Pyramid on which it stands.

Tablet of Hieroglyphics.   Tablet of Hieroglyphics.
Longitudinal Section.

Front Elevation.

South.

Room.   Tablet of Hieroglyphics.   Room.

Tablet of Hieroglyphics.   Tablet o Hieroglyphics.
Outer Corridor.

North.

59. Plan of No. 1, CASAS DE PIEDRA, PALENQUE.

Scale o feet.

F. Catherwood.

G G

1.6. Catherwood's architectural record of the Temple of the Inscriptions at Palenque (see Figure 7.11).

the frontispiece to Volume 2 of his book on their journey, claiming it to be "the most perfect and most interesting monument in Palenque."

While praising the art of the ancient Maya, Stephens minimized the difficulties and dangers of working at Palenque, and differed from previous visitors in the sobriety of

1.7. The sculptured tablet in the Temple of the Sun at Palenque, with a hieroglyphic inscription that has been interpreted as a dynastic text.

his conclusions. "There was no necessity for assigning to the ruined city an immense extent, or an antiquity coeval with the Egyptians or any other ancient and known people.

Page 20, Fig. 1.7 caption should read: The sculptured tablet in the Temple of the Sun at Palenque. Its hieroglyphic inscription has been interpreted as a dynastic text, detailing both the mythical and the historical ancestry of the ruler Chan-Bahlum (reigned A.D. 684-702).

...d re-...ated, ...gh all the stages incidental to the rise and fall of nations, reached their golden age and perished, entirely unknown." (By "stages" Stephens probably meant the social typology of hunter-pastoralist-farmer-urbanite that had been disseminated during the Enlightenment of the previous century, a model that has had widespread influence in the development of anthropology.)

With the rains now in full spate, they left Palenque on June 1, 1840, and sailed down the Usumacinta (see Chapter 3) to the Laguna de Terminos on the Gulf of Mexico, and thence north along the coast to Sisal, the port of Mérida, capital of Yucatan. Stephens had met the owner of the ruins of Uxmal and had accepted an invitation to visit them; but since their ship was now bound for New York, he was not sure that the diversion was going to be worthwhile. A few days later, however, his doubts were dispelled as they emerged from the low scrub forest and "came at once upon a large open field strowed with mounds of ruins, and vast buildings on terraces and pyramidal structures, grand and in good preservation, richly ornamented, without a bush to obstruct the view and in picturesque effect almost equal to the ruins of Thebes."

The scene was dominated by the Pyramid of the Magician overlooking the courtyard of the Monjas. (It was called thus a "nunnery" by the Spanish because of the similarity to European conventual cloisters; many Maya buildings have equally fanciful names, used by archaeologists out of convention rather than conviction.) The building "grandest in position, the most stately in architecture and proportions, and the most perfect in preservation of all the structures remaining at Uxmal" was the Palace of the Governors, standing on a massive triple platform six hundred feet long with the building itself more than half that length. Stephens noted the wooden lintels, one of which bore carved hieroglyphics similar to those of Palenque and Copan. The exploration of Uxmal was abandoned, however, when Catherwood fell sick; they returned to Mérida, and on June 24 sailed for Havana. Their adventures were not yet over, for they lay becalmed for two weeks until an American brig passed by and brought them in to New York at the end of July. They had been away for less than ten months, and less than two of these had been spent on full-time exploration of Maya sites: two weeks at Copan, three at Palenque, a few days at Uxmal, and short stops at other sites en route. They had visited the three major sites already reported abroad, and Catherwood had visited a fourth, Quirigua. In spite of his original antiquarian interest, Stephens had devoted a substantial part of his time to his official, though abortive, mission of diplomacy; when in June 1841 the two volumes of *Incidents of Travel in Central America, Chiapas and Yucatan* appeared, somewhat less than 200 of their 900 pages were devoted to archaeology, although most of the full-page engravings were of Maya sculpture and buildings.

Nevertheless, the book was a landmark in the history of Maya studies. It raced through twelve printings in three months, and the combination of spirited narrative and fine illustration brought the sites and their monuments to the attention of a wide audience. Equally valuable was Stephens's restraint in speculation; there were "not sufficient grounds for the belief in the great antiquity that has been ascribed to these ruins. . . . They were constructed by the races who occupied the country at the time of the invasion by the Spaniards, or some not very distant progenitors. It seems impossible that after a lapse of two or three thousand years a single edifice could now be standing." He met objections by examining, and rejecting, comparisons with China and Egypt, concluding that the Maya ruins were "different from the works of any other known people, of a new order, and entirely and absolutely anomalous. They stand alone: we have a conclusion far more interesting and wonderful than that of connecting the builders of these cities with the Egyptians or any other people. It is the spectacle of a people skilled in architecture, sculpture, and drawing, not derived from the Old World but originating and growing up here without models or masters, having a distinct, separate, independent existence; like the plants and fruits of the soil, indigenous."

With this assessment of ancient Maya sites as the remains of a native American culture of recent rather than antediluvian antiquity, lacking inspiration from or connection with Egyptians, Lost Israelites, Vikings, or Celts, and a wide public interest in and acceptance of Stephens's work, a new phase of Maya studies began. It originated, appropriately, with the same protagonists. Stephens had made a lot of money, rumored to be in excess of $15,000, from the 1841 book, and he used it to finance a second expedition. This one, however, was confined in area to the northern part of the Yucatan Peninsula, and was explicitly archaeological and scientific in its objectives.

On October 9, 1841, fourteen months after their return and while the book was still a best seller, Stephens and Catherwood sailed for Sisal on the *Tennessee*, accompanied by Dr. Samuel Cabot, Jr., a 26-year-old Harvard graduate and amateur naturalist. (On the previous journey Stephens had bemoaned the lack of a specialist to identify the strange animals and plants they had seen.) They departed without fanfare, wishing "to complete what we have begun before others can interfere with us," but became local celebrities in Mérida as the result of Catherwood's daguerreotype equipment, a form of early camera, and Cabot's ability to cure squint with a simple operation.

Eventually they set off for Uxmal by way of Mayapan, the last pre-Hispanic Maya capital and a site still unexplored. At Uxmal they settled into rooms in the Palace of the Governors and resumed their research, mapping the site, and on Catherwood's part, drawing the great panorama of the Palace from the east which became the frontispiece for Stephens's *Incidents of Travel in Yucatan* when that appeared in 1843. The play of light along the ornate facade was such that Catherwood abandoned his daguerreotype and returned to pencil and camera lucida.

Next to the Palace stood the small and severe House of the Turtles, lacking "the rich and gorgeous decoration of the former, but distinguished for its justness and beauty of proportions, and its chasteness and simplicity of ornament. Throughout there is nothing that borders on the unintelligible or grotesque, nothing that can shock a fastidious architectural taste; but unhappily it is fast going to decay. With a few more returns of the rainy season it will be a mass of ruins, and perhaps on the whole continent of America there will be no such monument of the purity and simplicity of aboriginal art." Luckily, the prognosis was wrong; the House of the Turtles, now restored, survives.

Catherwood stayed at Uxmal while Stephens rode around the region seeking other ruins and making copious notes on contemporary settlements. In many cases ruins lay ad-

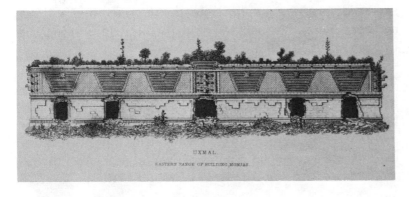

UXMAL.
EASTERN RANGE OF BUILDING MONJAS.

1.8. Uxmal: facade of the east range of the Monjas, showing the characteristic Puuc-style decoration on the upper part, with stiff, conventionalized double-headed serpents or saurians superimposed on a trellis-work background (see also Figure 9.1).

jacent to existing villages, and Stephens surmised that the Spanish had settled at the edge of a Maya town, and by a combination of killing the Maya leaders and providing alternative ritual in their church made their own buildings the political and religious focus of the settlement. Habitation then concentrated around those buildings, leaving the old temples abandoned in the fields around the town.

Catherwood plotted the Monjas courtyard, and drew elevations of the facades, "each ornamented from one end to the other with the richest and most intricate carving known in the art of the builders of Uxmal, presenting a scene of strange magnificence" (Figure 1.8).

Midway between the Palace and the Monjas were "two ruined edifices facing each other, and seventy feet apart, exactly alike in plan and ornament. In the centre of each facade, at points directly opposite each other, are the fragments of a great stone ring four feet in diameter, secured in the wall by a stone tenon of corresponding dimensions. Excavation satisfied us that these great parallel edifices consisted merely of four great walls, filled up with a solid mass of stones. It was our opinion that they had been built expressly with reference to the two great rings facing each other in the facades, and that the space between was intended for the celebration of some public games." Again, Stephens was accurate in judgment: a ball court for playing the sacred *pok-ta-pok* had been recognized for the first time in the Maya Area.

Although their work was presented as "incidents of travel," only the most archaeologically informative of Catherwood's drawings were eventually published, apart from small vignettes of modern settlements. One group of ruins, called Nohpat, "the most touching and interesting" they saw, did "nothing to illustrate the architecture and art of these unknown people," and the drawings remained unused.

From Uxmal they went to Kabah, a site then unexplored. They were struck by "the extraordinary richness and ornament," recalling Uxmal, "alike complicated and incomprehensible," on the building called the Codz Pop, where "the cornice running over the doorways, tried by the severest rules of art recognized among us, would embellish the architecture of any known era." The monument that aroused the most feeling was "a lonely arch . . . on a ruined mound, disconnected from every other structure, in solitary grandeur. Darkness rests upon its history, but in that desolation and solitude among the ruins around it stood like the proud memorial of a Roman triumph."

Some of the carvings of Kabah renewed Stephens's interest, dormant since their visit to Copan two years before, in shipping a collection of representative sculptures to New York as the nucleus of a museum. A carved sapote-wood lintel depicting a richly accoutred lord was reckoned worth acquiring "at any trouble or cost." When they had removed it from the doorway, with some effort, it was seen that the face of the figure was "scratched, worn and obliterated" although the rest was well preserved. (This has been noted on many recently discovered stelae also, and may be evidence of discontent with the ruling group; see Chapter 4, p. 141.) Luckily Catherwood drew the lintel as soon as it had been removed, for although it reached New York safely, it was consumed together with the rest of their sculpture collection by a fire on July 31, 1842, which destroyed Catherwood's Panorama building. (Some stone sculptures arrived late at New York and survived; after several decades they were found by Sylvanus Morley, built into a modern "ruin" on the banks of the Hudson, and now can be seen in the American Museum of Natural History).

Many other ruins had been reported by the helpful priest at Nohcacab, so the trio set off with only light luggage, each on a suitable horse; Catherwood could sketch on his, Cabot shoot from his, and Stephens's "could be pushed into a hard day's journey for a preliminary visit." After a stop at Sayil, where the south front of the Palace was cleared for Catherwood to take a view, they arrived at the ruins of Labna, also unknown and unexplored.

"We reached a field of ruins which, after all we had seen, created in us new feelings of astonishment. Since our arrival we had not met with anything that excited us more strongly." One striking structure was "an arched gateway, remarkable for its beauty of proportions and grace of ornament, passing through which we entered a thick forest growing in what had once been the courtyard. The doors of the apartments on both sides of the gateway opened upon this area; over each doorway was a square recess in which were the remains of a rich ornament in stucco with marks of paint still visible, apparently intended to represent the face of the sun surrounded by its rays" (Figure 1.9). To the north lay the "principal building, without extravagance really magnificent," Catherwood's panorama of which was used as the frontispiece for the second volume of *Incidents of Travel in Yucatan* as a companion to that of the Uxmal Palace in Volume 1.

Illness struck again: Catherwood and Cabot both went down with malaria, and Stephens set off alone for Ticul to explore. There he had a singular stroke of luck: a local anti-quary, Don Pio Perez, had written an account of the "An-cient Chronology of Yucatan," based on documentary and folk sources. In reading it, Stephens was impressed by "the fact that though the inhabitants of Yucatan and Mexico speak different languages, their calendar is substantially the same. It shows common sources of knowledge and pro-cesses of reasoning, a link in a chain of evidence tending to show a common origin in the aboriginal inhabitants of Yucatan and Mexico." Here we have the first glimmerings of the present model of a Mesoamerican culture area em-bracing southern Mexico and the Maya lands and sharing many aspects of material and intellectual culture.

Pio Perez is one of the unsung heroes of Maya studies, a man who without formal training and with no encourage-ment beyond his own interest preserved priceless frag-ments of the past, and when the chance came shared his discoveries with others without thought of credit. It is pleasant to record that not only was Perez's work published as an appendix to *Incidents of Travel in Yucatan*, but Ste-phens ensured that it appeared under its author's own name as an independent piece of work.

Journeying to Maní, where Diego de Landa had burned many Maya books three centuries earlier, Stephens was shown the municipal records, which included "an old painting on cotton cloth" recording the murder of the am-bassadors of Tutul Xiu in the period before the Spanish conquest, the "first and only instance" of a pre-Hispanic document that they encountered.

On March 7, 1842, the three travelers set off at last for Chichén Itzá, the great site to the east which had been reported to Stephens by a German, Baron Frederichstahl.

1.9. The archway at Labna, with the party of explorers. Note the miniature houses in relief flanking the arch (compare Figure 9.1). This illustration comes from a set of colored lithographs issued by Catherwood in 1844 as a separate venture from Stephens's books.

The baron had visited the ruins in 1840 and was responsible for their becoming known outside Yucatan, although in 1838 a New York engineer, John Burke, had celebrated the Fourth of July by climbing the major structures. Stephens's enthusiasm "was raised to the highest pitch by the ruins: the buildings were large and some were in good preservation; in general the facades were not so elaborately ornamented as some we had seen, seemed of an older date, and the sculpture was ruder, but the interior apartments contained decorations and devices that were new to us, and powerfully interesting." What Stephens had distinguished was the Toltec-Maya hybrid style for which the buildings of Chichén Itzá are now famed; this style, however, was later, not earlier than that of the buildings they had already explored at Uxmal and Kabah. The name of the site, "mouth of the well of the Itzá" (a Maya tribe), comes from the great *cenote*, "an immense circular hole, with broken rocky perpendicular sides and at the bottom a great body of water of an unknown depth, always about the same level." This collapsed limestone cavern, a principal water source at Chichén, was later called the Cenote of Sacrifice because of the discoveries made in it.

Near the hacienda buildings where the explorers stayed were a number of buildings with fanciful Spanish names, including the *iglesia* ("church") where music was reputed to sound on Good Friday; Stephens noted dryly that although they were using the daguerreotype in the building that day, nothing was heard. Just to the north was an edifice "conspicuous for its picturesque appearance, circular in form and known by the name of the Caracol [snail] on account of its interior arrangement. It is twenty-two feet in diameter and has four small doorways which give entrance to a circular corridor. . . . The inner wall also has four doorways . . . to a second circular corridor. The walls of both corridors were plastered and ornamented with paintings. The plan of the building was new, but instead of unfolding secrets it drew closer the curtain that already shrouded, with almost impenetrable folds, these mysterious structures" (see Figure 9.11).

1.10. The great ball court at Chichén Itzá in 1842. The court, built ca. A.D. 900, is the largest in the Maya area.

GYMNASIUM, CHICHEN ITZA.

Less mysterious were "two immense parallel walls, each two hundred and seventy-four feet long, thirty feet thick and one hundred and twenty feet apart [Figure 1.10]. In the centre of the great stone walls, exactly opposite each other and at the height of twenty feet from the ground, are two massive stone rings four feet in diameter; the diameter of the hole is one foot seven inches. These walls we considered identical in their uses with the parallel structures at Uxmal, intended for some public games." Stephens backed up his identification by quoting from the sixteenth-century Spanish historian Herrera's description of the Aztec game of *tlachtli*, noting the use of "certain stones like those of a mill, with a hole quite through the middle just as big as the ball, and he that could strike it through there won the game." From the similarities of Aztec and Maya ball courts Stephens traced "an affinity between the people who erected the ruined cities of Yucatan and those who inhabited Mexico at the time of the conquest," again adumbrating the cultural unity of Mesoamerica.

Stephens described the sculptures and murals of the ball court (the latter having now almost vanished) and then turned to the most spectacular building at the site, "the grandest and most conspicuous object that towers above the plain," the great pyramid known as the Castillo with its fourfold staircase. "On the ground at the foot of the [north] staircase, forming a bold, striking and well-conceived commencement to this lofty range, are two colossal serpents' heads, ten feet in length, with mouths wide open and tongues protruding."

After nearly three weeks at Chichén Itzá they set out east for the town of Valladolid, the major Spanish settlement in eastern Yucatan, in order to try to reach "two places on the coast called Tancar and Tuloom," and were directed north to the port of Yalahao. As they sailed down the coast of Quintana Roo in a 35-foot canoe, "rather unpromising for a month's cruise," they were told of ruins off in the jungle at Coba, with a *sacbe* or paved road running away to an unknown destination, said by some to be Chichén Itzá. This may be the first report of the longest of the Maya *sacbeob*, mapped in the 1920s, which runs 62 miles from Coba west to the small site of Yaxuna not far from Chichén.

Arriving at Tulum, they made camp in the main build-

ing, the Castillo, which rose "on the brink of a high, broken, precipitous cliff, commanding a magnificent ocean
view." Nearby was a small building with a curious figure
over the doorway, "with the head down and the legs and
arms spread out," similar to one they had seen at Sayil—the
"diving god" of later explorers.

Exploration brought a surprising discovery: "this forest-
buried city was encompassed by a wall, still erect and in
good preservation. We set out without much expectation
and all at once found ourselves confronted by a massive
stone structure running at right angles to the sea. Following its direction we soon came to a gateway and watch-
tower. The character of this structure could not be mis-
taken; it was in the strictest sense a city wall, the first we
had seen that could be identified as such beyond all question. We immediately set about a thorough exploration, and
without once breaking off measured it from one end to the
other.

"It forms a parallelogram abutting on the sea, the high
precipitous cliff forming a sea wall 1500 feet in length. The
wall is of rude construction and composed of rough flat
stones, laid upon each other without mortar or cement of
any kind. At the angle, elevated so as to give a commanding
view, is the watch-tower . . . but no guard sits in the watch-
tower now, trees are growing around it. Within the walls
the city is desolate and overgrown and without is an unbroken forest. The battlements, on which the proud Indian
strode with his bow and arrow and plumes of feathers, are
surmounted by immense thorn bushes and overrun by poi-
sonous vines. The city no longer keeps watch: in solitude it
rests, the abode of silence and desolation." So dense was
the undergrowth that on the very morning of their departure Cabot found, still within the walls, another unknown
building hardly a hundred yards from the Castillo. It was of
unusual interest, having two floors of rooms and walls covered with murals.

Stephens thought that at Tulum they "had seen, abandoned and in ruins, the same buildings which the Spaniards saw entire and inhabited by Indians and identified
them beyond question as the works of the same people who
created the great ruined cities over which, when we began
our journey, hung a veil of seemingly impenetrable mys-

tery." He was right, or almost so: Tulum has been dated to the centuries just before the conquest, while just to the north at Tancah direct continuity of settlement into the colonial period has recently been demonstrated.

From Tulum the party sailed back to the north coast of Yucatan on their way to Mérida, noting as they passed immense pyramids at Silan and Izamal. At the latter town Diego de Landa's convent stood on top of one of the principal structures, but the name would have meant little to Stephens: the rediscovery of Landa's invaluable account of sixteenth-century Maya culture lay twenty years in the future.

The last site visited was Aké, near the scene of an epic battle between Maya and Spaniards. The huge columned hall was "a new and extraordinary feature entirely different from any we had seen, and at the very end of our journey, when we supposed ourselves familiar with the character of American ruins, it threw over them a new air of mystery."

In mid-May of 1842 they embarked for Havana, where in changing ships they paid tribute to a great precursor in the discovery of America: "after dark, by the light of a single candle, with heads uncovered we stood before the marble slab enclosing the bones of Columbus."

Within nine months of their return *Incidents of Travel in Yucatan* was written, illustrated, and published, with enduring success. It contrasted with the earlier volumes in being almost totally concerned with archaeological exploration, and in the intelligent use of Spanish colonial authors such as Herrera and Cogolludo; the long appendix by Pio Perez, "The History of the Peninsula of Yucatan before the Conquest," made it as much a work of scholarship as a book of travels.

John Lloyd Stephens in 1839 had been a dilettante, an intelligent and enthusiastic amateur, combining antiquarianism with diplomacy, and very much an author in search of a book. The Stephens of 1841 was a dedicated, well-read, and resourceful scholar, directing the first planned archaeological reconnaissance in the Maya area.

The year 1840 was a watershed in Maya studies, preceded by three centuries of sporadic, sometimes surprisingly competent exploration of a very few sites (Palenque alone accounting for the bulk of the published material), and succeeded by a widening interest and deeper probing into the Maya past. In this change the writings of Stephens, one of the last romantic explorers and one of the first objective scholars, and the fastidiously accurate drawings of Catherwood were a vital catalyst.

2

Precursors and Successors

ALTHOUGH Stephens and Catherwood revolutionized the study of the ancient Maya, making it both
fashionable and scholarly, they neither were, nor
pretended to be, the first workers in the field. Stephens ac-
knowledges in his books the prior work of others, from the
Spanish explorers of Palenque in the eighteenth century
down to his own contemporaries, and an interest in Maya
ruins had in fact existed from the time of the conquest onwards. Before examining the lost civilization of the Maya
and its setting, we should perhaps glance at those scholars
who have, over the past four centuries, brought that civilization to light. Attitudes toward the ruins and their builders changed during this period, which can conveniently be
divided into several phases.

The Spanish Travelers

The first phase, that of the Spanish travelers, lasted from
just after the Spanish invasion of the Maya lands, from
about 1550, to 1759, when Charles III of Spain came to the
throne and instituted a policy of deliberate archaeological
exploration. During this period of 1550–1759 we find a
number of casual mentions and descriptions of Maya ruins,
as well as careful accounts of the way of life of the contemporary Maya, which contained many survivals from the
pre-Hispanic past. There was, however, no planned exploration of sites, and little antiquarian theory building compared with what was happening in Europe.

The earliest mention of a Maya site seems to be that of
Fray Lorenzo de Bienvenida, a Franciscan monk of Mérida,
the Spanish capital of Yucatan built on the ruins of the
Maya settlement of Tihoo. The old name, wrote Bienvenida
in 1548, was "after the beautiful buildings [Tihoo] contains: in all the discoveries in the Indies none so fine has

been found. Buildings of big and well-carved stones—there is no record of who built them. It seems to us they were built before Christ, because the trees on top of the buildings were as high as the ones around them. Amongst these buildings we, monks of the Order of St. Francis, settled."

There are several interesting things in this brief note: admiration for the vanished builders and acknowledgment of their skill, but no attempt to attribute the ruins to any known people; intelligent deduction of a great age for the ruins from the size of the trees growing on them (more than two centuries before Thomas Jefferson used a similar deduction to date Indian mounds in Virginia), and an attribution to a period before the time of Christ when the age of the whole earth was thought to be only some six thousand years; and the fact that by the sixteenth century the ruins had already been long abandoned, thus not being part of Tihoo but of a precursor. The ruins were probably, in the light of subsequent research, of the Puuc style, dating to the eighth and ninth centuries A.D.; Bienvenida did not appreciate the rapidity with which tropical vegetation can grow.

The year after Bienvenida wrote his note, another Franciscan friar arrived in Yucatan; Diego de Landa's rise was rapid and he soon became the provincial of the order, exerting more power than the bishop who was titular leader of the church (Figure 2.1). He was a severe and narrow-minded man, who appointed himself to lead the Inquisition in Yucatan and then carried out a notorious program of floggings and imprisonment that contravened even the instructions of Pope Paul III. His final act was to destroy, at the famous auto-da-fé at Maní in July 1562, several thousand "idols" and dozens of hieroglyphic books, which he claimed contained "superstitions and falsehoods of the devil," although he also acknowledged that the Maya used them to record "antiquities and their sciences."

His behavior was too extreme; he was summoned back to Spain for trial and was severely censured by the Council of the Indies. For eleven years he remained in Spain, his case remitted on appeal to a committee of scholars; this, since it included his friends, naturally acquitted him when the furor had died down, and allowed him to return to Yucatan as bishop in 1573. While he was on trial he pre-

2.1. Diego de Landa: a modern bronze statue in the plaza of Izamal, based on the eighteenth-century portrait in the convent there, where Landa lived for some years.

pared as part of his defense a background document describing the people whom he was accused of oppressing, their customs, culture, and antiquities, calling it *Relación de las cosas de Yucatan* ("an account of the things of Yucatan"), based on his own observations and on what Maya informants had told him. This document was destined to remain unread in the Madrid archives until 1863, but its contents show us a Spanish attitude to the Maya past in more detail than any other source of the period.

Noting that the ruined buildings in Yucatan reflected a former prosperity not apparent to the Spanish conquerors, Landa canvassed various theories that had been put forward to explain their construction: that they were built as make-work projects to keep the population occupied; that they were built from religious devotion; or that settlements were frequently moved, necessitating new temples on each site. Whatever the reason, Landa concluded, the ruins were certainly built by the Indians themselves, because there were stucco sculptures in Maya clothing on some of them; also, he had found in a demolished structure a pottery jar containing the ashes of a cremation and "three counters of fine stone, such as the Indians today use as money, all showing the people were Indians."

Landa noted that the bones were those of a larger person than the sixteenth-century Maya, and linked this with the height of the steps on ancient Maya staircases. In the past

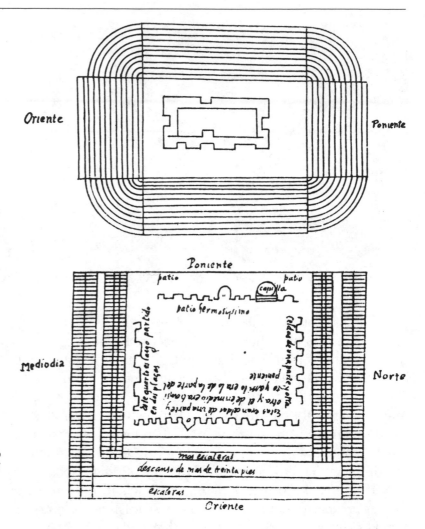

2.2. Landa's plan of the Castillo at Chichén Itzá and a sketch of the layout of a plaza at Tihoo (Merida), from the *Relación de las cosas de Yucatan.*

few years scientific evidence has shown that the Preclassic and Classic Maya were indeed taller on average than their descendants.

In the manuscript of Landa's *Relación* were a number of sketches, including rough diagrams of the ruins of Izamal, where Landa's monastery was built atop one of the great platforms; a large courtyard surrounded by ranges of buildings at Tihoo (Mérida) which seems to have included a circular structure like the Caracol at Chichén Itzá; and a plan of the Castillo at Chichén which Landa made on the spot (Figure 2.2). This last noted correctly the nine tiers of the pyramid and their rounded angles, the ninety-one steps on each staircase and the serpent heads at their bases. The sketches and some of the phraseology show that Landa in fact kept notes on Maya ruins, which he took to Spain and incorporated into his description.

The *Relación* is best known, however, not for its fragments of antiquarian topography, but for the key it offered (when it was finally published in the mid-nineteenth century by Brasseur de Bourbourg, of whom more later) to the decipherment of Maya hieroglyphic writing. Section 41 of the manuscript described in summary form the working of the Maya calendar, and also attempted a transliterated Maya alphabet, giving the Maya equivalents for the Spanish *a*, *b*, *c*, and so on (which would have been pronounced *ah*, *bay*, *say* by Landa). The Maya informant simply gave a hieroglyphic sign that corresponded with this sound, so that *b*, pronounced *bay*, yielded a drawing of a footprint between two lines, the Maya sign for *be* ("road"). Although for a long time this misconception on Landa's part was thought by scholars to make his alphabet useless, recent research has shown its value in establishing some of the phonetic characteristics of Maya writing.

The survival and discovery of Landa's *Relación* (even as an incomplete copy of the original) has been blessed by Maya scholars (though doubtless with only one-hundredth of the fervor with which its author was cursed by the Maya themselves); it is the best description we have of a vanished culture that was being eradicated even as Landa wrote.

Other Spanish clerics have also left us their impressions, however, and their ascription of the ruins was also to the local Maya, as in Antonio de Ciudad Real's description of the travels of Father Ponce in 1588 to Uxmal, where in the Monjas quadrangle "there are shapes of naked Indians with their loin cloths . . . which would seem to indicate the building to be Indian." He suggested that the ruins were 900 years old, a not inaccurate guess.

Far to the south, in 1576, Diego García de Palacio visited the ruins of Copan and noted the resemblance to the ruins of Yucatan: "They say that in ancient days a great gentleman arrived from the province of Yucatan and built these buildings. . . . It seems among all the rubbish they talk this is the most certain." Here we have a notion of the cultural unity of the Maya realm nearly three centuries before Stephens made a similar deduction on the basis of the hieroglyphic inscriptions. Garcia's description of Copan was so remarkable that Alfred Maudslay, exploring the site again in the late nineteenth century, said that "it might have been written by any intelligent visitor within the last ten years." Unfortunately, Garcia's manuscript suffered the same fate as Landa's and remained buried in an archive until 1840, after Stephens's later explorations.

The Spanish travelers made many laudatory references to the quality of ancient Maya buildings: "sumptuous . . . crowded with well carved figures . . . with porches of great exquisiteness"; "beautiful buildings, so much art and sumptuousness . . . carefully carved stone"; "the grandeur and beauty of Yucatan's buildings . . . for it excels in these. . . . It is the most remarkable of all the things discovered in the Indies because it has so many of these buildings and in so many places . . . so good is the masonry work . . . it is frightening"; "Uxmal deserves great and special admiration." In all of these references we find also a hardheaded ascription of the ruins to the ancestors of the sixteenth-century Maya, and not to any biblical, classical, or other Old World migrants. In 1688 López de Cogolludo summarized this view: "Some people have said they may be the work of Phoenicians or Carthaginians, but this can generally be refuted by the argument that there is no history telling us that such nations ever came to this region."

Attribution of the buildings to the Maya was accompanied by a recognition of the hieroglyphic signs as writing. Landa not only describes the books he burned so enthusiastically, but notes stone stelae at Mayapan "that contain characters that they use," while Ciudad Real refers to "some characters and letters of those used by the Maya Indians in the old times," and Palacio at Copan notes "letters of unknown meanings."

This first phase of European discovery of the Maya past, down to 1759, thus comprises a series of intelligent, if brief, descriptions of sites, monuments, and objects, together with notes on contemporary Maya life; the intellectual attitudes include the use of material remains to document Maya prehistory, appreciation of their artistic quality, and the explicit assumption that the Maya were indeed the builders of the forest-clad ruins. None of the descriptions, with the possible exception of some of Landa's topographical notes, was archaeological in method or historical in intent: they are factual, often incidental, notes of interesting phenomena in writings that place no particular emphasis on the past.

The Spanish Explorers

The second phase of discovery began in 1759 with the accession of the antiquarian Charles III of Spain (who sponsored the excavation of Pompeii, at that time within his dominions), and ended in 1840, the year between the first and second expeditions of Stephens and Catherwood.

About the time of Charles III's accession, Ramon Ordoñez y Aguiar, a student at the town of Ciudad Real in highland Chiapas (now the city of San Cristobal Las Casas, named after the "Apostle of the Indies," Bishop Bartolomé Las Casas, another great student of Mesoamerican anthropology and as much a protector of his Maya flock as Diego de Landa was a persecutor) learned of "stone houses" at a place called Palenque, far to the north in the tropical lowland forests. Years later, in 1773, Ordoñez organized an expedition to the site, and reported on it to the governor of Guatemala, José de Estachería; he in turn demanded further information from his local subordinate, one José Calderón, who in December 1784 sent off a description, accompanied by some poor sketches, attributing the ruins to the Romans. He listed more than two hundred buildings, including one that "given its construction and magnitude could not be less than a palace." Estachería was intrigued, and dispatched an official expedition to Palenque led by the royal architect Antonio Bernasconi (who happened to be in Guatemala rebuilding the capital after the disastrous earthquake of 1773). His orders included an investigation of the age of the site, its size and former population, where its builders had come from and why it had been abandoned, whether it was fortified, and the size, materials, and styles of the buildings.

Bernasconi's report, in August 1785, described the style as "somewhat Gothic," but then more honestly said, "this architecture does not have any of the architectural patterns that I know, either old or modern." The report was sent to Charles III, who insisted on further exploration, doubtless exhorted by the royal historiographer Juan Bautista

Muñoz, who was at that time working on the history of the
Spanish-American empire. The royal command demanded a mass of specific data—a distinction "between doors,
niches and windows . . . study any stones that are found
like those described or walls of stoned mortar or of similar
mixed materials . . . make detailed descriptions and drawings of shapes, sizes and the cut of the stones and bricks,
particularly in arches and vaults . . . bring samples of plaster, mixture, stucco, bricks (baked or otherwise), pots or
any other utensils or tools that may be found, digging
where necessary." In the orders given by Estachería and
the king we see an interest in both the processes of cultural
development and in specific architectural detail, a spirit of
judicious inquiry fully in tune with the philosophical Enlightenment and growth of science in eighteenth-century
Europe.

Thus instructed, Estachería sent a second expedition
to Palenque, led by Captain Antonio del Rio. It arrived on
May 3, 1787, and included an artist, Ricardo Alméndariz.
Del Rio reported extensive excavation: "no window or
blocked door, room, corridor, patio, tower, prayer room or
crypt . . . has not been excavated." (Luckily for Palenque,
and later archaeologists, the claim was somewhat inflated.)
He determined that these ruins and the ruins of Yucatan
were the remains of the same civilization, and collected
and sent to Spain a number of artifacts. In both its instructions and their execution Del Rio's expedition bordered on
the explicit practice of archaeology to the degree that such
studies were being carried out elsewhere in the world at
that time.

The report and Alméndariz's drawings, instead of following the earlier reports into archival oblivion, reached London by a circuitous route, and in 1822 were published as
"Description of the Ruins of an Ancient City," with sixteen
plates engraved from the drawings by Jean-Frédéric Waldeck, who was working in London at the time (Figure 2.3).

Charles IV of Spain maintained his father's interest in
antiquities, and in 1804 he commissioned Guillermo Dupaix, a retired captain of dragoons with antiquarian inclina-
tions, to survey the principal pre-Hispanic ruins of Mexico.
Dupaix worked his way eastward from Mexico City, and on
his third and last expedition in 1807 he reached the Maya

Opposite:
2.3. The tower of the Palace at
Palenque seen through eighteenth-century eyes: Waldeck's
engravings of Ricardo Almen-
dariz's drawings of 1787. This
example comes from a pirated
German edition belonging to
Lord Kingsborough, who sent it
to Waldeck in Mérida in 1836
for his comments, which he
added on the plate.

Dans le mois de May 1787 Antonio del Rio dessina cette tour composée de trois corps
comme elle l'est encor aujourd'hui 1836, mais Dupaix et Castañeda à la fin de 1806 levèrent
et en firent des plans coupes et élévations, depuis le temps de Delrio la tour avait grandi
car Castañeda lui donna 5 étages ou corps et près de 40 marches intérieures, elle a diminué depuis
ce temps car en 1832.12. May j'ai vu que trois corps et 18 marches dans les deux étages, car la
base est solide et a servi de sépulture. Dupaix quoiqu'Autrichien était devenu Espagnol
dans la force du terme

Tab. II.

Gez. von F. Gadow.

lands, accompanied by an artist, José Castañeda. Both were conscientious recorders of detail; while Castañeda drew, Dupaix classified the reliefs of Palenque according to the techniques employed. He described the stucco panels in technical detail, noting the use of a core and the traces of red paint in the folds of the drapery. The stucco did "not appear to contain either sand, powdered marble or any other form of adulteration; it is hard in the extreme, besides being beautifully white. Most of the figures are erect and well proportioned; all of them are in profile, portly, and almost colossal, their height exceeding six feet. Their dress, though sumptuous, never wholly covers the body; their heads are decorated with helmets, crests and spreading plumes; and they wear necklaces, from which are suspended medallions."

Examining the Temple of the Cross and its great carved slab, Dupaix noted that "closer examination convinced me that it was not the holy Latin Cross which we adore, but a Greek Cross disfigured with various fantastical ornaments . . . neither do these whimsical embellishments correspond with the venerable simplicity . . . of the True Cross: we must therefore refer this allegorical symbol to the religion of the country. . . ." His overall conclusions followed the same line, that the art of Palenque was probably original, with no clear European ancestry and not even any close resemblance to the pre-Hispanic art of Mexico, that of the Aztec and their predecessors.

Dupaix's report, like Del Rio's, was sent circuitously to England, where it appeared as part of Lord Kingsborough's massive nine-volume *Antiquities of Mexico* in 1829–1831 and thus came to the attention of the learned world. It was also published in Paris in 1834, with a number of commentaries by French savants; the most interesting is that of Alexandre Lenoir, who proposed a three-phase chronology for Mexico with the Aztec being preceded in the twelfth century by the Toltec and others, and earliest of all, "Antiquities of Palenque and others of the same nature . . . the origins of which go so far back in time and are totally unknown."

The Paris publication of Dupaix won a competition for a description of Palenque set by the Société de Géographie, frustrating another hopeful candidate, Jean-Frédéric Waldeck, who in late middle age had just spent many months in 1832–1833 at Palenque, making numerous drawings and molds of the stucco sculptures. The accuracy of his drawings, some of which are preserved in the Bibliothèque Nationale in Paris, is sometimes far greater than his modern reputation for imaginative invention allows.

In 1838 Waldeck published *Voyage pittoresque et archéologique dans . . . Yucatan* which, although it contained little solid archaeology, was the book that stimulated John Lloyd Stephens into undertaking his first expedition. Most of his drawings were not published until 1866, when *Recherches sur les Ruines de Palenque* appeared with a text by the Abbé Brasseur de Bourbourg, Waldeck's text being thought unsuitable. Waldeck himself died in 1875, at an indeterminate but ripe old age (he claimed to be 109), allegedly from turning too quickly to admire a passing mademoiselle; his life seems to have been full and entertaining, but his impact on Maya studies was small.

One of the last explorers of the Spanish period, who in fact lived during the period when New Spain took its independence, was Juan Galindo; he was, in spite of his name, a British subject, born in Dublin in 1802 and killed during the civil war in Central America in 1840, only a short distance from where Stephens and Catherwood were beginning their explorations; they never met. At the age of 29 Galindo had been appointed governor of Petén, the vast rain-forest province in northern Guatemala, and given a large grant of land; both title and estates proved insubstantial, but during his sojourn in the Petén, Galindo reported on and possibly visited the standing ruins of Topoxte on a series of islands in Lake Yaxha. In 1831 he visited Palenque, which he saw with presciently modern eyes as a focus of interregional trade contacts, and sent a small collection of artifacts to the Royal Society in London.

Galindo then moved south into the highlands, and in 1834 explored the ruins of Copan. His conscientious report identified "writings always placed in almost square blocks containing faces and hands and other identical characters," and included twenty-six illustrations. Although his brief summaries sent to journals in England and the United States were published (the latter probably sent Stephens and Catherwood first to Copan), his official report to the

government of Central America and the copy of it sent with
the illustrations to the Société de Géographie in Paris were
not, and it remained for the British scholar Ian Graham to
bring him the credit he deserves by publishing his material
in 1963.

The Major Scholars

The third phase of Maya studies might be characterized as
that of a succession of individuals working alone or with
only incidental support from museums or universities,
whose achievements were essentially individual rather
than collaborative. This period began with the second expedition of Stephens and Catherwood in 1841–1842, their
first being effectively the culmination of the series of otherwise Spanish-inspired expeditions directed almost exclusively to Palenque, and the year 1840 is a useful date to use.
The period ended with the beginning of multidisciplinary
archaeological study under the aegis of the Carnegie Institution of Washington in 1924, and thus spans more than
eighty years.

Just after *Incidents of Travel in Yucatan* had been published in New York, a young French priest became honor-
ary vicar-general in Boston, where he was introduced to
the recent work of the local author William Prescott, the
History of the Conquest of Mexico. Stimulated by this, in
1849 Charles Etienne Brasseur de Bourbourg traveled to
Mexico, and thereafter devoted the rest of his life to studying the pre-Hispanic cultures of the country. When he was
recalled to France in 1851 he had access for three years to
J. M. A. Aubin's superb research library of Mexican manuscripts and books, and later helped to found the Société des
Américanistes, which had among its aims the publication
of the manuscripts.

In 1854 he obtained leave to travel through Central
America, and beginning in Nicaragua went west into Guatemala. There he spent two years, including one as parish
priest of the Quiché town of Rabinal. Here he found that a
pre-Hispanic drama was still passed down in oral tradition,
and transcribed it: the *Rabinal-Achí* is one of the few surviving fragments of pre-Hispanic Maya literature.

Another fragment turned up in the capital, where a
Quiché manuscript of the *Popol Vuh*, the Book of Counsel,

including part of a lost epic cycle of legends, was preserved. Other scholars had also had access to the manuscript, and it was published by Karl Scherzer in Vienna and by Francisco Ximénez in Spain, the first including the Quiché text, in 1857, four years before Brasseur's parallel Quiché and French edition appeared.

Ending his travels in 1857, Brasseur brought together his accumulated knowledge in the *Histoire des nations civilisées du Mexique et de l'Amérique central* which, as its four volumes came out over the next two years, made his international reputation as a scholar. He remains best known, however, for a discovery made in 1863, prosaically in the files of the Academy of History in Madrid—the copy of Diego de Landa's missing *Relación de las cosas de Yucatan*. He was also responsible for the discovery of part of one of the three surviving Maya hieroglyphic manuscripts, the Madrid Codex.

Brasseur was, in fact, essentially a library scholar, a man who found documents more exciting than artifacts or ruins. He stands at the beginning of a line of similar major scholars of the later nineteenth century, whose contributions were made at the desk rather than in the field, and most of whom were concerned with the elucidation of the Maya calendar and Maya hieroglyphic writing, for which Brasseur's publication of Landa had provided the vital catalyst.

Research on Maya writing proceeded on both sides of the Atlantic. In 1882 the American scholar Cyrus Thomas showed that the correct way to read the hieroglyphics was from top to bottom in pairs of columns, and from left to right, so that an inscription began like the modern printed English page, in the top left-hand corner (Figure 1.7). Already the Frenchman Léon de Rosny had in 1876 deciphered the directional glyphs for north, south, east, and west, and had used the Madrid Codex and a second Maya book, the Paris Codex, in his work.

Study of the calendar began with the publication between 1880 and 1887 of a series of papers by Ernst Förstemann, librarian to the Elector of Saxony, in whose collection at Dresden lay the best-preserved of the three Maya books, the Dresden Codex. Förstemann had read Landa, and also the work by Pio Perez that Stephens had so as-

tutely brought to publication; the latter contained the information that the Maya used a dot for *1* and a bar for *5*, and
Förstemann was able to show that the Maya had used a
place-notation, to a base of 20 rather than our own base of
10, to express numbers larger than 19. He also deciphered
the signs for zero or completion (as we regard the 0 in *10*
as completing the higher grouping, but also expressing
zero in terms of left-over units). With the basis of Maya
mathematics established, he was able to unravel the tables
of multiples in the Dresden Codex and to work out the
complex records that established the movements of the
planet Venus.

Landa had mentioned a "calculation of ages" using the
katun, a period of about twenty years, and said that it was
easy for an old man "to recall events which he said had
taken place 300 years before." Although Landa probed no
further into this claim, Förstemann was able to demonstrate the existence of the great cumulative counting of
years known as the Long Count, and its beginning on a
date 4 Ahau 8 Cumhu in what is now accepted as 3114 B.C.
With this information, Förstemann in 1894 was able to
read the Long Count dates contained in the Initial Series
inscriptions (see Chapter 4) on seven of the stelae at
Copan.

Although the internal structure of the Long Count was
now clear, it had not been linked to the Christian calendar,
so that the absolute age of the Maya inscriptions was still
problematical. The correlation, using items of historical information recorded by Landa and others, was finally made
by Joseph T. Goodman in 1905. Goodman, a middle-aged
newspaper proprietor on the West Coast, had been the first
to recognize the talents of the young Mark Twain; in Maya
studies his major contributions were the calendric correlation that bears his name and the identification of the
numbers 0–19 expressed as profile heads instead of bars
and dots (see Chapter 4, p. 109).

The copies of inscriptions used by both Förstemann and
Goodman were drawings of the monuments, made from
plaster casts taken by Alfred Maudslay (Figure 2.4) between 1883 and 1894. Maudslay, who had fallen by chance
into a diplomatic career in the south Pacific, was visiting
Guatemala for health and pleasure when he first saw the

2.4. Alfred Maudslay at Chichén Itzá in 1886.

sculptures of Quirigua and Copan, and "it began to dawn upon me how more important were these monuments . . . than any account I had heard of them led me to expect." He returned equipped with paper and plaster of Paris for making casts, a large plate camera, and surveying apparatus. His molds, shipped to London, were used to produce copies of the monuments which now, because of subsequent erosion, show more detail than the stelae, altars, and zoomorphic carvings do themselves. From the copies drawings were made, mostly by Annie Hunter, and these were published, together with Maudslay's superb photographs, in the sixteen paperbound volumes of *Biologia Centrali–Americana: Archaeology* that appeared between 1889 and 1902.

Maudslay returned to the Maya area again and again, exploring Tikal, Palenque, and Chichén Itzá after Quirigua and Copan (Figures 2.9, 7.5, 7.6, 9.20, 9.21, 10.6, 10.7). One of his earliest expeditions was to the newly reported site of Yaxchilan on the Usumacinta River, where he removed, with government permission, a number of sculptured lintels from fallen buildings and dispatched them to the British Museum. He also encountered the French explorer Désiré Charnay, 22 years older than himself, the man who had pioneered photography of Maya ruins in 1858, when he had recorded Palenque and Uxmal. Charnay wryly tells how he, hoping to be the first to reach the site of Yaxchilan, found "le jeune homme fort blond" already there, who graciously ceded to him the right of discovery with the remark that he, Maudslay, was only an amateur, and that Charnay was free to "name the town, claim to have discovered it . . . and even dispense with mentioning my name if you please." Maudslay modestly recorded only that Charnay had kindly shared his rations with him.

Alfred Maudslay matched John Lloyd Stephens in assiduity, and explored his sites with a thoroughness and skill that have never been exceeded. He carried the study, as opposed to the mere exploration, of Maya ruins to a new degree of competence, and his photographs and the drawings he published are still a primary research tool of Maya scholars. He also encouraged the work of others, making sure that Goodman's work on Maya dates was published by having it included in *Biologia Centrali–Americana*, and sending the indomitable Adela Breton to make watercolor copies of the fading and crumbling frescoes at Chichén Itzá. Although for the last thirty years of his life he had little to do with active Maya research he remained interested until the end; in the late 1920s both *The Times* of London and the Royal Geographical Society published his comments on matters of current discussion. The importance of his contribution is undiminished, and he remains, in the words of H. E. D. Pollock, "the first modern archaeologist in the Maya field."

Slightly older than Maudslay, but a much later entrant into the field of Maya exploration, was Teobert Maler, a German-born Austrian national who had come to Mexico with the Hapsburg army to prop up the ill-fated empire of Maximilian. With the collapse of the empire in 1865 Maler chose to stay in Mexico, and he wandered east through Oaxaca to Palenque, where in 1877 he spent a week and decided to devote his time to Maya archaeology. While at Palenque he met the Swiss botanist Gustave Bernoulli, who is noted for having removed (Maler says with official permission) one of the magnificent carved lintels of Tikal, which is now in the museum at Basel.

In 1884, after some years in Europe, Maler returned to buy a house in Mérida and fulfill his intention of studying the Maya. He began a series of explorations, traveling light with his local workmen under what Ian Graham has called "vile conditions," which resulted in the discovery of several important sites in the Usumacinta basin, including Piedras Negras (Figure 7.3), Altar de Sacrificios, and Seibal, and the great site of Coba in northern Quintana Roo. The "romance of archaeology" had little effect on Maler: "Wandering about from one year's end to another in these inaccessible wildernesses in search of remnants of bygone civilizations . . . constitutes a kind of immolation," he remarked in one of his monographs, *Explorations in the Upper Usumatsintla and Adjacent Regions.* This and other studies were published between 1901 and 1911 by the Peabody Museum of Harvard University (which followed up Maler's work at Altar de Sacrificios and Seibal in two major projects between 1959 and 1968); but sadly Maler quarrelled with the Museum, which he decided was making a profit by selling his reports, and much work remained unpublished. He died in 1917, during the First World War, and as Robert Brunhouse has pointed out, the anti-German jingoism of the time left his contribution to Maya studies insufficiently appreciated.

Another lone explorer working for the Peabody Museum was Raymond Merwin, who carried out a series of expeditions between 1910 and 1915 in the eastern part of the Maya lowlands, including Quintana Roo, Petén, and British Honduras (Belize). He was the first man to explore or make accurate records of a number of important sites, including

Lubaantun, from which he sent back three ball-court markers carved with scenes of the game being played (Figure 9.26). These he had found in the alley between two parallel mounds in the southern part of the site, and had thus identified for the first time a Classic period ball court in the tropical forest zone (although they were known in Yucatan from the time of Stephens onward). Merwin's most significant discovery came, however, at the site he called Holmul, in the northeastern Petén. In a series of superimposed buildings that he excavated there he isolated the first ceramic sequence known in the Maya Area, and also found for the first time evidence of the Holmul I or Protoclassic phase at the end of the Preclassic, a flowering especially of ceramic art, which seems to antedate the full development of Classic Maya civilization and to bring elements of highland culture into the lowlands at this crucial time (see Chapter 4, pp. 124–127).

Merwin unfortunately fell ill, and died without publishing his significant discoveries. The Holmul work was eventually edited by George C. Vaillant and appeared in 1932, after the ceramic sequence at Uaxactun had already been established in outline, but his description of Lubaantun was not published until 1975 and the rest of his work remains in typescript at Harvard.

The Peabody Museum also sponsored the work of Edward H. Thompson, a Massachusetts youth whose enthusiasm was fired by reading Stephens and Brasseur de Bourbourg, and who came to the notice of the influential antiquary Stephen Salisbury, Jr. The post of American consul in Mérida was obtained for Thompson, with the implicit duty of carrying out Maya research for the Peabody Museum. His first assessment was that the Maya "ruins indicate a considerable civilization . . . above the communal pueblos of the Southwest, but not of that advanced state of progress that sends forth a far-reaching influence." It was a modest and reasonable conclusion not belied by subsequent work.

Thompson worked initially at Labna, a site little disturbed by looters or tourists (both existing even in 1885). He early on concluded that the bottle-shaped chambers dug into bedrock, called *chultunob*, were used for storage, and was also the first to appreciate the significance of what is now called "settlement archaeology," using ethnographic comparisons drawn from contemporary Maya dwellings to support his deductions. The small platforms called house-mounds were "once covered by the mud-walled, palm-thatched houses of these humbler classes. . . . Excavating these sites I find the ever-present *koben*, the three-stone fireplace, the broken pottery in the ashes, the fractured *metatl* and roller with which the corn was ground, and children's toys in the shape of polished sea-shells and bits of figured clay, hard burned." The number of corn-grinding stones he found to be similar in ancient and modern Maya houses, and he therefore calculated that like the modern, the pre-Hispanic Maya diet must have consisted of some 80% maize, 12% other vegetable crops, and 8% meat.

The identification of houses similar to those of the modern Maya led him to conclude in a paper that the "Ancient Structures of Yucatan [were] not Communal Dwellings," the title of a presentation to the American Antiquarian Society in 1892. This early interest in the everyday life of the Maya was subordinated in the field at large to studies of hieroglyphic writing, art, and architecture, and it is only since the Second World War that settlement archaeology has again become a major focus of research.

Thompson made a number of molds of architecture and sculpture at Labna and Uxmal for the 1893 Chicago World's Fair, where their display led to Thompson's acquisition of the money to buy the hacienda and ruins of Chichén Itzá, where he had already assisted Maudslay in 1889. He began a program of excavation there, including the small simulacrum of the Castillo known as the High Priest's Grave (the work on which was eventually published after his death by his unrelated namesake, Eric Thompson). In 1904 he started to dredge the Cenote of Sacrifice, the deep, water-filled hole with vertical sides that lay north of the Castillo, and after modest initial results, began to find carved jades, worked gold plaques, copper and wooden objects, human bones, and many balls of copal incense. Many of the more precious objects were sent quietly to the Peabody Museum, where scholars such as Alfred Tozzer, Samuel Lothrop, and Tatiana Proskouriakoff worked on them for many years (the jades, for instance, being published only in 1975), and where they became the object of demands from the Mexican government for their return.

The objects from the cenote proved an invaluable source of information: the metalwork had come from as far to the east and west as Panama and Oaxaca, and the human remains were for decades the best evidence on the physical characteristics of the ancient Maya themselves. Although Edward H. Thompson was perhaps not a major scholar, he made a substantial contribution to our knowledge, and his was among the last individual enterprises in the history of Maya archaeology.

The Institutional Period

The fourth phase of exploration is in strong contrast, an institutional period in which the field was dominated by teams of scholars working in concert on a given site or area. The dominant institution was the Division of Historical Research of the Carnegie Institution of Washington (C.I.W.), until its dissolution in 1958, and the period began with its entry into the Maya field, taking over Edward Thompson's work at Chichén Itzá in 1923. It ended with the completion of two major university museum projects, that of the University of Pennsylvania Museum at Tikal, and that of the Peabody Museum of Harvard University at Altar de Sacrificios and Seibal, the latter ending in 1968.

The C.I.W. involvement at Chichén began entirely as the result of a proposal by Sylvanus G. Morley (Figure 2.5), a young Harvard graduate who had been brought into Maya archaeology as an assistant to Edgar L. Hewett on the School of American Research project at Quirigua, just before the First World War. Morley's proposal had in fact been accepted in 1914, but it was nearly a decade before fieldwork began. After the first seasons the project broadened into a multidisciplinary investigation of the natural and human ecology of Yucatan, in addition to the excavation and restoration of the ruins of Chichén. Much of the credit for this breadth of approach must go to Alfred V. Kidder, who became Morley's superior as head of the newly created Division of Historical Research in the late 1920s, but the practical execution of it remained Morley's.

Morley had two major influences on Maya studies. First, he was a planner and manager par excellence, who brought together the C.I.W. and the governments of Mexico and Guatemala (the latter for the second major project, at Uax-

2.5. Frances and Sylvanus G. Morley (left) with Eric and Florence Thompson at Chichén Itzá in 1930.

actun) to establish long-term research projects in those countries, and then recruited a staff of such quality that most became noted scholars in their own right—Oliver Ricketson, H. E. D. Pollock, Eric Thompson, Tatiana Proskouriakoff, Robert and Ledyard Smith. The greatest monument to Morley's managerial skill is the site of Chichén Itzá, which he turned from a ruin into a national monument of Mexico.

Morley's second major influence, and his governing passion, was in the field of hieroglyphic studies. He had begun, during the First World War, a project to collect and publish all known Maya inscriptions and to seek new ones, and in pursuit of this objective the C.I.W. sent a series of expeditions to the Petén and Yucatan. At one point Morley had a notice printed and put up all over Petén: *¡Ojo! ¡Ojo! ¡Ojo!* "Look! Look! Look!" it said, offering a reward of twenty-five dollars for each new inscription reported to Morley or his agents.

The project at Uaxactun resulted from the discovery there of Stela 9, for long the earliest dated Maya monument, A.D. 328. In addition to a number of early stelae the excavations yielded for the first time stratified pottery of the Preclassic or Formative period that preceded the Classic period during which the dated stelae were erected. Robert Smith, who worked on the pottery from Uaxactun for many years, divided this Formative period into an earlier

Mamom and a later Chicanel phase, the two together spanning the period from 500 B.C. to A.D. 300 (Figure 4.1). Although more recent work has pushed the beginnings of the
Formative period farther back in time, Smith's classifica-
tion and ceramic terminology remain at the heart of Maya
pottery studies.

Morley's obsession with hieroglyphic writing resulted in
two massive compilations, *The Inscriptions at Copan*,
which appeared in one volume in 1920, and *The Inscriptions of Petén*, which came out in five volumes in 1937–
1938. They remain a most valuable research tool, but Morley's conviction that "the Maya inscriptions treat primarily
of chronology, astronomy and religious matters . . . they are
not records of personal glorification, they are so completely
impersonal that it is unlikely that the name glyphs of specific men were ever recorded on the monuments," was an
error that sent Maya epigraphy off on the wrong track for a
quarter of a century.

A scholar who shared Morley's views on the nature of
Maya inscriptions until nearly the end of his life was Sir
Eric Thompson (Figure 2.5), knighted in the year of his
death, and the first British Mayanist to receive public recognition. Thompson's career began in 1926 with a season
working under Morley at Chichén, followed by a season in
1927 with the British Museum Expedition to British Honduras, working at Lubaantun under Thomas A. Joyce. He
was also recruited by the Field Museum at Chicago and
directed two important projects in British Honduras before
being hired by the C.I.W., where he remained until his
retirement.

Thompson is remarkable for having integrated archaeological fieldwork, hieroglyphic decipherment, and the use
of ethnographic observation and ethnohistoric documents
into his scholarship; his breadth of approach can be seen
from the publications during only the first four years of his
career, from 1927 to 1930. He wrote a guide for the Field
Museum, *The Civilization of the Maya*, which in its seventh edition still sells many copies each year; he published
his correlation of the Maya and Christian calendars, a correction of that advanced by Goodman and Martínez Hernández, which is still widely accepted (and is used in this
book); he published the newly discovered stelae from Pu-

silha in southern British Honduras, which he had been
the first archaeologist to see; he contributed to the 1927
Lubaantun report compiled by Joyce; and he produced a
monograph on the ethnography of the Maya of central and
southern British Honduras which emphasized the survival
of pre-Hispanic traits in modern Maya culture.

In the early 1930s Thompson undertook excavations at
San José, a small site in central British Honduras, with the
explicit intention of studying a small center that would
yield a different kind of information than that from the
large sites that had until then been the focus of attention.
He hoped that it would be an "average" site, characteristic
rather than unique, and coined the term "ceremonial center" to describe Maya sites instead of "city," which begged
too many questions about structure and function.

After the last season at San José in 1936 Thompson did
little excavation, but became the leading Maya epigrapher, specializing in attempts to decipher the noncalendric
glyphs. Like Morley, he was convinced of the esoteric and
ahistoric content of the Maya inscriptions, but when in the
1960s contrary evidence appeared, he admitted his mis-
take. Thompson was also convinced that Maya writing was
not phonetic, and in the 1950s and 1960s pursued a vigorous dispute with the Russian epigrapher Yurii Knorosov.
Further work in the 1970s by linguists such as Floyd
Lounsbury seems to indicate that Knorosov was in principle correct, and Thompson wrong: many Maya glyphs do
represent syllables, and can be combined to form words
that do not necessarily reflect the sum of the meanings of
the individual glyphs.

Apart from the C.I.W., a number of other institutions carried out fieldwork in the Maya area. The newly founded
Department of Middle American Research at Tulane University in New Orleans sent Frans Blom and Oliver La
Farge on an expedition to Veracruz, Tabasco, Chiapas, and
highland Guatemala, and after Blom became director of
the department several other expeditions followed. In the
1930s the University of Pennsylvania Museum carried out
several seasons of excavation at Piedras Negras, but only
preliminary reports were ever published; and the British
Museum, between 1926 and 1931, carried out six seasons
of work in southern British Honduras, mainly at Lubaan-

tun and Pusilha, under the direction of Thomas A. Joyce.

One of the doyens of Maya studies during the institutional period was Alfred M. Tozzer, the first Bowditch Professor of Mexican and Central American Archaeology and Ethnology at Harvard University; in 1940 he was honored by a volume of papers, *The Maya and Their Neighbors*, with contributions from many Carnegie staff members and others in the field. An exception to the generally factual nature of the papers, and a trenchant criticism of them and the C.I.W. approach, was the contribution by the social anthropologist Clyde Kluckhohn. He accused Mayanists of being obsessed with factual detail at the expense of a whole picture of an extinct society, an accusation that eight years later was to be brought by Walter Taylor against the whole establishment of American archaeology. Kluckhohn had a valid point: the history of Maya studies until then had consisted of the acquisition of information, and few scholars had begun to do anything with it.

The next major innovation in approach did not come until 1953, when Gordon R. Willey, Tozzer's successor at Harvard, brought into the Maya area the techniques of settlement archaeology he had used to analyze pre-Hispanic occupation of the Virú Valley on the north coast of Peru (Figure 2.6). Willey selected a portion of the Belize River valley in central British Honduras for a regional project. The focus of investigation was an area of river terrace cleared of bush at Barton Ramie (Figure 5.8), where sev-

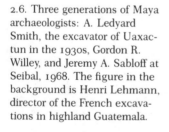

2.6. Three generations of Maya archaeologists: A. Ledyard Smith, the excavator of Uaxactun in the 1930s, Gordon R. Willey, and Jeremy A. Sabloff at Seibal, 1968. The figure in the background is Henri Lehmann, director of the French excavations in highland Guatemala.

eral hundred small house-mounds had been noted. No major ceremonial structures lay in or near the site, and this fitted in with Willey's plan to study an area of residential development. It was an unusual approach—Thompson's San José project had explored a small ceremonial precinct, but had not sought its surrounding settlement, while Ricketson's settlement survey around Uaxactun in the late 1920s had been centered on the ceremonial precinct.

For the first time, at Barton Ramie a large sample of house-mounds was investigated and an attempt at total excavation was made on several structures. A long cultural sequence, estimated to run back to at least 600 B.C. (now known to be several centuries longer than that), and a regional site survey were integrated into a study, published in 1965, that has become a landmark in Maya archaeology.

The Barton Ramie project was followed by two other major Peabody Museum excavations, both in the Pasión valley at sites explored by Maler—Altar de Sacrificios and Seibal —and both directed by Willey and Ledyard Smith (Figure 2.6). At both sites specific problems were addressed: at Altar the nature of highland-lowland interaction, and at Seibal a Late Classic florescence of an unusual nature; the settlement survey at Seibal, by Gair Tourtellot, was among the most ambitious yet achieved in the Maya lowlands.

A project on an even larger scale was carried out at Tikal, in northeastern Petén, by the University of Pennsylvania Museum under Edwin Shook and then William Coe from 1955–1966 (Figure 2.7). Large-scale excavation and restoration of the huge temples and acropoles in the ceremonial precinct, which was a square mile in area, were accompanied by a mapping program and excavations in the surrounding settlement on an unprecedented scale. So much information was produced that even by 1981 the final reports had not begun to appear; the Tikal Project trained an entire generation of Maya archaeologists and they and the data so far released in interim reports and specialized papers have had an enormous impact on the field.

Although these two institutions dominated the Maya field in the 1950s and 1960s, two other projects were on a substantial scale: at Dzibilchaltun, in the flat plain of Yucatan northwest of Mérida, extensive mapping and excavation were carried out by a Tulane University–National

Geographic Society project under E. Wyllys Andrews IV. Andrews claimed that the site was extremely large, bringing within its bounds groups of buildings that other archaeologists thought should be defined as being separate sites. He also felt that the development of Maya architecture in the late first millennium A.D., exemplified by Dzibilchaltun among other northern sites, was so complex that a longer span of time had to be allowed for it than most other Mayanists were prepared to concede. To this end Andrews argued in favor of a correlation of Maya and Christian calendars in which the date 12.9.0.0.0. of the Long Count fell in the mid-sixteenth century; most scholars accepted, and still accept in preference to this Spinden correlation (named for Herbert Joseph Spinden, a noted art specialist and epigrapher whose career spanned the first half of this century), the Goodman-Martínez-Thompson correlation in which the Long Count date 11.16.0.0.0. falls in 1539. On the Spinden scheme all Maya dates, and therefore the florescence of Classic Maya civilization, would fall 260 years earlier (roughly A.D. 40–640) than with the G-M-T correlation in which they cover ca. A.D. 300–900. Argument over the correlation question continued well into the 1960s, until a long series of radiocarbon dates from inscribed wooden lintels at Tikal favored the 11.16. version; over the past decade there has been general acceptance of this, although some noted scholars such as David H. Kelley still dispute it, and new correlations are occasionally proposed.

Another Mexican site where significant work has been carried out in the period since World War II is Palenque, where the Mexican archaeologists Alberto Ruz L. and Jorge R. Acosta successively directed operations. Ruz made one of the most famous and spectacular discoveries of the century when working on the Temple of the Inscriptions in 1949; he noted stone plugs set into holes in the floor slabs in the inner room, and reasoned that these had been used to lower the slabs on ropes. When he raised them, he found a descending stairway, choked with rubble, which over the next four seasons he removed. At the bottom of the stair, below the ground surface on which the pyramid was raised, the skeletons of six slain youths lay outside a great stone door. Within was a tomb chamber with elaborate stucco decorations around the walls, which was almost filled by a

Opposite:
2.7. Tikal: the University of Pennsylvania excavations in the north acropolis in the early 1960s. The large pyramid in the foreground, Structure 5D-33-1st, was totally removed in 1965 during the project, arousing some dissension among scholars.

stone sarcophagus with an elaborately carved lid (Figure 2.8), and the sarcophagus contained the jade-decked skeleton of a man who has since been identified as Pacal, the first great ruler of Palenque in the seventh century A.D.

One of the last projects in this period was that at Becan, a large site in the center of the lowlands with a moated ceremonial precinct; the project began under E. Wyllys Andrews IV, but on his death was concluded by Richard E. W. Adams. It, like that at Dzibilchaltun, was notable for the long-term participation of the National Geographic Society with Tulane University. The results were of great importance: the backdating of the moat, presumed to be Terminal Classic, to the end of the Preclassic period led to a theory of warfare as a cause of complex social entities and thus of lowland Maya civilization, and demonstrated the great resources at the call of rulers in the Late Preclassic period. The project also included a survey of settlement and subsistence patterns, and the discovery and mapping of many square kilometers of terraced and walled fields has led to a drastic revision of our ideas about Maya agriculture in the Classic period. The site also yielded a long ceramic sequence, beginning in the early part of the Middle Preclassic period, and evidence of direct contact with Teotihuacan during the Early Classic period. Overall, the Becan project changed accepted notions about Maya civilization to a substantial degree.

All of the projects of the late institutional period were devoted to the excavation of major sites, and except for Altar de Sacrificios included substantial restoration work to prepare the sites for visitors, as tourism began to have an increasing economic impact. They were also, however, devoted to problems of what came to be called "culture process," understanding the how and why of Maya civilization as well as the when and where and what.

The projects thus far described (Figure 2.9) were carried out in the lowland zone (see Chapter 3); the highlands, although not devoid of interest, have received comparatively little attention because of the unspectacular nature of the sites: lost cities in the jungle are far more appealing to the explorer than dusty mounds amid farmland. Most of the highland sites lack the carved monuments and the romance of the lowland centers, and there has been a great

Opposite:
2.8. Palenque: the carved lid of the sarcophagus of Pacal, ruler of Palenque in the seventh century A.D., discovered by the Mexican archaeologist Alberto Ruz L. in the early 1950s. From a rubbing by Merle Greene Robertson.

deal of erosion, making already unspectacular sites even more so. Nevertheless, some early recording was carried out—at Utatlan by Miguel Rivera y Maestre in 1834, a study that Stephens used, and by Brasseur de Bourbourg around Rabinal in 1855–1856. In 1894 Maudslay devoted part of his last expedition, which was more a leisurely holiday with his wife, to recording highland sites, and he brought together his notes in published form as part of their joint book *A Glimpse at Guatemala* (1899).

Most of the substantial work in the highlands has been done since the Second World War: in the late 1940s the United Fruit Company sponsored the excavation and publication of the findings at Zaculeu, the Postclassic capital of the Mam at Huehuetenango, and also had the buildings restored; it was a rare example of corporate sponsorship in Maya archaeology. The work at Zaculeu was carried out by North American archaeologists Richard Woodbury and Aubrey Trik, but another late highland capital, Iximche, was excavated and restored in the 1960s by the Guatemalan Society for Anthropology and History, under the direction of Jorge Guillemin. A third such site, thought at the time to be Mixco Viejo, was the first of three French projects in the Maya Area. Like Zaculeu and Iximche, it was a fortified hilltop site, and the ceremonial precinct was excavated and restored by Henri Lehmann. A second project, under Alain Ichon, has been working at the important Preclassic and Classic site of Lagunita in the highlands of El Quiché, and a third has been investigating the large ceremonial center of Tonina in highland Chiapas, with results that include one of the latest Initial Series stelae known (Figure 4.18). North American activity in the highlands has also continued, with a study of the Quiché based on excavation of their capital at Utatlan, but embracing all branches of anthropology and linguistics as well as archaeology. Probably the most important projects, however, have been the salvage excavations at Kaminaljuyu during the 1970s, as more and more of the site disappeared under the expanding suburbs of Guatemala City, and the excavations at Abaj Takalik on the Pacific piedmont near Retalhuleu. At this latter site a number of early sculptures have been found, including Maya inscriptions with dates going back to at least the first century B.C. and late Olmec works; the site has also yielded a number of early, if confusing, radio-carbon dates. The results promise to revise our ideas about the origins of Maya writing and also to provide the high-land zone with the Early Preclassic sequence that has proved elusive at so many sites.

Problem Orientation

The economic climate at the end of the 1960s precluded further massive investigations on the scale of those at Tikal, and although academic institutions, mainly in North America, and government departments in the Maya coun-tries continued to sponsor fieldwork, it was on a smaller scale and with more attention to specific problems. In this, Maya archaeology was reflecting some of the changes brought about by the "New Archaeology" in North Amer-ica, in which the formulation and testing of explicit hy-potheses was a dominant theme and the use of the com-puter for detailed statistical work a necessity.

Thus the fifth, problem-oriented phase of Maya studies is one in which smaller budgets and less excavation have been augmented by more detailed notions of why a particu-lar project should be undertaken. A greater underlying confidence that the broad outlines of Maya cultural history are now known has been a major factor in the conceptual reorientation of the subject toward specific problems, al-though in fact large areas in space and time remain little known and the traditional project of exploration, mapping, and excavation, simply to add to our range of knowledge, still has its place.

One of the first of the problem-oriented projects was that carried out on the island of Cozumel, off the east coast of Yucatan, in 1972–1973 by Jeremy Sabloff of Harvard and William Rathje of the University of Arizona. Their research design advanced a specific model of a trading settlement and its functions, and suggested ways in which hypotheses about varying functions could be tested archaeologically. The project was also notable as one of the first occasions on which large numbers of undergraduate students were used as a labor force with only a few local workmen, instead of the traditional pattern of a large local force directed by pro-fessionals, with or without the assistance of a few graduate students.

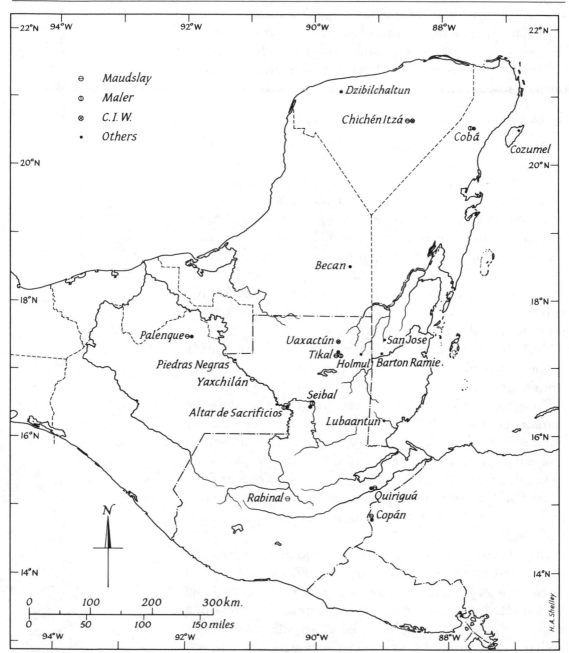

2.9. Explorations in the Maya
Area in the late nineteenth and
twentieth centuries: some important sites.

In other problem-oriented projects the natural sciences
were used extensively, as in Robert Rands and Ronald
Bishop's study of the manufacture and trading of pottery
vessels in the area around Palenque and the use of these
data to define an area of economic dominance for the site.

The application of such techniques as neutron-activation analysis to determine the source, and hence the distribution patterns, of materials as diverse as pottery, obsidian, and jade have become commonplace, and for obsidian in particular a detailed picture of changing source exploitation and trade-route utilization is emerging.

Some problems are more practical: the increase in market value of looted Maya sculpture in the 1960s led to the devastation of both known and previously unknown sites; some scholars and many museum directors collaborated in the destruction by allowing the purchase of the stolen material. In the face of this, Morley's dream of a complete corpus of Maya monuments, with the sculpture receiving as much attention as the inscriptions, was revived under the direction of Ian Graham at Harvard. The first few volumes of the corpus have already appeared, but the project may well last until the end of this century.

While Graham's project has, like Maudslay's, concentrated on providing epigraphers with accurately recorded inscriptions, the decipherment of Maya writing has been revolutionized over the past twenty years. The major change has been the demonstration that the content of the inscriptions is historical and mundane, as Stephens and Maudslay thought, and not astronomical, ritual, and esoteric, as Morley and Thompson asserted.

The process began in 1958, when Heinrich Berlin showed that emblem glyphs were site-specific and could be dynastic or place names. Then in 1960 Tatiana Proskouriakoff, in a famous paper in *American Antiquity*, demonstrated that the pattern of erection of stelae at the site of Piedras Negras was consonant with the lifetimes of several rulers, commemorating their births and accessions. She then showed that a similar pattern of life-spans could be adduced in the inscriptions of Yaxchilan, and David Kelley used the same methods at Quirigua; since then the inscriptions of Tikal, Copan, and Palenque have been partially deciphered. Probably the most extensive work has been at Palenque, where Floyd Lounsbury, Linda Schele, and Peter Mathews have suggested a complete dynastic sequence for the seventh to the ninth centuries.

Thus the present phase of Maya studies comprises several kinds of intellectual activity: one group of workers concentrates on the recovery, publication, and decipherment of hieroglyphic inscriptions and their associated iconography; another deals with the economic foundations of Maya civilization—its agriculture and settlements; a third is concerned with the chronology, trade, and other kinds of information that may be extracted from the study of pottery and stone artifacts; and a fourth is adding to our range of knowledge by continuing to excavate sites of all periods throughout the Maya lands. Some individuals work in more than one of these groups, although the groups themselves are less interdependent than might be expected in a relatively small discipline, and interact surprisingly little with the similar groups of scholars working in other parts of Mesoamerica.

Nevertheless, the sum of these efforts has begun to give us a broad picture of Maya civilization and how it operated, from its emergence in the early centuries A.D. to its collapse and partial revival. We now know the names of some individual Maya rulers and can follow their careers, while the undocumented efforts of farmers, artisans, and merchants can be elucidated by the archaeologist and scientist to give us an understanding of the way in which Maya agriculture, economy, and trade functioned. The Maya are being dragged from prehistory into history, and in the process are losing some of their mystery, though none of their interest.

3

The Maya Lands and Their People

WHERE are the Maya lands? And if we can define them on a map, what is our justification for doing so? Is it the present distribution of those who call themselves Maya, or whom scholars define as such, or should we bear in mind the great changes that have taken place since the Spanish conquest, and define the Maya lands by the distribution of archaeological sites of Maya cultural type? In other words, do we work from the world of the living Maya, or from the ruins of their ancestors?

Luckily we can take both approaches: the general distribution of ancient Maya sites coincides with the pattern of languages linked into an overall linguistic group that we call Mayan, even though some formerly populous areas are now dense forest and in others post-Hispanic immigrants have pushed out the indigenous peoples. There is general agreement that the territory defined culturally as the Maya Area (Figure 3.1) consists basically of those parts of Mexico and Central America bounded on the west by the narrowing of the Isthmus of Tehuantepec, on the north by the Gulf of Mexico and the Caribbean coastline, on the south by the Pacific shore, and on the east by the Ulua and Lempa basins draining respectively north and south from the highlands of Honduras. No Maya speakers (apart from the Huastec far to the north on the Gulf of Mexico) and no culturally Maya sites lie beyond these boundaries, although conversely the area has been penetrated both linguistically and culturally by non-Maya groups at various times in the pre-Hispanic and historic past.

The whole area lies between 14° and 22° North, entirely within the Tropics, and between 87° and 93° West; it is some 900 kilometers (550 miles) from north to south— roughly the same distance as from St. Louis to New Orleans—and from east to west is some 550 kilometers (350

3.1. The Maya Area, showing
modern political boundaries.

miles) along the continental divide, close to the Pacific
coast, and about 400 kilometers (250 miles) across the peninsula of Yucatan. The overall area of the Maya lands is
comparable to that of New Mexico or the British Isles.

   In terms of modern frontiers, about half the Maya Area
lies within Mexico, including most of Chiapas and Tabasco

and all of Campeche, Yucatan, and Quintana Roo (the last three forming the peninsula of Yucatan); the central part of the area is occupied by Guatemala, flanked by Belize (formerly British Honduras) on the east; and the southeastern part of the area falls within Honduras and El Salvador. The eastern parts of these two republics are both linguistically and culturally part of Central America, a region reaching south and east to Panama, while the Maya Area forms the eastern part of a cultural entity known as Mesoamerica, first defined by Paul Kirchoff in 1943 and embracing the area west and north to beyond Mexico City, into the arid plateaus of northern Mexico. The region of Mesoamerica immediately to the west of the Maya Area consists of the central Mexican highlands, including Oaxaca, and the northern piedmont and coastal plain of Veracruz. These two areas saw the rise of Olmec culture on the coast in the late second millennium B.C., followed by that of Classic Veracruz, and in the Oaxaca highlands the burgeoning of Zapotec and Mixtec cultures from the mid-first millennium B.C. onward. Still further northwest lie the highland basins of Central Mexico proper, where the urban civilizations of Teòtihuacan, Tula, and Aztec Tenochtitlan flourished from the time of Christ until the Spanish conquest, from time to time extending their influence eastward into the Maya lands. In both historic and prehistoric times the Maya had external contacts as far west as the Central Mexican Plateau and as far east as Panama. North of Yucatan, across a relatively narrow channel, lies Cuba, the westernmost island in the Antilles, with which some contact has been suggested but not proven.

The Landscape

Geologically the Maya Area forms part of "Middle America," a region that stretches from central Mexico to Colombia and forms a geological bridge between the North and South American continents. It is internally diverse (Figure 3.2), with four major geological zones of contrasting age and history: some of the mountain ranges of central Guatemala are of pre-Paleozoic date, while the flat limestone plateau of the northern Yucatan Peninsula emerged from the sea as late as the Tertiary period, hundreds of millions of years later. In the eons in between, parts of the area were

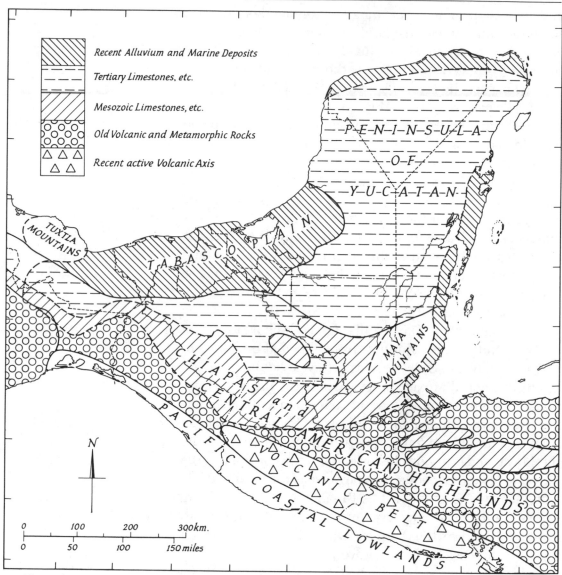

Recent Alluvium and Marine Deposits

Tertiary Limestones, etc.

Mesozoic Limestones, etc.

Old Volcanic and Metamorphic Rocks

Recent active Volcanic Axis

3.2. The geological structure of
the Maya lands.

so deformed and faulted by earth movements that the Guatemalan mountains have been called "the meat-grinder of
the gods," and the southern part of the highlands continues to be unstable, with numerous active volcanos forming
the continental divide from the Chiapas border southeast to
Nicaragua. The end result of these geological processes is
a landscape that can be divided into five basic physiograph-
ic regions, four of which coincide with the geological zones
noted above (the peninsula of Yucatan, the mountains of
central Guatemala and western Honduras, the volcanic

belt of southern Guatemala, and the Pacific coastal lowlands), and a fifth, the Tabasco plain, which is the eastern
end of the Mexican Gulf Coast lowlands (Figure 3.2).

Tabasco, the Pacific lowlands, the Caribbean coast of
northern Yucatan, Quintana Roo, and Belize are strips of
geologically recent alluvial deposits; the northern third
of the Yucatan Peninsula is of Tertiary limestone and marl
(*sascab*), while the southern part and the areas of Chiapas,
Petén, and Belize are of older limestones with greater elevation and relief and more developed drainage. Still further
south, older and more elevated are the Cretaceous and
Jurassic limestones, Triassic shales, and other sedimentary
rocks forming the hills of southern Petén, the Alta Verapaz,
and the foothills around the Maya Mountains in southern
Belize. (These mountains are a northern isolated block of
much older rocks, separated from the Guatemalan highlands.)

The three areas of limestone, becoming successively
younger in age and lower in elevation and relief from south
to north, form the land mass known to geologists as the
Yucatan Platform, which has been thrust by the movements of the earth's crust southward against the immov-
able body of the ancient highlands; as a result its southern
end has buckled slowly into high ridges, which have eroded into steep, forest-shrouded hills resembling, in Michael
Coe's words, "a Chinese landscape."

Beyond the ancient highlands to the south lies the belt of
Tertiary and Quaternary volcanic uplands, in which are a
number of basins filled with rich soil derived from volcanic
dust; some of the basins, such as those of Guatemala, Que-
zaltenango, and Huehuetenango, have been important
centers of human settlement from the early Formative period. The ancient and more recent mountain blocks are
separated by two major valleys, their rivers flowing in opposite directions out of a long geological depression: the
Motagua runs east and northeast to the Gulf of Honduras,
while the Grijalva flows through the central valley of Chiapas before turning north to the Gulf of Mexico.

This variable and complex geology provided the raw material from which the soils of the Maya Area were formed;
since climate, relief, and vegetation also contribute to the
nature of the soil, they are like the tesserae in a compli-

cated mosaic, with each change of slope, rainfall, and parent material resulting in a different soil. For example, near
the site of Lubaantun in southern Belize a single eight-
kilometer (five-mile) transect of the foothills crossed ten
distinct soils belonging to six different larger sets; as a result any generalization about the soils of the Maya Area
founders on a multitude of exceptions—not all volcanic
soils are rich in minerals, and not all of those in the lowlands
are calcium-rich. Nevertheless, some broad classifications
can be made: the limestone in Petén and Belize yields red-
dish-brown and yellowish-brown lateritic soils, while the
drier climate and underground drainage of northern Yucatan yield soils of the terra rossa and rendzina groups from a
parent limestone. The rendzina or similar black, calcium-
rich soils also occur in parts of Belize and Petén, however,
and in all areas an association between these soils and the
presence of ancient Maya sites has been noticed. A similar
association of sites with alluvial soils, especially those of
river levees, has been documented not only in the Maya
Area but in other parts of Mesoamerica—for instance,
around the major Olmec site of San Lorenzo in Veracruz.
The Maya themselves have a detailed terminology that recognizes the properties of different soils, with terms such as
tzekel ("stony land bad for sowing"), *ekluum* ("black
earth"), and *kankab-cat* ("potter's red earth").

The rocks and soil form only the solid component of the
Maya environment: the relief of the landscape, the drainage patterns that this governs, the climate that determines
the amount of rainfall, and the vegetation that the soil supports all interact on a continuous or seasonal basis.

Relief is determined principally by the geological structure of the landscape, and may be said to rise, at first slowly
and then rapidly, from the northern margin of Yucatan at
sea level southward through the peninsula and then the
Petén, into the highlands of Alta Verapaz and upward again
to the volcanic continental divide before descending swiftly
into the narrow Pacific coastal plain (Figure 3.3). Northern
Yucatan is so flat that Maya pyramids are the most prominent features in the landscape; the first hills are the Puuc
range just north of Uxmal, which begin a broad region of
rolling and undulating topography that reaches south into
Petén and Belize. The rise into Alta Verapaz occurs in sev-

Opposite:
3.3. Relief and drainage of the
Maya lands.

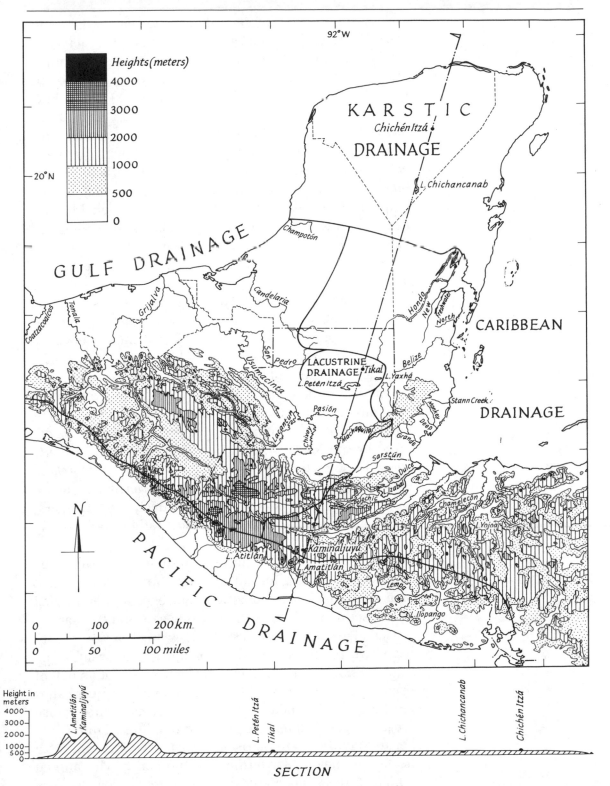

eral ascending tiers of steep limestone hills, which give place to the broken ranges of the Sierra de Chuacus and the Sierra de las Minas, the first of the ancient metamorphic uplands, rising to more than 3,000 meters (10,000 feet) elevation. The volcanic axis, with peaks such as Fuego, Agua, Pacaya, and Izalco, reaches more than 4,200 meters (14,000 feet) elevation, and contains several highly active peaks: Izalco erupted for the first time in 1770 and has done so twelve times since, while Fuego has erupted nine times since the Spanish conquest. Some ancient eruptions have left high lake basins of exceptional beauty, including Atitlan in western Guatemala and Ilopango in El Salvador, the latter formed by a cataclysm that occurred in the third century A.D., near the beginning of the Classic period.

The climate of the Maya Area (Figure 3.4) is as varied as its landscape, with startling changes of temperature and rainfall within fairly short distances, but the closeness of the sea, nowhere more than 250 kilometers (160 miles) away, and the tropical location together ensure a generally warm and humid regime. Altitude is the main factor in determining regional climates, and topography in establishing local variations within regions; these factors are recognized by the Maya, who classify land into *tierra caliente* below 1,000 meters elevation (3,300 feet), *tierra templada* between 1,000 and 2,000 meters and *tierra fria* above 2,000 meters (6,600 feet), with relatively cold temperatures for most of the year, subtropical rather than tropical in nature.

Both the Pacific and Caribbean shores are bathed by warm currents, and moisture-bearing winds blow inshore on both coasts. Those from the Pacific expend their rainfall on the southern slope of the volcanic axis and the narrow coastal plain, but the easterly trade winds from the Caribbean sweep across the whole of the lowland zone. The rainy season lasts from May to December, and at its height from August to October tropical cyclones or hurricanes reaching 180 kilometers (113 miles) an hour often cause great damage to forests, crops, and buildings. From October to May there are occasional *nortes*, cold storms with heavy rain moving down from North America. This annual rainfall pattern has resulted in most archaeological work

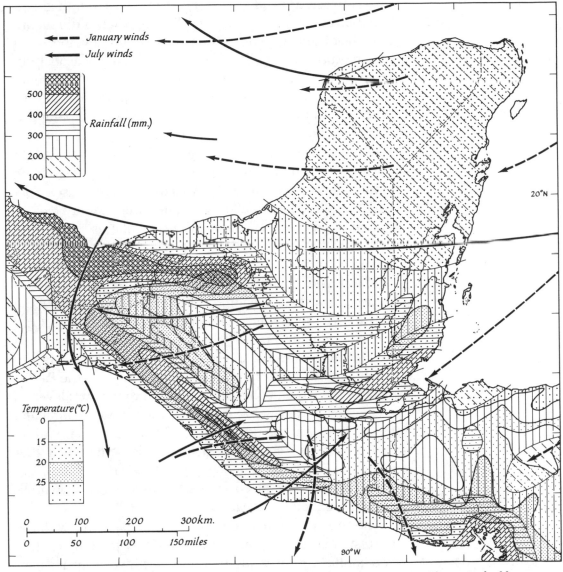

3.4. Climate in the Maya lands—rainfall, temperature, and winds.

being carried out during the dry season of January–May in the lowlands, although in some years it is possible to work through the summer without excavations being too much damaged by heavy rain.

The hottest part of the year is also, unfortunately, the dry season, because there is very little cloud cover to keep temperatures low during the day. (This also creates problems for archaeologists attempting to photograph their excavations without harsh shadows.) Temperatures are governed mainly by altitude, with the mean annual lowland tempera-

ture between 25° and 30° C. (77°–86° F.), that in the highland plateaus 15°–25° (59°–77° F.), and that in the mountains below 15° C. The difference between day and night
temperatures is usually far greater than the seasonal difference, and nights even in the tropical forest can be chilly,
while the daytime temperature rises to more than 38° C.
(100° F.). In the *tierra templada*, dry season temperatures
of 35° C. (95° F.) are common, but in the *tierra fria* they
rarely rise above a comfortable 27° F., and frost at night
during the winter can be severe enough to kill growing
plants. Throughout the Maya Area in the rainy season relative humidity remains above 80%, but drops toward 60% in
March in northern Yucatan and the highlands.

Rainfall (Figure 3.4), a factor of crucial importance to
the Maya farmer, is governed by the winds and the lie of
the land: hills facing the coast get high rainfall and may
create a rain shadow behind. The three wettest parts of the
Maya Area, receiving more than 3,000 millimeters (120
inches) annually, are the Chiapas mountains facing north
to the Gulf of Mexico, the scarp of the Alta Verapaz facing
north and east toward the Gulf of Honduras, and the Pacific
slope of the volcanic highlands. Most of the central lowland
area of Petén and Belize has more than 2,000 millimeters
(80 inches), but the deep valleys of the Grijalva and Motagua are in rain shadow and receive less than half that
amount. The driest zone is northwestern Yucatan, between Mérida and the coast, which has less than 500 millimeters (20 inches) a year.

The seasonal rainfall follows the same patterns, with the
wettest areas having the highest monthly total, more than
500 millimeters (20 inches) and northwestern Yucatan
less than 100 millimeters (4 inches) even in the wet season. Almost the whole of the projecting platform of the
Yucatan Peninsula receives less than 2,000 millimeters (80
inches) a year, with less than 200 millimeters (8 inches)
in September and less than 50 millimeters (2 inches) in
March, and these isohyets define a distinct ecological and
cultural region of the lowlands, which will be discussed
later in this chapter. The seasonality of rainfall governs
the agricultural cycle—now as it must have done in pre-
Hispanic times (see Chapter 5).

Rainwater, be it much or little, must go somewhere and although evaporation in parts of the Maya Area is high, there are many lakes and rivers that contain water throughout the year, acting as focuses of settlement, sources of fresh water and fish protein, and avenues of communication. These Maya waters drain from the continental divide in various directions, so that five major drainage zones can be defined: the Pacific, Caribbean, Gulf, karstic, and lacustrine (Figure 3.3).

The Pacific drainage area is small, since the divide runs close to the coast, and its largest river, the Lempa in El Salvador, lies at the eastern margin of the Maya Area. The streams of the Guatemala and Chiapas coast are short, steep, and markedly seasonal, often drying up completely in March and April, but some are fed by perennial springs or have eroded back into the mountains to tap lake basins such as those of Amatitlan and Ilopango. The Pacific coastal plain, now between 25 and 40 kilometers (16–25 miles) in width, has been built up by the silts and gravels deposited by these streams as their steep courses flatten out and the flow loses momentum.

On the Caribbean shore the northernmost river is the Hondo, the frontier between Mexico and Belize, which drains northeast from Petén and southern Campeche. It is a sluggish river with a fairly constant level, navigable far upstream by canoe and undoubtedly a major corridor from the coast into the Petén in Classic and Preclassic times. Its straight lower course is due to a fold in the earth's crust, and similar folds channel the other rivers of northern Belize. The next major stream to the south, across central Belize, is the Belize River, like the Hondo draining out of Petén and similarly important as an ancient line of communication. It loops around the north end of the Maya Mountains to drain their western slopes, while the eastern, coastal slope has a number of short rivers, each with a major Maya site at the head of its navigable portion (which was also where a land trail along the mountains crossed the rivers). The southern border of Belize, the Sarstoon River, opens a corridor between the Maya Mountains and the Guatemalan highlands, which provides access by land and water into southern Petén.

In Guatemala the short Rio Dulce gives access to the large inland lake of Izabal, defended by a Spanish fort and for long the point of entry for Guatemala City; the lake itself is fed by the Rio Polochic. Beyond the mountains that border the lake on the south lies the deep trench of the Motagua, running back west in a long depression that includes some of the few patches of semidesert in the Maya Area. The eastern frontier of the Maya Area lies somewhere between the Motagua and the next major river, the Ulua. In late pre-Hispanic times the Maya had trading settlements in the valley of the Ulua's tributary, the Chamelecon, and occupied at least part of the basin.

On the western side of the Maya Area the rivers drain into the Gulf of Mexico. The largest, with a basin that includes most of Petén and a major part of the Quiché–Verapaz highlands, is the Usumacinta, once dubbed the "River of Ruins" from the many Maya sites along its banks. The Usumacinta is thus named from the confluence of its two major tributaries, the Rio de la Pasión and the Rio Negro or Chixoy; the former rises near the Maya Mountains and drains southern Petén, while the latter originates in the same small area of the continental divide as the Motagua and the Grijalva and zigzags north through the mountain ranges of western Guatemala, along part of its course forming the frontier with Mexico.

The Usumacinta proper is joined by the rivers of highland Chiapas, the Lacantun and Jatate, and flows past the great sites of Yaxchilan and Piedras Negras before crossing the flat plain of Tabasco in a series of gigantic meanders bordered by swampland. The lower course of the Usumacinta lies not far north of that of the Grijalva, which drains out of the central valley of Chiapas, a deep trench that forms a dramatic interruption in the landscape of highland Chiapas. Parts of the Grijalva have been flooded in recent years for hydroelectric power schemes, and salvage archaeology by the New World Archaeological Foundation has made the valley one of the best-known parts of the Maya Area.

North of the Usumacinta the Candelaria and Champoton drain the southwestern sector of the Yucatan Peninsula, but north of the Champoton there exists an entirely different pattern of karstic drainage in which the water percolates underground to flow through caverns and buried channels in the limestone. Sometimes the roofs of the caverns collapse, leaving deep cylindrical sinkholes called cenotes, from the Maya *dz'onot*, which often contain fresh water. Since there is little surface water in the peninsula, these cenotes have acted as magnets for human occupation for thousands of years. One of the earliest known settlements in the region is at the cenote of Maní, and the

3.5. An underground water source in the karstic Yucatan Peninsula: the deep cavern at Bolonchen, drawn in 1842 by Frederick Catherwood.

greatest late center, Chichén Itzá, has two cenotes, one of them the famous Cenote of Sacrifice.

The other major source of water in the peninsula is the *aguada*, a shallow pond formed where impermeable clay has stopped rainwater from percolating underground (found in the wetter areas to the south also). A third way of getting water was from caves that extended down to the water table, such as the cavern at Bolonchen (Figure 3.5), so dramatically described and illustrated by Stephens and Catherwood. Caves were used even in well-watered areas such as Petén for the collection of *zuhuy ha* ("virgin water") for use in ritual.

To the south of the karstic zone, and between the Gulf and Caribbean drainages lies the lacustrine drainage zone, an area of inland lakes of which the largest are Petén Itzá, 36 kilometers (23 miles) long, and Yaxha-Sacnab. They are rich in fish and amphibians, and it is surprising that relatively few large sites lie on their shores. The Petén, like much of the southern lowland region, has many low-lying swamps, *bajos*, filled with clay, and it has been argued that these were once lakes, even in the Classic period of just over a millennium ago.

Overall, the drainage pattern of the Maya Area thus radiates out from a fairly small area of the Guatemalan highlands, with short rivers flowing south to the Pacific, longer ones traversing the Petén forests to the Gulf and the Caribbean, and in the Yucatan Peninsula a small lake district and an extensive area of karstic underground drainage. Because of this, the lowland regions of riverine and karstic drainage have very different potentials for settlement, subsistence, and communications, although their geology and climate lack this abrupt distinction.

The pattern of vegetation is the product of geology, relief, soils, climate, and availability of water, all interacting. The precise combination of these in a given place will determine the nature of the plant aggregation present, and the structure of two neighboring aggregations may differ either subtly, if the environmental change is small, or dramatically if it is abrupt, with a change in a major factor such as soil parent material, aspect, or elevation. Changes in temperature and rainfall tend to be gradual, while those in the soil may be very sharply defined.

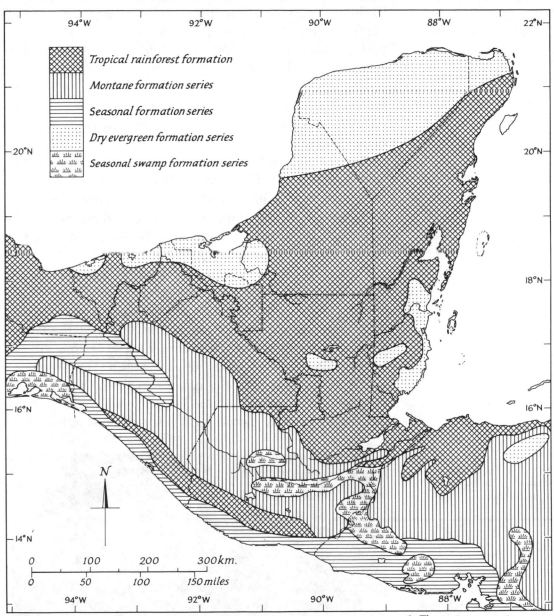

3.6. The major vegetation zones of the Maya lands: the local pattern of vegetation is extremely complex within these broad divisions, depending on soil and relief as well as geology.

The central part of the Maya Area is covered with tropical rain forest (Figure 3.6), the product of high temperature, high rainfall, and high humidity; this zone occupies the whole of Petén (apart from some areas of savanna) and most of Quintana Roo, Belize, Campeche, and lowland Chiapas. The dry area of northwestern Yucatan has an evergreen, low scrub forest, found also in areas of the lower Usumacinta and northern Belize. Throughout the highlands the vegetation is montane, a low, often open, forest, except for the deep trenches of the Grijalva and Motagua where seasonal forest and swamp occur, and the damp, luxuriant cloud forest of the Alta Verapaz. Pine is a major constituent of the highland forest; it occurs also in isolated parts of the lowlands, but as the result of poor acid soils rather than altitude, as in the Petén savannas and the pine ridge of the Belizean coastal plain.

All of these plant formations occupy a landscape long exploited and modified by man, so that the present pattern of vegetation is one influenced by human activity. Even the deep rain forest, apparently so primeval and permanent, is in many cases only a thousand years old, as we can tell from the Maya ruins buried in it.

The forest (Figure 3.7) does not deserve the popular name of jungle, except where recent regrowth has left an almost impenetrable tangle of small trees and vines, most of them, to the traveler, apparently equipped with sharp spines pointing in his direction. The forest proper is like an underwater cathedral, with a deep green gloom resulting from the sunlight diffusing through the canopy more than 60 meters (195 feet) above the floor. The floor is relatively clear, with little undergrowth, and visibility often extends to half a ki-

3.7. Tropical rain forest in the center of the lowlands at Tikal (compare the vegetation with that in Figure 3.11).

lometer or more. The trees include many species useful to man, such as mahogany, breadnut (*ramón*), rubber, sapodilla, and palms, and the towering ceiba or cottonwood with its branchless trunk soaring to the sky was to the Maya *yaxche*, the "tree of heaven." Modern man has extracted from the forest chicle for chewing gum, rubber for tires, and mahogany and rosewood for fine furniture. The ancient Maya likewise used it, taking the hard sapodilla wood, resistant to termites, for the lintels of their temples, the leaves of the guano or corozo palm to thatch their houses, the wood of the Santa Maria tree for canoes, and the small hard fruits of the *ramón* as a protein- and carbohydrate-rich food in times of hardship.

The structure of the forest canopy is complex, a world in itself, but man rarely penetrated there. The height of the canopy, the number of tiers of plants within it, and the dominant species vary with local conditions, but the same basic range of trees characterizes the rain forest from the Gulf of Mexico southward into South America. The present extent of forest in the Maya lowland area is much greater than it would have been in the pre-Hispanic period, when population density was great and settlement and cultivation more widespread.

It has been argued that some other kinds of vegetation—such as the seasonal forests, the swamp forests, and the savannas—were once rain forest, until man disturbed the ecosystem, but there is substantial evidence to suggest that many of these areas have simply reverted to their prehuman pattern of plant aggregations. Some variant vegetation patterns, such as the dry, evergreen forest of northwestern Yucatan with its water-storing succulent plants or the open pine ridge of Belize, are very clearly the result of local environmental conditions.

The animal population of the Maya Area, like that of the rest of Mesoamerica, reflects the position of the isthmian lands as a bridge between the North and South American continents. In the rain forest the opossums, bats, anteaters, armadillos, and sloths are all of southern origin, while the squirrel family and the small rodents come from North America.

The distribution of animal species closely follows the pattern of vegetation, as might be expected. The faunas of the

Yucatan Peninsula and the rain-forest zone of Petén-Belize are very similar, with a gradual change westward into the Isthmus of Tehuantepec and the Veracruz Gulf Coast. In the highlands, however, the faunal pattern, like that of the vegetation and the landscape itself, is fragmented and changes rapidly from valley to valley. We may simply accept the existence of lowland and highland regions, each with its different overall range of animals, although sharing some species. Maya interest in the local fauna was twofold: as a source of food, skins, and other natural products, and as inspiration for legend and art; both of these will be discussed in later chapters.

Environmental Zones

All of the factors considered briefly above, which form the natural backdrop against which and by using which the ancient Maya developed their culture, can be considered together to define a series of contrasting environmental zones, each with its characteristic advantages and drawbacks for the Maya. A traditional division has been into three areas: the northern arid Yucatan Peninsula, the central rain-forest zone, and the southern highlands and Pacific slope. The frontier between the northern and central areas has always been rather vaguely defined, using varying criteria such as the northern boundary of surface drainage, or just a straight line across the map from the Laguna de Terminos to Chetumal Bay. The lowland/highland frontier has by contrast always been fairly clear, along the northern edge of the Verapaz highlands, but even here the extension of lowland Classic Maya culture into Verapaz, into highland Honduras, and into southeastern Guatemala as far as Asunción Mita and the Ixtepeque obsidian source has led to some semantic confusion.

The suggestion advanced here (Figure 3.8) is for a division at two levels, into basic highland and lowland zones, and for each of these to be divided into three regions with equally real but less immediately obvious differences. The highland/lowland frontier lies along the edge of the Chiapas and Verapaz uplands, where the limestone platform of Yucatan thrusts against the ancient metamorphic mountains of central Guatemala and its neighbors. The bulk of the lowland zone is below 1,000 meters (3,300 feet) eleva-

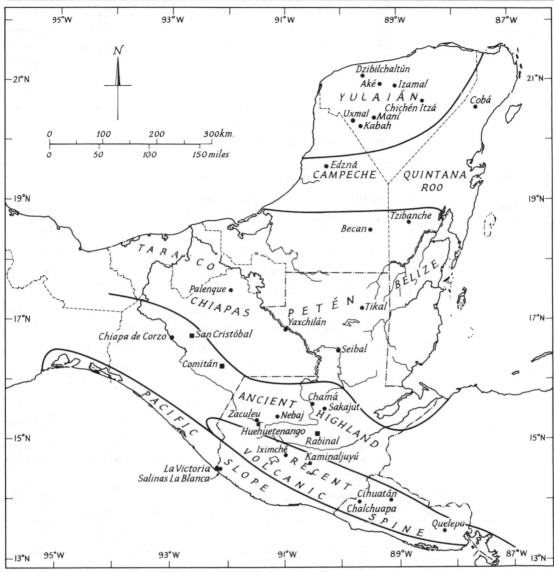

3.8. Major environmental divisions within the Maya Area.

tion, the bulk of the highland zone above that height; the geology of the lowlands is sedimentary, that of the highlands metamorphic and igneous. Deciduous, mixed, and pine forests in the highlands, with rapid local transitions, contrast with huge uniform areas of rain forest or scrub forest in the lowlands.

In the highland zone the three regions are

- the Pacific slope
- the volcanic axis
- the ancient metamorphic uplands.

The first of these, the Pacific slope, is partly below 1,000 meters elevation, but its rich soils derive from the volcanic axis and make it qualitatively different from the limestone lowlands. The Pacific plain is a narrow strip, a steep skirt fringing the Sierra Madre of Chiapas and the volcanic chain stretching east through Guatemala to Nicaragua. At its western end the plain runs into the Isthmus of Tehuantepec, a low saddle that links it to the similar Gulf Coast plain of Veracruz. Along the Pacific it ranges in width from 25 to 40 kilometers (16–25 miles), with rain forest on the upper slopes and seasonal forest on the lower, where sugar and coffee plantations have not removed the natural vegetation. The strip is crossed by numerous short, swift rivers, the deposit from which forms bars enclosing lagoons and supporting mangrove swamp along the coast, although some places have sandy beaches. There is a rapid succession of distinct ecological niches inland from the seashore. The economy of early settlements exploiting their resources was investigated at La Victoria and Salinas La Blanca, close to the Mexico-Guatemala border, by Michael Coe and Kent Flannery, while a preceramic settlement system among the lagoons and mangroves of the Chiapas coast has been studied at Chantuto by Barbara Voorhies. On the upper part of the slope a site at Abaj Takalik with early carved and inscribed Maya monuments has been excavated by John Graham.

The second highland region, the volcanic axis north of the Pacific slope, is the highest part of the Maya Area. The volcanos, geologically recent, are part of a chain extending to Nicaragua that makes Central America one of the most volcanically active regions of the world in terms both of eruptions and of earthquakes. The thick deposits of lava, tephra, ash, and obsidian resulting from these eruptions form useful raw materials both for soil forming and for the manufacture of tools.

Human settlement occurs mainly on the lower slopes of the volcanos and on the floors of the intermontane basins, where there are often lakes. Cultivation extends far up the mountain slopes, particularly on dormant or extinct volcanos. The climate has the same alternation of wet and dry seasons as the lowlands, and oak-pine forest is the natural climax vegetation below 2,000 meters (6,600 feet), with cloud forest above that elevation. Many rivers originate in the volcanic axis, which is the continental divide, including the Usumacinta, Grijalva, Motagua, and the short Pacific streams; only the lakes, however, are navigable.

Several notable sites have been excavated in this region, the best-known sequence being that at Kaminaljuyu, in the valley of Guatemala City, where a long Preclassic sequence was followed by an Early Classic heavily influenced by the great city of Teotihuacan in central Mexico. Recent destruction of many of the mounds of Kaminaljuyu in the course of suburban development led to a major project directed by William Sanders and Joseph Michels. Farther east, the sites in the Chalchuapa valley were investigated over a long period by Stanley Boggs and then by Robert Sharer, yielding a sequence that reached back to the early Preclassic phase, while on the eastern border of the Maya lands the Quelepa site was excavated by E. Wyllys Andrews V, and the Postclassic center of Cihuatan has been studied by a number of scholars.

The earliest site known in the Maya Area, that of Los Tapiales in El Quiché in western Guatemala, lies north of the volcanic axis on the edge of the ancient metamorphic uplands, while some of the latest pre-Hispanic sites to have been investigated, including several fortified towns actually stormed by the Spaniards, such as Iximche, lie in the intermontane valleys or on the northern fringe of the region.

The third region of the highlands, lying north of the volcanic axis, consists of the ancient metamorphic mountains and plateaus of Verapaz and Quiché, extending beyond the Motagua trench into Honduras on the east, and on the west abutting the limestone highlands of Chiapas. It is a region of great geomorphological complexity, rich in mineral resources. The upper courses of the major rivers flow across it in deep valleys, and there are large intermontane basins, usually occupied by colonial towns (San Cristobal Las Casas, Comitán, Huehuetenango, Rabinal). Apart from the Los Tapiales site near Chichicastenango, some ten thousand years old, and numerous Archaic sites recently reported from the same region, human settlement of the region goes back at least as far as the Early Preclassic period, with important excavations in recent years at Chiapa de Corzo (in the Grijalva trench), San Isidro in Chiapas, and Sakajut and El Portón in Alta Verapaz. Classic period sites such as Nebaj and Chamá are best known for their art, of lowland rather than highland Maya affiliation; of the few late sites to be investigated Zaculeu is probably the best known.

The mineral resources of this region included jade, serpentine, cinnabar, and hematite, and the cloud forest of Alta Verapaz was the home of the quetzal, a bird with long, iridescent, green tail feathers much in demand among the Classic lowland Maya for the raiment of their chiefs.

The lowland zone also consists of three regions:

- Tabasco-Chiapas-Petén-Belize
- Campeche-Quintana Roo
- Yucatan.

The first of these includes the whole lowland basin of the Usumacinta, the lower Grijalva and the other Gulf Coast rivers, and the basins of the Caribbean rivers from the Hondo southward to the Chamelecon. It also includes the inland lake district of northern Petén. The characteristics of this region include abundant surface drainage, potential for canoe transport except at the height of the dry season, and available domestic water for much of the year except on minor streams and away from watercourses. The topography is rolling to hilly, descending to alluvial plains near the coasts and in the main river valleys, and covered with a tropical rain forest dominated by palms, ramon, mahogany, sapodilla and ceiba. Rainfall is high, usually over 2,000 millimeters (80 inches) annually. This region holds many of the best-known Maya sites, including Palenque, Yaxchilan, Seibal, Tikal, and Quirigua. On the basis of the radiocarbon dates from the Cuello site in northern Belize, it is estimated that farming settlements began by, at the latest, 2500 B.C., following a long period of occupation by more mobile gatherers, hunters, and fishermen (see Chapter 4).

The Campeche-Quintana Roo region occupies most of these two states of Mexico, although southern Campeche properly belongs in the Tabasco-Chiapas-Petén-Belize region. There is much less surface drainage in this area, which is separated from the Petén-Belize region on a line running roughly from the Laguna de Terminos to Chetumal Bay. Only the Champoton River reaches the coast, others disappearing underground as the karstic topography becomes dominant, but there are a number of lakes in folds in the limestone, as at Bacalar and Chichankanob, or in isolated regions with less permeable subsoils, as at Coba. Northward the vegetation changes gradually, with decreasing rainfall, the canopy becoming lower and the hilly relief decreasing in elevation and amplitude.

The coast of Quintana Roo is low-lying and swampy, with a deep band of mangrove making the shore inhospitable. Offshore in the north lies the island of Cozumel. Important sites in this region include Coba, and San Gervasio on Cozumel, but it is an area in which comparatively little excavation has been done: recent field survey, especially in southern Quintana Roo, has revealed the existence of many further sites, some of great size, of which we still know little. Culturally there is a northeastern extension of Petén-style sites down the Rio Hondo corridor and north through Quintana Roo to Coba.

The northernmost lowland region embraces almost all of Yucatan and a small area of northern Campeche. Geologically it is the most recent part of the peninsula, porous, flat, and low-lying. It has scant rainfall and a highly karstic landscape supporting only a low scrub forest trending to a xerophytic scrubland. The soil is thin, with bare rock showing in many places, but both soil and vegetation have been modified by man for so long that the environment has itself become an artifact. There is no surface drainage and there are no lakes; the major sources of water lie in the deep cenotes and more shallow aguadas. In spite of these constraints, the region was occupied by man at an early date: recent excavations in the Loltun cave yielded a preceramic sequence that must date to before 2500 B.C. in calendar years, and pottery of close to that age was excavated at the Maní cenote in 1942 by George Brainerd. In the later first millennium A.D. some of the most famous Maya sites flourished on the thin soil of Yucatan: Uxmal, Kabah, Chichén Itzá, Dzibilchaltun, Ake, and Izamal. Their elaborate buildings bespeak a large and organized population, and while the rain-forest zone to the south became depopulated in and after the tenth century A.D., northern Yucatan supported an urban society until the Spanish conquest.

One common characteristic of all six regions is that they were occupied by settled farming peoples at a relatively early date. Village agriculture in Mesoamerica has not yet been traced back beyond the third millennium B.C.; but there were settlers in several parts of the lowlands before 2000 B.C. and in the highlands before 1000 B.C., while on the Pacific slope occupation is as early as in the lowlands. Clearly the environment of the Maya Area, whatever limitations we may perceive, offered sufficient resources and encouragement for people to settle there, and sufficient potential for their descendants to develop a unique civilization.

The Modern Maya

One way in which we can learn how the first settlers adapted to their environment, and how the Maya have continued to flourish to the present day, is to study the present inhabitants of the Maya Area, most of them direct descendants of the pre-Hispanic peoples of the same regions. More than two million Maya still live in their ancient homelands, in two major blocs: Yucatan, and the Chiapas-Guatemala highlands. The intervening rain-forest region has only a low population level, and many of the modern inhabitants have migrated in from other parts of the Maya Area.

Physically, the Maya are Amerindians, derived from the original migrants who crossed the land bridge from Siberia to Alaska more than twenty thousand years ago. They form part of the Mongoliform division of mankind, which includes most of the peoples of eastern Asia, although by now the Asian and American branches are genetically quite distinct.

The Maya are most closely related, as might be expected, to the other Amerindian groups of Mexico and northern Central America, and since their physical characteristics overlap those of these other groups to a substantial degree, a Maya may not always be distinguishable from them. The Maya are, however, among the shortest of Mesoamerican peoples, the men averaging 155 centimeters (62 inches) and the women 142 centimeters (57 inches) in Yucatan and some 2 centimeters (0.75 inches) less in highland Guatemala. (There is archaeological evidence that the Preclassic period Maya were rather taller, and that stature declined during the Classic period.) Their legs are relatively

3.9. Lowland Maya man, a Mopan in his mid 30s, and Highland women, Cakchiquels in their 20s and late 30s.

short, which accounts for most of the difference from other Mesoamericans. Maya are notably brachycephalic, with broad heads and long narrow noses that make Yucatecans, in particular, easily recognizable. Blood grouping follows the usual Amerindian pattern with, for example, a high incidence of Group O. Within the Maya Area the Yucatecan and highland groups are the most distinct from each other genetically; they are also the most distant geographically, suggesting that this may reflect the maximum genetic divergence from a common proto-Maya ancestor.

Other features are common to Amerindians, including a high basal metabolic rate, low pulse rate, and low blood pressure; a highland sample also had low serum cholesterol—all desirable characteristics. Maya eyes are brown, hair black and straight, skin color ranging from medium blond/ light brunette in the highlands to medium/dark brunette in Yucatan. The darkening is thought to be genetic, and not just the result of stronger sunlight in Yucatan, since skin measurements are taken on the protected skin on the inner side of the arm. The exposed facial and hand skin is often much darker than the standard measurement, and equal in highland and lowland Maya.

The average Maya (Figure 3.9) is thus of compact, sturdy build, with short, muscular legs, broad shoulders and head; many of the figures shown on ancient Maya sculpture and vase paintings could be duplicated in the modern population. Physical unity between Maya groups is greater than their combined similarity to other Amerindian groups, and a common physical ancestry is generally accepted, albeit with some outside infusions from time to time.

A similar diverse unity is seen in the Maya languages (Figure 3.10), which are still spoken by some two and one-half million people, according to the anthropological linguist Terrence Kaufman, who has made one of the most recent and widely accepted classifications of the Maya tongue. He recognizes twenty-four languages, including Huastec, which is spoken by an isolated group of perhaps 60,000 persons in northern Veracruz, and twenty-three others clustered into ten groups and three main divisions. These divisions are the Yucatec complex, spoken by the Maya of the peninsular region, lowland Chiapas, Petén, and Belize; the western division, including the Cholan groups of the Tabasco lowlands, the now-separated Chorti in Honduras around Copan, and the Tzeltal-Tzotzil in highland Chiapas; also of the Chuj and Kanjobal groups just to the east in northwest Guatemala; and the third division, the eastern, consisting of the greater Mamean and Quichean branches that occupy the rest of the Guatemalan highlands, and in the case of the Kekchi have now begun to move northward down into the underoccupied lands of southern Petén and Belize. The largest Maya groups now are the Quiché, estimated at 500,000, the related Cakchiquel (400,000), the Mam and Yucatec (350,000 each) and the Kekchi (300,000); the smallest are the Itzá of Petén (500) and the Lacandon of the Chiapas rain forest, of whom perhaps 200 had survived in the early 1970s.

It is accepted that all Maya languages derive from a single extinct ancestor, known as proto-Mayan, and the antiquity of this ancestor has been estimated by a technique known as glottochronology or lexicostatistics, developed and applied to Mesoamerican languages by the late Morris Swadesh. The basic assumption (not universally accepted by linguists) is that over a given period, say 1,000 years, all languages will change to approximately the same extent, in this case 14%: two languages of common parentage, separated for 1,000 years, will *each* have changed 14% of their vocabulary, and since the same words need not have been changed in each language they will in fact share 74% of cognate, related words (74% being 86% of the 86% remaining unchanged in each language), according to the calculations of Terrence Kaufman. Thus the Mayan language family began to break up from the common proto-

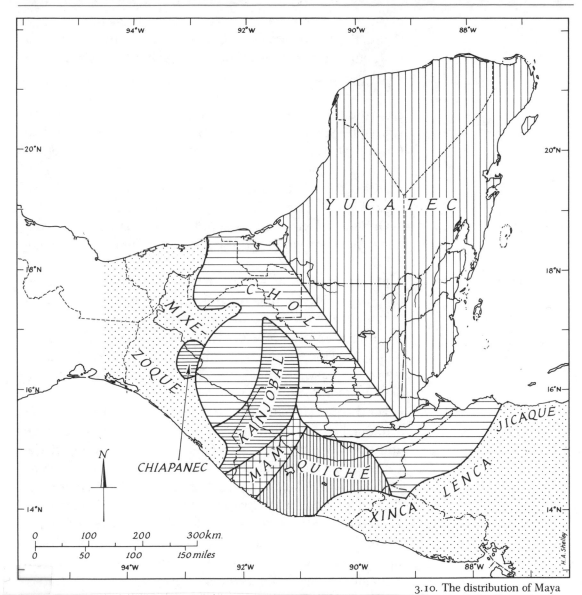

3.10. The distribution of Maya ~~~es (after Terrence~~ ~~n).~~

Page 93, Fig. 3.10 caption, add: The Classic Maya inscriptions were written in both Yucatec and Chol, and much of the southern lowlands seems to have been bilingual.

Mayan before 2000 B.C., and retains a common 26%–35% of cognate words; the linguistic reconstruction suggests that the Maya came into existence as a separate entity more than four thousand years ago, and recent archaeological work (see Chapter 4) not only confirms this, but indicates an even greater antiquity for the Maya as a cultural entity.

The Maya languages are related more loosely to others in Mesoamerica, and there has been suggested a large-scale grouping into a Mesoamerican language phylum that includes the languages of Veracruz and Oaxaca to the west across the Isthmus of Tehuantepec. Less controversially, it has been established that these languages have given "loan words" to the Mayan family, and that Mayan has donated words to the Xinca-Lenca-Jicaque languages on the eastern frontier of the Maya Area. Mayan has also received words from the Nahuatl (Aztec) languages of highland Central Mexico, and all of these linguistic contacts reflect physical contact among the peoples concerned (and essentially reflect what is independently known from archaeological evidence).

One distant contact, proposed in 1961 by Ronald Olson, is between Mayan and the Chipaya language of the Lake Titicaca region in Bolivia in the high Andes of South America. Terrence Kaufman suggests either a direct local contact, occurring perhaps in the context of the diffusion of maize agriculture or technology between Mesoamerica and the Andes, or a more widespread relationship and contact of Mayan with the languages of northwestern South America in the past, of which the Chipaya case is the only evidence so far documented.

For the pre-Hispanic period it seems reasonable to accept a major bloc of Yucatec speakers in the peninsular zone and another major bloc, of Chol-Chorti speakers, in the Usumacinta basin and across southern Petén and southern Belize into the Motagua valley and the hills of Honduras. The split between the two groups may well have occurred after their initial settlement of the Maya lowland zone, while the boundary between them probably lay much farther north than it has done since the conquest. Archaeological evidence suggests a southward move of Yucatec-speakers into the power vacuum created by the collapse of the rain-forest centers in the tenth century, and it is likely that Yucatec-speakers were in the Classic period confined to the Campeche-Quintana Roo and Yucatan regions discussed earlier in this chapter. It is even possible, again from archaeological evidence, that the Chol speakers occupied eastern Quintana Roo as far north as Coba during the Late Classic period.

Thus it would seem that the Classic Maya inscriptions of Tikal, Yaxchilan, Palenque, Naranjo, and Copan were all expressed in languages of the Cholan group, but the earliest inscriptions currently known, from Abaj Takalik on the Pacific slope of western Guatemala, are probably in Ma-mean, while those from other early sites to the east, El Baul and Kaminaljuyu, are probably in Quichean.

Language is only one part of the culture of the living Maya that can be utilized to understand the civilization of their ancestors. The social structure and material culture of the present inhabitants of Yucatan and the Guatemala-Chiapas highlands have also been extensively document-ed, and the notable conservatism of many aspects of Maya life means that we can, with due care, use the present to illuminate the past.

It has been calculated that even under optimum condi-tions of preservation only some 15% of the characteristics of a culture would survive archaeologically, and even then the artifacts would be shorn of their significance within the living society. Conditions of preservation in the Maya Area, especially in the lowland zone, are far from optimum: the only materials that usually survive to be recovered in an ex-cavation are stone and pottery, and, rather less often, bone and shell. Thus the platforms of houses, some tools and or-naments, some containers and culinary vessels, and some food remains form the bulk of our evidence for daily life. Objects made of wood, bark, basketry, leather, textiles, gourds, feathers, and cordage have vanished entirely, with very rare exceptions when a dry cave or waterlogged *bajo* has fortuitously preserved a discarded or deliberately de-posited object, or when a sudden fire has burned things *in situ* and left them as charcoal.

There is therefore a strong temptation to make use of the culture of the living Maya to study the dead, but we have to allow for the enormous impact of the Spanish conquest on even the most fundamental aspects of that culture, and also for the impact of other Mesoamerican groups—of Teo-tihuacan at the beginning of the Classic period, of Tula at its end, and of the Aztec in the period just before the con-quest. These two latter influences made the Maya culture observed by Landa, for example, arguably different to an unknown degree from the culture of the Classic period.

The culture of the modern Maya is as varied as their lan-guages, and we must restrict ourselves to just two exam-ples, one each from the highlands and the lowlands.

3.11. The Tzotzil village of
ʔApas and its maize fields in
the highlands of Chiapas.

Page 96, Fig. 3.11 caption, add: Highl Maya commune commonly ized in wa
groups (*sna*), the homes of related lin s.

about one hundred and twenty
thousand strong, living in the central highlands of Chiapas
(Figure 3.11) around the colonial capital of San Cristobal
Las Casas, have been exposed to more, and more intensive,
anthropological observation over the past two decades than
any other group of Maya. Robert Laughlin described them
as being "bombarded with anthropologists," and the villag-
ers of Zinacantan must be among the best-known Indians in
Mesoamerica. The ideas anthropologists have formed as a
result of the Zinacantan project have guided the minds of
the present generation of Maya archaeologists more than
we perhaps realize or care to admit.

The Tzotzil economy is based on the Mesoamerican
"holy trinity" of maize, beans, and squash (a pumpkinlike
plant grown for both its flesh and its seeds). Between December and February a *milpa* field is cut from the secondary vegetation on a hillside, and the cut bush left to dry out;
in March or April it is burned to clear the ground, and between March and May the farmer plants seed corn with a
pointed digging stick in anticipation of the rains. Beans
and squashes are planted together in the same hole, and a
wide variety of other crops is also grown, including tomato,
avocado, and sweet potato.

Introduced domestic animals are now important: horses,
mules, and burros are used for carrying goods and oxen for

ploughing. Cattle are also raised for beef and milk, which are sold to the *ladino* (non-Indian) population in the local towns. Sheep are kept mainly for wool, chickens and turkeys for meat and eggs. Much of the meat supply comes from hunting, especially jackrabbits, but including deer, armadillo, and birds; domestic dogs and cats are common.

Maize is the main food, eaten as flat grilled cakes called tortillas, or as a fine paste enclosing beans or meat—tamales—cooked by steaming in a banana leaf or corn husk. Maize can also be mixed with water to make the drinks *atole* and *posole*, with flavorings including cinnamon, pepper, mint, coriander, and other herbs. Maize is initially prepared by soaking in limewater, which softens the kernel and liberates the important amino acid lysine, and is then ground to a paste on the stone *metate* with a cylindrical *mano*; both the soaking and the grinding introduce gritty particles into the food, and teeth become worn down at an

3.12. A ceremonial *huipil* from Magdalenas, Chiapas, with complex embroidery affirming its owner's identity and place in the cosmos. The design around the neck maps the universe, while that on the bottom edge includes motifs specific to the village, lineage, and wearer of the *huipil*. The richly intermeshed information in such perishable artifacts is totally lost in the archaeological record.

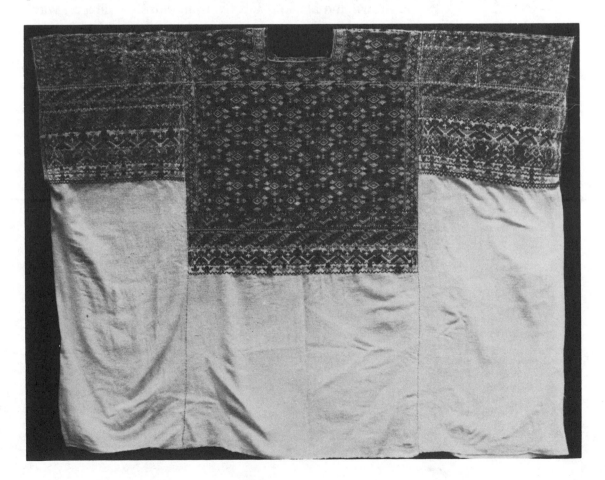

early age. Beans, the most common accompaniment to
maize, are stewed whole or mashed to a paste and fried, in
which form they keep for several days. Meat is a luxury.

The major craft practiced by women is weaving, using
the backstrap loom of pre-Hispanic origin which can be set
up anywhere there is a tree or post. Cotton and wool are
woven and ornamented by dyeing or embroidery, in elaborate designs that are not only restricted to one community
but often indicate the social position of the wearer as well
(Figure 3.12). Plant fibers are used to make hammocks,
baskets, and nets, and palm leaves are woven into hats, by
men. Other handicrafts have become concentrated in single villages, so that the market of San Cristobal Las Casas
(Figure 3.13) finds Chamula wooden furniture, pottery,
leather, and stone goods being traded, as well as salt from
Zinacantan and food products from other villages.

Women wear a blouse (*huipil*) and skirt, white and blue
or brown and black, respectively, in different villages, with
a red sash and a rectangular cloth used as a shawl or for
carrying a baby. The man's outfit includes a palm hat with a
heavy broad brim, festooned with ribbons; a white shirt

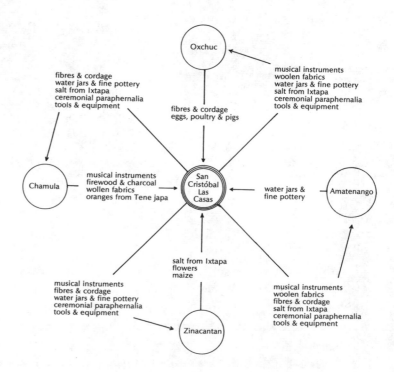

3.13. The regional market system based on San Cristobal de
Las Casas, the principal center
of the Tzotzil country in highland Chiapas, showing how local craft specialities are
integrated into the overall economy (after Siverts).

with red or blue stripes; white calf-length trousers with a woolen sash; a woolen poncho in black, white, or both colors. Some men wear heavy leather sandals, and the whole costume is, like that of the women, village-specific.

The Tzotzil house consists of a single rectangular room, with a thatched or shingled pitched roof overhanging the walls to provide storage space outdoors. The pole or mud-daubed walls have a single door and no windows, and there is an open hearth on the stamped earth floor. A sweathouse for bathing and a maize store may be atached to the house. Women work mainly in and around the house, tending poultry, hauling water, preparing food, and growing some plant foods and flavorings in the yard. Building and maintaining the house, repairing tools, and most crafts are men's work, as is the cultivation of the *milpa*. Most potters are women, and both sexes sell their produce in the market.

Marriage is usually within the local community, and a man will seek a wife with a different family name. (Such names descend patrilineally, from father to son, and inheritance of property is also in the male line.) In the Zinacantan hamlet of Paste about 80% of the marriages recorded were within the same small "waterhole group" of families, or with a neighboring waterhole group.

Social standing is attained by participation in the *cargo* system, a series of offices held for a year at a time, which can be held only by married men and which must be purchased. Several years between offices are usually needed to recoup the necessary funds to pay for the obligatory alcohol and fireworks, and the periodic draining-off of surplus capital prevents too great an economic distance developing within the community (although it also prevents constructive investment), and thus contributes to social solidarity.

A *cargo* position involves participation in frequent ritual activities, and the ceremonial and religious part of Tzotzil life is intimately interwoven with the fabric of society and the relationship among men, maize, earth, and gods. The Maya gods themselves have become syncretized with Catholic theogony, but a considerable body of pre-Hispanic belief survives: the world is envisaged as lying between the sky— a pyramid supported by the *yaxche* tree—and the underworld of the dead. Thirteen sky gods survive in some villages, a direct Classic survival, while in others, the earth is an all-embracing goddess and the ithyphallic black bat-man is a regional demigod.

The pre-Hispanic Calendar Round, with intermeshing cycles of 365 and 260 days, survives as part of the agricultural cycle, and in a Chamula house some years ago, the anthropologist Gary Gossen found a wooden board still being used to mark the passage of days (Figure 3.14). The cultivation of the *milpa*, including clearing, weeding, and harvest, is attended by ritual observances, but in an even-handed way the Tzotzil also devote three- or four-day fiestas to the major Christian festivals, with what is considered an appropriate excess of food and liquor.

The upper levels of the *cargo* hierarchy form the internal government of the community, and after a man has passed up the ladder of formal offices he becomes a member of the group of respected elders who act as collective conservators of the traditions and practices of the Tzotzil.

Yucatec. The Maya of the Yucatan Peninsula occupy the Mexican states of Campeche, Quintana Roo, and Yucatan, and the northern part of Belize; they are considered to have expanded southward within the past millennium from the northern part of this area. The most recent estimate places their number at about three hundred and fifty thousand.

Like the Tzotzil, the economy is based on *milpa* cultivation of maize and other plants, in a field cut every two years or so from the low scrub forest, in a landscape as flat as that of the Tzotzil is hilly. Some 85% of the calories in the diet are estimated to come from maize in various processed forms, and the *milpa* also produces beans, sweet potato, manioc, watermelons, and squashes. The yard around the house is cultivated by the women, who grow peppers, onions, tomatoes, and herbs in earth-filled boxes or hollow logs (the soil being very thin), as well as fruit trees including *guayaba*, *guava*, *guanabana*, *annona*, orange, and banana. Some tobacco is grown, the leaves being twisted into simple cigars, and henequen (century plant) is cultivated for its stiff fibers, which are twisted into nets and bags.

The domestic animals are mainly chickens and pigs (which are fed surplus maize and now form an important cash crop), occasionally turkeys, and in some places cattle as a cash crop. Deer and wild pig (peccary) are hunted, together with small animals such as armadillo and *tepez-*

3.14. A wooden calendar board with charcoal marks recording the passage of the days and months; the folk equivalent of the sculptured inscriptions of the Classic Maya in its notation of the passage of time.

cuintle, a large rodent. Bees are kept for honey and wax, a survival of a famed pre-Hispanic industry.

The Yucatec settlements, spread across the limestone plain rather than scattered in waterhole groups across the hills, as are the Tzotzil hamlets, range from compact grid-plan towns of Hispanic foundation to small clusters of houses in the fields. In 1936 Alfonso Villa Rojas studied the village of X-Cacal and recorded "some thousand individuals distributed in eight small hamlets plus a sanctuary which served as the center. The huts without exception are built of palm leaves and bajareque, and are scattered around the public well or *cenote*. There are neither streets nor fences around domestic plots; another characteristic is the grouping of huts by families, those of the married children standing next their parents'. The *milpas* are only a short distance from the settlements, so that the owners can come and go to them the same day." This ease of access typifies Maya communities, although in Petén in the 1960s Reuben Reina recorded men traveling many miles by canoe along Lake Petén Itzá to reach their fields.

The houses in Yucatan are apsidal in plan, tending to become rectangular farther south, with a single room (Figure

3.15. A characteristic Yucatec Maya house with perishable superstructure of poles and palm thatch on a timber frame set into a low stone platform base. The early buildings at Cuello (Figure 4.8) used similar bases with plastered floors and must have had similar superstructures; Figure 9.1 shows a Classic period representation of such a house at Uxmal.

3.15). Subsidiary structures may include a separate kitchen, granary, pigpen, chicken coop, and laundry shelter, with hollow-log beehives kept in a roofed apiary—if the native bees are kept; introduced Italian bees live in the European box-shaped hive.

As in Chiapas, certain communities are noted for their crafts: pottery was made at Ticul, Lerma, and Becal, and Ticul and Becal were also noted for palm-leaf hats. Potting has ceased in some communities in recent years, and weaving is no longer practiced, commercial linen being purchased and embroidered at home. Henequen hammocks are widely made, ranging from rough cord examples in Belize to multicolored, very fine, and very large *matrimonios* or *familiales* in Yucatan.

With the decline of crafts, male dress is becoming very Westernized, a shirt and trousers being the common garb; women still wear the long *huipil* with an underskirt and sometimes several petticoats. Although festal dress is more elaborate, there are no intercommunity distinctions such as those that remain among the Tzotzil. Regional markets and market days have also vanished, and the Yucatec have become in many communities what Manning Nash has called "Machine Age Maya."

These two brief sketches give some indication of the comparable, yet contrasting, ways of life among living Maya groups. Detailed studies of many of these groups have been carried out (summarized most recently in the *Handbook of Middle American Indians*), but this book, with its concentration on the Maya past, is not the place to discuss them: I wish merely to note that like the land they live in, the modern Maya offer so much evidence for investigating their forebears that we cannot afford to ignore it.

GREGORIAN CALENDAR	RADIOCARBON DATES: C¹⁴ yrs	MAYA LONG COUNT		HIGHLANDS	SOUTH & CENTRAL LOWLANDS	NORTHERN LOWLANDS
AD 1700		—12.0.0.0.0.	COL	C O L O N I A L		
1500			POSTCLASSIC	Iximché LATE	LATE	
1300	—1300 a.d.	—11.10.0.0.0.			Santa Rita MIDDLE	DECADENT Mayapan
		—11.0.0.0.0.				
1100				E A R L Y		MODIFIED Chichén Itzá
	—900	—10.10.0.0.0.			Nohmul	
900						
		—10.0.0.0.0.	CLASSIC		TERMINAL	PURE
700					LATE	II
	—500	—9.10.0.0.0.			MIDDLE	
500						I
		—9.0.0.0.0.			EARLY	
300		—8.10.0.0.0.			(P R O T O C L A S S I C)	
100	—100 a.d.		PRECLASSIC			
AD/BC		—8.0.0.0.0.			LATE	
100	—100 b.c.	—7.10.0.0.0.		Abaj Takalik		
300		—7.0.0.0.0.				
500	—400					
700						
900	—700				M I D D L E	
1100						
1300	—1000			Kaminaljuyú	Tikal	Dzibilchaltun
1500				Ocós		
1700				E A R L Y		
1900	—1500			Altamira		Maní cenote
2100						
2300						
BC 2500	—2000 b.c.				Cuello	Loltun cave
			ARCHAIC	Los Tapiales	Belize sites	
BC 9000						

COLONIAL (Northern Lowlands)

FLORESCENT — EARLY PERIOD

—H.A.S—

4

The Flowering and Fall of the Maya

THE ruins and monuments that Stephens, Catherwood, and others recorded at Copan, Palenque, and elsewhere all date to what is known as the Classic period of Maya civilization, the period during which that culture attained its greatest degree of sophistication and of political and artistic development (Figure 4.1).

The Classic period has been generally defined as the time during which monumental stone inscriptions were carved and erected in the lowlands, particularly in the rainforest zone, using a hieroglyphic script and a method of reckoning the passage of time known as the Long Count. The Long Count forms part of the rather complex Maya calendric system, outlined below; its most striking feature is that events are dated to the precise day and, provided the calendar can be correlated with our own, we can accurately place any event recorded in the Maya inscriptions.

There is still some dispute about the correlation, but most Maya scholars are at present content to accept the one put forward by Joseph Goodman and refined by Juan Martínez Hernández and Eric Thompson, known as the G-M-T acronymically, or as the 11.16 correlation; this latter notation derives from the fact that the date 11.16.0.0.0. in the Long Count is argued to correspond to the Christian date November 13, 1539, on the basis of a reference in a Spanish colonial document. On the 11.16. correlation the Classic period spans A.D. 250–900 (on another correlation, that of Herbert Spinden, it would fall 260 years earlier), so that the florescence of Maya civilization parallels the later Roman Empire, the early Byzantines, and the wildfire spread of Islam around the Mediterranean and east to India. The apogee of Tikal in the eighth century is coeval with the great Tang capital of Chang-an, with its population of over a million, and with the empire of Charlemagne in Western Europe.

Opposite:
4.1. The chronology of Maya culture and civilization.

Page 105, Fig. 4.1 caption, add: Recent studies suggest that the Cuello site was not permanently occupied until the end of the Early Preclassic.

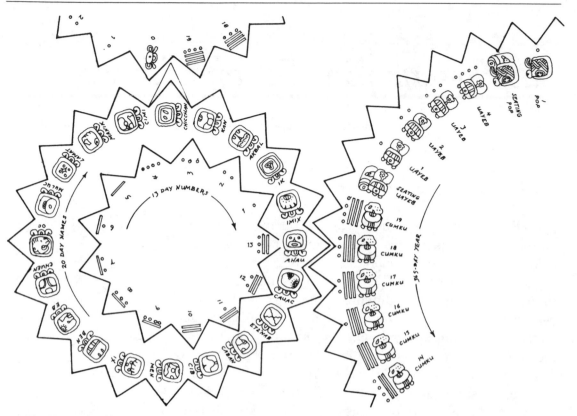

4.2. The Maya calendar: inter-
locking cogs of time moving at
different speeds (after
Thompson).

In this chapter we will examine how Maya civilization
rose and declined, providing a chronological framework in
which we can consider various aspects of the culture in
later chapters. In order to understand the chronology of the
Classic period, as well as many aspects of Maya thought,
we need to appreciate at least in outline the structure of the
ancient Maya calendar (Figure 4.2).

4.3. The glyphs for the 20 day
names in the Sacred Round of
260 days (after Thompson).

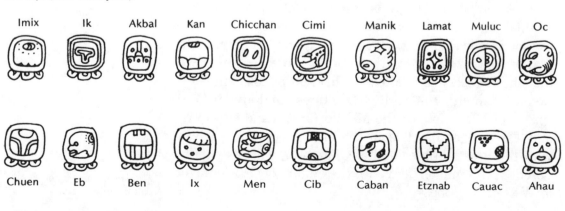

This structure has two basic forms: repeating cycles of days, each of a different length; and a cumulative count of days from a single base in the past. Our own calendar is comparable: the days of the week form a repeating cycle of 7, Sunday to Saturday, followed again by Sunday; the days of the month form another repeating cycle from 1 to 31 (or 30, or 28/29 in February), after which the next month begins with 1 again; and the months of the year form a third cycle, from January to December and back to January. Parallel with these repeating cycles, each moving like the cogs of a clock mechanism at different speeds, we have a cumulative count of days beginning with the official date of the birth of Christ nearly two thousand years ago. In this count, year succeeds year, so that 1981 follows 1980 and neither will ever repeat: we can use the repeating and the cumulative counts to fix a single day forever in time—"Friday, April 16, A.D. 1982" defines a unique and unrepeatable fragment of eternity.

The Maya used several cycles of days, of which the two most important were the Sacred Round of 260 days and the approximate solar year of 365 days. The Sacred Round combined the repeating cycle of numbers 1–13 with 20 day names (Figure 4.3), so that any particular combination would recur in 13 × 20 or 260 days; the day name and the number changed together: 1 Imix, 2 Ik, 3 Akbal, . . . as we might say Monday 1, Tuesday 2, Wednesday 3, and so on. The approximate solar year consisted of 18 months (Figure 4.4), each of 20 days, plus a terminal period of 5 days. Each of these months had an internal sequence of changing numbers: 1 Pop, 2 Pop, 3 Pop, . . . comparable with our January 1, January 2, and so forth. The first day (or perhaps the last) of each sequence of 20 days was called the "seating" of the following month, so that instead of 20 Pop we have the seating of Uo.

The two cycles proceeded simultaneously, so that any one day could be designated in both, as in 3 Akbal 1 Pop; since the two cycles are of unequal length, this pairing of 3 Akbal and 1 Pop could occur only once every 52 years, and this period needed for the complete repeating of the two cycles is known as the Calendar Round. Such a calendar was used over most of Mesoamerica, and the 52-year period was still of great importance to the Aztec and the Maya at

Pop	Xul	Zac	Pax
Uo	Yaxkin	Ceh	Kayab
Zip	Mol	Mac	Cumku
Zotz	Chen	Kankin	Uayeb
Zec	Yax	Muan	

4.4. The glyphs for the 18 months in the 365-day approximate solar year and for the 5-day terminal period Uayeb (after Thompson).

the time of the Spanish conquest. The use of it survives to this day among the highland Maya of Guatemala and Chiapas.

What does not survive, and seems to have fallen into virtual disuse with the collapse of Classic Maya civilization in the ninth and tenth centuries, is the cumulative count of days known as the Long Count, although parts of it including the *katun* (20 years) and perhaps the *baktun* (144,000 days, or 400 years) remained enough in use to be reported to Landa. The Long Count begins from a notional base date in August 3114 B.C., centuries before the first evidence of the Maya as a people or their movement into the Maya Area. This date may represent the latest creation of the world in Maya mythology, and forward from it the total number of days elapsed were counted by the Maya and then divided into periods of varying length. First they expressed the number of complete *baktunob* (*-ob* indicating the plural form); then from the remainder the number of completed *katunob*, the number of *tunob* (of approximately one year each), the number of months of 20 days each (*uinalob*), and finally the remaining single days from 0 to 19, *kinob*. It is as though we were to say on July 10, 1981, that since our base date, the birth of Christ, there had elapsed one millennium of 1,000 years, nine centuries of 100 years, four score years of 20 years each, no single years of 365 days, six months of 28–31 days, and finally 10 days of the seventh month.

As can be seen, the Maya used multiples of 20 instead of the 10 that we use—a vigesimal, not a decimal system of numeration—so that 20 *kinob* made a *uinal*, 20 *tunob* a *katun*, and 20 *katunob* a *baktun* (the 18 *uinalob* to a *tun* were to approximate a solar year). These numbers were expressed (Figure 4.5) by using a dot for *1* and a bar for *5*: a bar with two dots above or to the left stood for *7*, two bars and three dots for *13*; the highest number expressible in this way was *19*, three bars and four dots, because 20 was the completion of the lower unit and the entry instead of one higher unit. In our decimal system we count to 9, but the addition of a further *1* gives us 10, with a zero in the lower unit position and a *1* indicating a single unit of ten. The way in which we write numbers, Arabic notation, places higher units to the left of lower, so that our figure 423 means four units of a hundred (ten tens), two completed units of ten each, and three remaining ones; Maya notation placed the larger units at the top, so that a Maya count of 423 would appear as shown in Figure 4.5.

Because setting bars and dots in type is not very practical for us (although Morley's splendid book, *The Ancient Maya*, "recently revised."   by Robert Sharer, has the chapters numbered by Maya notation), we conventionally transcribe Maya numbers and dates into Arabic numbers, so that a period of nine *baktunob*, fifteen *katunob*, seven *tunob*, twelve *uinalob*, and six *kinob* (which would be expressed by a vertical sequence of four dots and a bar, three bars, two dots over a bar, two dots over two bars, one dot over a bar) is expressed as 9.15.7.12.6. This would then be followed by the days in the Calendar Round to give a date in this case of 1 Cimi 19 Uo.

The earliest date so far deciphered from the Maya lowlands is on Stela 29 at Tikal (Figure 4.14): 8.12.14.8.15., or July 6, A.D. 292, using the G-M-T correlation. A still earlier

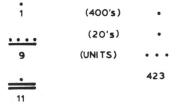

4.5. Maya bar-and-dot numeration: on the left are separate examples showing the use of the dot for 1 and the bar for 5; on the right is an example of positional notation, the higher quantities above the lower, for the number 423—one quantity of 400, one of 20, three of 1.

date may exist on a fragmentary circular altar from Polol, on which John Graham and Gary Pahl have suggested that a 7 is the first quantity. The latest Long Count date may be 10.5.0.0.0., in A.D. 928, from a site in Campeche; otherwise, there is a definite date of 10.4.0.0.0., A.D. 909, on a very small stela from the site of Tonina in highland Chiapas (Figure 4.18). Within this span of just over six centuries the Maya carved and erected hundreds of monuments with hieroglyphic inscriptions expressing such dates, exact to the day; this period, expanded to an arbitrary limit of A.D. 250 at its inception and terminated at A.D. 900 (before the discovery of the later monuments), is known as the Classic. It is followed, logically enough, by a Postclassic (or sometimes Decadent) period lasting from A.D. 900 until the Spanish conquest in the sixteenth century, and preceded, equally logically, by a Preclassic (or Formative) period reaching back from A.D. 250 to the first recorded settlement of the Maya Area (and before that a pre-agricultural Archaic).

Although the notion of a Classic period in the first millennium A.D., of maximum cultural florescence, spread to other parts of Mesoamerican archaeology, at the same time the appearance of earlier inscribed monuments in Oaxaca and Veracruz made it clear that "Classic" could be used only as a chronological designation and could not carry any imputation of comparative cultural development between areas of Mesoamerica. There have indeed been suggestions that the whole Preclassic-Classic-Postclassic temporal scheme should be discarded as inaccurate and irrelevant, but the problem is, first, that the scheme is so embedded in the literature of Maya archaeology that it would never really cease to be used (like the long outdated Neolithic, Bronze, and Iron Ages of European prehistory); and second, that any other such scheme of named and defined periods (such as the "horizons" and "intermediate periods" used in Andean archaeology) would be no more relevant and equally susceptible to anachronism. If we do discard the trinal designation, then it would seem more sensible to move immediately into a chronology expressed in terms of centuries A.D. or B.C., based on inscriptions and radiocarbon dates. In the Classic period, events (at many, but not all sites) can be placed in Long Count terms, but beyond the immediate reach of such documented dates we have at present only radiocarbon dates, even the most accurate of which has a built-in margin of error of nearly a century. Nevertheless, radiocarbon dating has formed a reasonable basis for the chronologies of other protohistoric civilizations, and a designation of "third century B.C.," based on implicit acceptance of the limitations of the radiocarbon method, would be at least as accurate as one of "early Late Preclassic." In reconciling the Long Count with this less precise but more extensively applicable method we would simply specify which correlation we were using, and at the same time, if we desired, specify which calibration scheme we would use to convert radiocarbon dates into calendar dates. (This is not the place to discuss the question of calibration, which is admirably summed up in an appendix to Colin Renfrew's *Before Civilization*, except to note that back to about 1000 B.C. calibration does not alter radiocarbon dates very much, but that a radiocarbon date of 2000 B.C. will calibrate at 2500 B.C. in solar years. I have calibrated all radiocarbon dates into calendar years, using the chart published by R. M. Clark in *Antiquity*, 1975.)

In spite of its inherent inaccuracies, radiocarbon dating is one of the few ways in which we can gain a notion of the absolute and relative chronology of Maya culture outside the Classic period, and a good example of its utility is the extension of the known length of the Preclassic by more than fifteen hundred years in recent research, described later in this chapter.

For the Postclassic period, radiocarbon dating is supplemented by a number of historical traditions, some recorded at the Spanish conquest, others entwined in the gnomic formulas of the native records known as the Books of Chilam Balam. Although some progress has been made in correlating these traditions with the observed archaeological sequence in Yucatan, Postclassic chronology is still far from precise.

Maya Prehistory in Outline

There is at present little evidence of the existence of Pleistocene hunters and gatherers anywhere in the Maya Area, although the first Americans must have passed through it on their way to South America more than eleven thousand years ago. They may have traveled along the coastline, which during the ice age was much farther seaward than it is now as a result of lower sea level; any evidence of such passage will have been drowned by the rising sea level as the glacial icecaps melted.

The earliest site so far known in the Maya lands is Los Tapiales (Figure 4.6), a small hunters' camp in the western highlands of Guatemala, dated by radiocarbon to as much as eleven thousand years ago. Its inhabitants ranged widely over the mountains, as can be seen from their utilization of obsidian: trace-element analysis of this has shown that they had collected it from three different outcrops, all between 50 and 75 kilometers (30–45 miles) from the site. Among the artifacts from Los Tapiales was the base of a fluted projectile point, a distinctive kind of weapon known from several sites of this period in North and South America, as well as from an undated site at San Rafael near Guatemala City, and recently from Belize.

Recent survey in the Quiché basin north of Los Tapiales has yielded more than 100 sites of the period from 8000–1000 B.C., including another fluted point and many stone tools similar to those known from the same period in the Tehuacan Valley in highland central Mexico. Also, a survey of the coastal zone of Belize by Richard S. MacNeish and S. Jeffrey K. Wilkerson has located dozens of sites of the Archaic period, before 2000 B.C. and perhaps as early as 9000 B.C. It appears that the coastal adaptation of preagricultural populations detected by Wilkerson in Veracruz extends southeast along the Caribbean coast to include the Maya lowlands. In 1978 excavations in the Loltun cave, in the Puuc hills not far northeast of Uxmal, penetrated a deep deposit with pottery in the upper levels back to about 2000 B.C., and below that several feet of aceramic levels with flaked stone tools. Taken together, the new evidence from the El Quiché basin in the highlands, from coastal Belize, and from the Yucatan peninsula shows widespread human penetration for thousands of years before the first appearance of a distinctly Maya cultural tradition. Whether these early hunters and gatherers are the ancestors of the Maya is a matter of debate.

The beginning of settled life in Mesoamerica occurs after 5000 B.C., when the domestication of maize, beans, and

4.6. Important sites in the Maya Area: Preclassic through Postclassic periods (1000 B.C.– A.D. 1500+ in calendar years).

other plants allowed an agricultural economy to develop. The investment in crops tied people to certain locations, and with the beginning of such settled villages new kinds of artifacts began to appear. The most striking innovation was the manufacture of pottery vessels for storage, cooking, and serving of food; pottery, because of its weight and fragility, is not often used by mobile groups and its appearance is often a good indication of long-term settlement.

The first pottery known in the Americas has been found in northwestern South America, dating to at least 3500 B.C. In Mesoamerica pottery of about 2500 B.C. has been found in the Tehuacan valley of highland central Mexico, and on the Pacific coast near Acapulco perhaps of several centuries earlier; in the valley of Oaxaca and on the coastal plains of Chiapas and Veracruz accomplished potters were at work by about 2000 B.C. Until recently the Maya Area was thought to share in this phase of early village development only marginally, if at all, since no sites earlier than about 900 B.C. were known in the lowlands and none earlier than 1200 B.C. in the highlands. Also, some anthropologists considered the tropical forest of the lowlands to be environmentally unsuited to an advanced culture, so that Classic Maya civilization had to be interpreted as a secondary development from prior advances in the highland plateaus of Mesoamerica.

Over the past five years more than thirty radiocarbon dates have become available for the site of Cuello, in northern Belize, where a series of stratified building and trash deposits more than 3 meters (10 feet) deep is associated with well-made pottery from the earliest levels up. The dates indicate continuous use of the site from about 2500 B.C., and not long after this early date there were buildings of timber frame on a low basal platform surfaced with white plaster (Figure 4.7). The earliest building platforms include one subcircular structure some 5 meters (16 feet)

4.7. Early plaster-surfaced structure excavated at Cuello, Belize, in 1980. Several sets of post holes can be seen, the earliest dating to perhaps 1000 B.C A plaster lined shallow basin or hearth lies off center within the building.

in diameter, with a fired clay hearth at the center of a ring of post holes, and a long oval platform about 13 by 6 meters (42 by 20 feet) that had a timber-framed building at its northern end. The size and layout of these two structures, dating to between 2500 and 2000 B.C., suggest possible ceremonial rather than domestic use. By 2000 B.C. the platforms were set around a plastered courtyard or patio, a plan that remained common in Mesoamerica down to the Spanish conquest. These early buildings stood on platforms with rounded ends, in which the postholes of the timber superstructure survive to indicate their layout and dimensions; between the major posts the walls would have been of light poles, perhaps covered with mud and plastered over, and the roof of palm thatch, much like Maya houses today (Figures 4.8, 3.15).

Some of the people who used these structures were buried close by; among the earliest burials found so far is one of a woman, relatively young but with her teeth worn down by gritty particles in her food. Her skull seems to have been deformed by using the forehead sling called a tumpline, still utilized by the Maya for carrying heavy loads. She lay in a shallow grave cut into the limestone bedrock, a pottery bowl over her face and another at her feet, and wore a necklace of roughly chipped shell beads.

In later burials of about 600 B.C. small jade beads were found, the first use of this semiprecious green stone in the Maya Area. It was brought from sources at least 400 kilo-

4.8. A building of about 900 B.C. (1550 B.C. in radiocarbon years) excavated at Cuello in 1980. The apsidal ends are partly unexcavated, but the overall dimensions of the building can be accurately gauged at 8 by 4 meters (26 by 13 feet). The major post holes can be seen around the perimeter, together with the low step and T-shaped ramp at the entrance. The latter suggests a ceremonial function. The two depressions are later intrusions.

meters (250 miles) away to the south, probably in the Motagua Valley, and shows that valued luxury goods were
being procured over very long distances even at this early
date. Whether the route ran overland through Petén and
down the Rio Hondo or up the Caribbean coast is uncertain, but in either case the use of canoe transport is plausible. The use of canoes can be argued for a yet earlier date,
about 900 B.C., because by then the inhabitants of Cuello
were acquiring corn-grinding *manos* and *metates* made of
pink sandstone from the Maya Mountains 150 kilometers
(94 miles) to the south, and the most direct route for the
movement of these heavy objects would have been by
water for a substantial part of the distance.

We can say with some confidence that these stone
utensils were used for grinding corn, because numerous
fragments of carbonized corn kernels and cobs have been
recovered at the Cuello site by the water-flotation technique. The earliest corn is small-cobbed and in many ways
comparable with the primitive corn found by Richard S.
MacNeish in the dry caves of the Tehuacan valley; it is,
however, a distinct breed, and clearly one that had adapted
to the humid tropical lowland climate. The Preclassic sequence at Cuello documents the gradual development of
this corn into larger-cobbed and higher-yielding varieties,
until by the Late Preclassic period the inhabitants were
cultivating a form of the Nal-Tel/Chapalote corn used in
Classic Maya times (Figure 4.9).

The earliest phases of occupation at Cuello are characterized
by pottery of the "Swasey" and "Bladen" complexes, the
latter contemporary with the "Xe" pottery found in early
Middle Formative sites in the southern lowlands. This
pottery is technically sophisticated even in the earliest
layers of the site, suggesting that earlier ancestors of the Cuello people lived somewhere in the region; the
buildings and stone tools at Cuello, as well as the pottery,
are in turn clearly ancestral to the later Preclassic Maya
cultural tradition. Whether the people of Cuello in the earliest phase spoke a language we would define as Maya we
can never know (although the lack of any other linguistic
group in the Maya lowlands in later times would suggest
that they did—see Chapter 3), but they were certainly *culturally* Maya: we have in northern Belize the earliest evi-

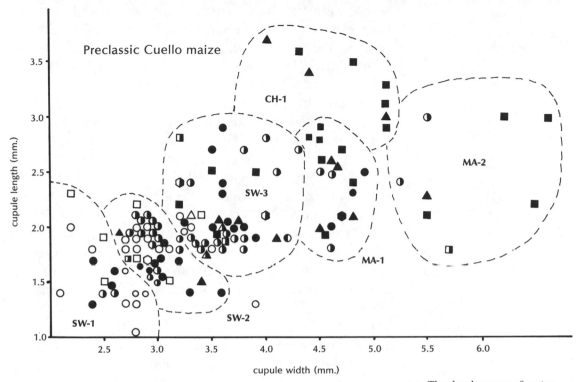

Preclassic Cuello maize

4.9. The development of maize over nearly 1300 years at Cuello, the longest sequence of preserved plant remains so far known in the Maya lands. The diagram shows the increasing size and changing shape through time of the cupules that hold the corn kernels, and, hence, the increasing size of the kernels themselves. The abbreviations are for Swasey types 1, 2, and 3, Middle Preclassic Mamom 1 and 2 and Late Preclassic Chicanel 1. Open symbols are specimens recovered from Middle Preclassic layers at Cuello, half-filled symbols those from late Middle Preclassic deposits, and solid symbols those from Late Preclassic contexts. The symbols' shapes correspond to different cupule shapes, and smaller symbols indicate transitional specimens.

dence so far of the development that culminated in Classic Maya civilization.

The next phase of Maya prehistory, the Middle Formative, is far more widely known, and has been documented since the Uaxactun excavations half a century ago. The pottery complex of this period is known from northern Yucatan southwest through Chiapas and southeast into El Salvador. It represents the first complete occupation of the Maya Area, and the uniformity of the pottery style (often called Mamom after the initially defined complex at Uaxactun) indicates considerable interaction among the various regions. Numerous sites of later importance were first occupied during the early Middle Formative period, including Tikal and Uaxactun in northeast Petén, Dzibilchaltun in northern Yucatan, Altar de Sacrificios and Seibal on the Rio de la Pasión, and Kaminaljuyu in the highlands of Guatemala. The Pasión sites have pottery similar to that from Chiapa de Corzo, in the deep trench of the middle Grijalva River in Chiapas, and there may have been a movement of people between the two regions down the valley of the Chixoy. The earliest levels at Seibal also yielded a ritual deposit of jades, including a "stiletto" or "blood-letter" in Olmec style; the Olmec, arguably America's first cultural group to attain the level of social complexity that we call civilization, had by 1300 B.C. evolved a relatively advanced society in the Gulf Coast lowlands of southern Veracruz and western Tabasco. Their sculptors carved giant stone heads from boulders brought from many miles away, and their procurement network extended south into the highlands of Oaxaca. The Seibal offering indicates contact between Olmec and Maya around 900 B.C., and blue jade beads at Cuello may document more distant links a century or two later, but whether the Maya contributed to the growth of Olmec culture prior to this, or whether the Olmec had any impact on the evolution of Middle Preclassic Maya society, remains unknown.

Human occupation of the Pacific coast of Chiapas had also begun by the fourth millennium B.C., with shellfish collectors living on low islands among the Chantuto mangrove swamps; the first pottery-using people settled further inland, on the coastal plain, where at sites such as Altamira and Paso de la Amada ceramics of the Barra complex from about 1700 B.C. are found, but the swamp site of Tlacachuero had a pottery-using occupation on top of the already ancient shell midden. Gareth Lowe, the excavator of the inland sites, has found parallels for the Barra pottery as far away as Ecuador, but admits its distinction from the Swasey pottery in Belize.

The Barra phase is followed by one named after the site of Ocós, also on the coastal plain; the pottery of this period, in the latter part of the first millennium B.C., is marked by rocker-stamping with the edge of a marine shell and by painting with iridescent red pigment. An occupation of this period precedes the major development at the first great Olmec site of San Lorenzo, to the north across the Isthmus of Tehuantepec, and Gareth Lowe would equate the Olmec people with the Mixe-Zoque linguistic group that still occupies the isthmian area.

From 1300 B.C. onward, down to perhaps 450 B.C., the Olmec cultural tradition dominated the region west of Tehuantepec, penetrating into the central basin of Mexico and spreading its influence east along the Pacific coast of the Maya Area. In the heartland of the Gulf Coast, at San Lorenzo and then at La Venta, massive public architecture and monumental sculpture appear, evidence of an organized and ranked, perhaps stratified, society with specialist artisans working to an ordained plan. Olmec pottery expresses a range of iconographic concepts complementing those found in sculpture, and both kinds of art mark the "Olmec diaspora" to the east and west. On the Pacific slope in the southern part of the Maya Area, Olmec low-relief stone carving is found at Tzutzuculi, and an Olmec pattern of offertory at San Isidro. Several sites have a formal plan close to that of La Venta, and the presence of ball courts at these sites toward the middle of the first millennium B.C. reflects another aspect of Olmec ritual activity and the beginning of a Mesoamerican tradition that survived into the colonial age. The most recent find has been a small version of an Olmec giant head, recarved into a figure seated in a niche, at Abaj Takalik on the Guatemalan piedmont, while the easternmost example of Olmec sculpture is still the carved boulder from Las Victorias, part of the Chalchuapa site in western El Salvador.

The Olmec also penetrated the Maya lowlands: a magnificent relief found at Xoc on the Rio Jatate in Chiapas in 1968 (and stolen by 1972) depicted a striding figure more than 2 meters (6.5 feet) high, with a grotesque mask, taloned feet, and a large bundle or plaque borne in its arms (Figure 4.10). Another large relief adorns one entry to the Loltun cave, a carving similar in scale to those at Tzutzuculi has recently been reported from Tenosique, and the Seibal jade cache mentioned earlier contained Olmec-style objects.

Thus three distinct elements have so far been detected as being possibly antecedent to the pan-Maya late Middle Preclassic horizon or as having a major coeval influence on it: the early occupation represented stratigraphically at Cuello, and at Loltun cave and the Maní cenote; the Barra phase of the Chiapas coast and the succeeding Ocós; and the Olmec civilization, arising on the Gulf Coast and spreading its artistic influence, if not its trade or people,

4.10. Olmec influence in the Maya lowlands: a striding figure carved in the rock at Xoc, Chiapas. The carving has now been looted.

east into the lowlands of the Pasión basin, Yucatan, and the Pacific coast.

The Middle Preclassic uniformity represented by Mamom pottery emerges first in the Maya lowlands, where it appeared at Cuello, Barton Ramie, and other sites by 600 B.C., and the westward spread through Chiapas did not occur until after 600 B.C., according to Arthur Demarest. A social model of the growth and fissioning of tribal societies as population expansion forced the Maya to seek and settle new ecological niches, to explain both the homogeneity and the expansion of Mamom ceramics, has been advanced by Joseph Ball.

Mamom pottery lacks specialized types for such functions as burial—people were interred with the same kinds
of vessels that they used in everyday life—but some differentiation in society is seen in the architecture. At Altar de
Sacrificios a platform 4 meters (13 feet) high faces onto a
planned plaza, and other platforms larger than would seem
necessary for an ordinary house foundation have been recorded at Nohoch Ek in the Belize Valley and Dzibilchaltun
in northern Yucatan. At Cuello in northern Belize the
early courtyard group, which had been reconstructed on
several occasions, was succeeded in the late Middle Formative period by a slightly expanded patio, on the north
side of which stood a rectangular building with stone walls
built of limestone cobbles and covered with plaster. A foundation burial beneath the threshold, and the ceremonial
pattern of demolition of the building, ca. 400 B.C., detected
by the excavators, both suggest that its function may have
been public rather than domestic; such a function has already been suggested for one or more of the buildings
around the preceding Early Preclassic courtyard and the
entire area of the Cuello site so far excavated is seen as the
ceremonial and elite residential core of the Preclassic village. If the interpretation is correct that architectural differentiation reflects social distinctions, then a ranked society may already have existed in the Early Preclassic
period, with special-purpose public buildings being constructed then or in the succeeding Middle Preclassic stage.

The southward routes that had been used since 600
B.C. for the procurement of jade were lengthened in the
late Middle Preclassic period into the volcanic highlands of
southern Guatemala, from which obsidian was for the first
time exported to the lowland zone in any quantity (although occasional pieces found their way through to
northern Belize in the preceding period. The
first source to be exploited was at San Martín Jilotepeque,
northwest of Guatemala City (Figure 4.6); obsidian from
there has been found in Middle Preclassic deposits at Edzna, Seibal, Barton Ramie, and Cuello, among other sites,
suggesting that the obsidian was taken over the mountains
into Petén and then shipped down the rivers (Figure 8.4).
The same routes could have been used for jade and other
highland mineral products.

The discovery of blue jade beads and a blue jade claw-shaped pendant at Cuello in layers dating to ca. 600 B.C. suggests direct contact with the Olmec world. Blue jade is not found with any frequency in the Maya Area, but at about this date the Olmec were carving superb objects from the material, the source of which is still unknown (it might possibly lie in Guerrero; another postulated source in Costa Rica has recently been found to be geologically improbable). The exchange of both jade and obsidian in the Middle Preclassic period has shown that much of Mesoamerica had already formed an interaction sphere within which the network of commercial and information transmission from region to region was highly complex. The Maya Area, although on the eastern margin of this sphere, was undoubtedly part of it, and the generic resemblance of many features of the intellectual and religious superstructure of Mesoamerican civilization probably dates from this time.

A division between Middle and Late Preclassic periods was suggested by Robert Smith on the basis of the Uaxactun pottery. He placed it by guess-dating at 300 B.C., and this has remained the formal limit until recently; calibrated radiocarbon dates for the Middle–Late Preclassic transition at Cuello suggest that it should be placed at about 400 B.C. The Late Preclassic is marked by the appearance of pottery of the Chicanel sphere, a clear development from Mamom in which widespread standardization of vessel form, finish, and decoration become apparent. Although pottery from different sites can be distinguished by minor details there is impressive uniformity of intention and accepted ceramic models. Most of the pottery is plain slipped ware, with a bright red predominant and a marked waxy finish that feels like a candle (this is found in Mamom also); vessel forms become more adventurous and some are true masterpieces of the potter's art (Figure 4.11).

Chicanel pottery has been found at almost every Maya site investigated, and there is a dramatic increase in the number of site occupancies known over those of the preceding Middle Formative period—in northern Belize a fourfold gain—and in the size of the area of each site over which Chicanel trash is found. Even if some of this increase is due simply to the greater accessibility of Chicanel

4.11. The Maya potter as artist: an elegant vessel of the Late Preclassic period, ca. A.D. 200, from San Antonio, Albion Island, Belize.

deposits, the expansion is too general to represent anything other than a substantial population increase and a concomitant increase in settlement size. Much of the uniformity of Chicanel pottery may result from increased contact among such larger and perforce more closely spaced settlements.

The sites of this period not only become more numerous and larger, but also undergo internal differentiation: specific areas of sites now have public architecture marking them off as ceremonial precincts rather than residential areas, and these public buildings display features anticipating later developments in the Classic period, including the use of corbel vaulting to roof burial chambers at Tikal and Holmul, among other sites. The tombs themselves contain a variety of grave goods indicating the importance of ceremonial luxuries such as stingray spines for bloodletting and decorative shells, while the differences in grave furnishings from one burial to another show that society was becoming divided into those with preferential access to these scarce and desirable goods and those without. Jade becomes a spectacular marker of status in death, both in the quantity of beads made into thick ropelike necklaces and in the quality of workmanship devoted to carving this refractory stone (Figure 4.12).

Tikal is a good example of a site that was transformed during the late Preclassic period: occupation is much more

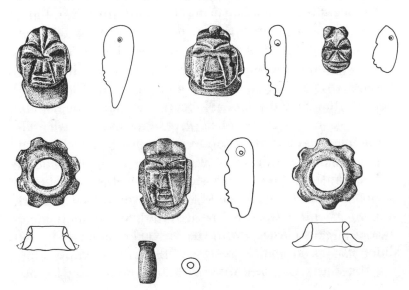

4.12. Maya jades of the Late Preclassic period: a set of four head pendants from Nohmul, Belize, depicting four distinct iconographic personalities; these may be gods or connected with the four world directions of Maya cosmology.

widespread after 250 B.C. than before that date, and at the
same time the ceremonial precinct of the North Acropolis
began to develop, with cut stone masonry instead of rough
boulders. The most striking building of this date at Tikal,
Structure 5C–54, is a pyramid more than 30 meters (100
feet) high, with four stairways flanked by huge masks, and
sides 80 meters (260 feet) long. Another colossal pyramid
of this period has recently been identified at Lamanai, in
northern Belize (Figure 9.4), and much of the huge site of
El Mirador in northern Petén is also known   to be Late Preclassic in date, including one of the largest pyramids in the
Maya world. The small site of Cerros, on the coast of northern Belize, has proved to be entirely Late Preclassic in construction, although until work began there the size of the
pyramids had led to the assumption that it was a Late Classic site. All of these recent discoveries dwarf the best-
known Late Preclassic building, Structure E-VII-sub at
Uaxactun, which is itself eloquent testimony to the skill of
architect, sculptor, and stucco worker (Figure 9.3), and to
the managerial control that brought their combined efforts
to fruition.

Members of this ruling elite may be portrayed on the
walls of the tomb of Burial 166 in the North Acropolis at
Tikal, where elaborately dressed individuals on the murals
accompany in death a person with rich grave goods; the
pottery in tombs is now often of forms specially made for
sepulture. Overall, the character of Late Preclassic society
is complex in its social layering, its community planning,
and its range of occupational specializations. It is no longer
implausible to suggest that Maya culture had by this date
already attained the level of civilization, and that the subsequent changes that mark the beginning of the Classic period (or that have traditionally been taken as doing so) are
superficial rather than substantive. Preclassic Maya civilization is not a contradiction in terms: it is the reality that
has emerged from the past two decades of field research.

The transition from Preclassic to Classic has a number of
curious features, and some scholars have dubbed the terminal part of the Preclassic period, roughly from A.D. 50 to
250, the "Protoclassic," with the implied characteristics of
differentiation from the Preclassic and in some way presaging the Early Classic. Among the differentiating factors

they see developments that apparently are not local, but seem to result from the injection into the Maya lowlands of cultural influence, perhaps accompanying human groups from the highland zone. There is no argument over the fact that most lowland sites so far studied were occupied during this period, whether it is called Protoclassic or Terminal Preclassic, nor that the period saw a dramatic increase in the cultural development of the lowlands. Dispute centers on the possibility of, and degree of physical intrusion by, new settlers who, like the Normans in Saxon England after 1066, imposed their own ideas on the existing society.

The late James Gifford was probably the most extreme of these invasionists, deriving not only the changes of the Protoclassic from a migration out of El Salvador, but also ascribing the Mamom-Chicanel transition six centuries earlier to another migration (an opinion not generally accepted). Gifford has been followed by Robert Sharer, on the basis of his work at the Salvadorean site of Chalchuapa, and by Payson Sheets (who also worked at Chalchuapa) who ascribes the postulated migration to the catastrophic eruption of the volcano Ilopango near San Salvador, and to the subsequent search of the people for new land. Richard Adams has accepted a similar intrusion in the lowland site of Altar de Sacrificios, but a number of Mayanists (among them Gordon Willey, who directed the Altar research) reject the invasionist explanation. They prefer a local evolution into a complex society, which then drew into itself artistic and other stimuli from the highland zone, with which it already had long-standing trade ties. The accumulating evidence of recent research supports this model of an indigenous emergence of civilization in the Maya lowlands and suggests that any migration from the highlands would have had a very local impact. That any such migration occurred is still only a matter of speculation, and the evidence of social recovery after other catastrophic volcanic eruptions (such as Vesuvius in A.D. 79, Thera in about 1500 B.C., and Krakatau in A.D. 1883) does not suggest that the Ilopango eruption would have caused regional depopulation.

Even if the causes were autochthonous, changes did occur in the lowlands during the final centuries of the Preclassic period and at the beginning of the Classic: a num-

ber of substantial and prosperous Preclassic sites were
abandoned or reduced to mere hamlets, while others went
on to develop into the great centers of the Classic period.
Tikal flourished mightily, while Seibal and Dzibilchaltun
experienced severe recession, and Cerros in northern
Belize was largely abandoned. No environmental cause
seems to explain this selectivity, and a human, political one
is the most likely—that increasing competition between
centers of expanding population and social differentiation
led to warfare, conquest, and the removal of the subjugated
settlement from further competition by forcible depopulation. The seriousness with which the prospect of war was
taken can be seen at Becan, in the center of the lowlands,
where the entire ceremonial precinct was surrounded by
a moat 1.9 kilometers (1.17 miles) long, dug into bedrock
and averaging 16 meters (52 feet) in width and 2.5 meters
(8 feet) in depth; the spoil from the moat was piled into a
rampart averaging 3.6 meters (12 feet) in height and 10
meters (32.5 feet) in width. The earthworks alone would
present an enemy with an obstacle more than 6 meters
(about 20 feet) high, while a timber palisade on the rampart would increase this by half again as much. The most
likely date for these massive fortifications, which must
have involved the organized labor of hundreds of men, is in
the Terminal Preclassic period between A.D. 100 and 250.
Recently an island site called Muralla de Leon has been
explored in a lake east of Tikal. It has a defensive wall,
smaller by far than that of Becan but possibly of the same
Protoclassic date, and it has been suggested that it was a
western outpost of the peoples making and using Protoclassic pottery, who are concentrated in Belize and eastern
Petén.

Certain sites selectively flourished during this period,
but only a few have yielded the innovative pottery that has
been held to characterize the Protoclassic phase. The pottery includes resist decoration in the Usulutan style of Salvador—produced by differential coating with several fine
clay slips or by painting the design in wax or honey before
firing to give contrasting colors—gloss surfacing and polychrome painting on other vessels, and a range of new
shapes including the swollen mammiform support. These
traits are found disparately in the Maya highlands, the

mammiform support in particular being of great antiquity and wide distribution—but the particular combinations in which they are found in the lowlands are not duplicated in the highlands, and each lowland site where Protoclassic pottery appears has its own set of local variations on the overall theme.

The distribution of this innovative pottery was limited, and only a few sites have yielded more than a few sherds or vessels; the center of distribution is in the Rio Hondo valley, with major collections from Holmul and Nohmul, and in central Belize immediately to the south at Barton Ramie and Tzimin Kax. Curiously, the major sites of northern Petén such as Tikal and Uaxactun have only a trace of Protoclassic pottery, and its presence is clearly no guarantee of subsequent Early Classic importance.

The work of Duncan Pring at Nohmul has shown that even within a site the distribution of Protoclassic pottery is uneven. Most of it is found in graves, but a deep deposit at a structure interpreted as the river port of Nohmul also yielded a complete range of Protoclassic vessels including utility storage types. The best explanation for the distribution within sites seems to be that this pottery was restricted to the use of a certain stratum of Maya society in the Late Preclassic period, both in life and in death, but there is no evidence that these people were immigrants into the lowland sites. Whatever the social significance of the new ceramic fashion, the florescence of many sites that lacked it indicates that the burgeoning of Classic Maya civilization was in no way linked with the localized adoption of exotic and innovative ideas in pottery, even though such features as polychrome ornament and gloss surfacing became universally used during the Early Classic period.

In the valley of Guatemala on the continental divide, the site of Kaminaljuyu, occupied from the early Middle, or even the Early Preclassic onwards, had developed into an impressive center by 500 B.C. and continued to expand during the Late Preclassic, with a ceremonial precinct growing up just north of a small lake. Mapping of the site by the Carnegie Institution of Washington and excavations between 1936 and 1942 demonstrated that at least a hundred of the impressive mounds, including some of the largest, were of Preclassic date. Numerous sculptures were also

4.13. Late Preclassic highland sculpture: Stela 10, a massive but fragmentary monument, from Kaminaljuyu. It has two figures with attributes in a clearly Maya style and an inscription in hieroglyphic writing of a style related to but not identical with that of the Maya lowlands.

Drawn by James Porter.

found, and though few bore inscriptions, there were palpable resemblances to the Classic Maya style (Figure 4.13). The C.I.W. work demonstrated that the Maya Classic in the lowlands was later than much of the expansion of Kaminaljuyu and also later than the initial growth of Teotihuacan (which occurred in the early centuries of the Christian era). Although, in recent years, the Late Preclassic has been recognized as a period of major development and change in the Maya lowlands, the relationship of this to the coeval florescence of the highlands from Teotihuacan through Oaxaca to Kaminaljuyu has not yet been ascertained.

The end of the Preclassic phase and the beginning of the Classic period have in the past been formally defined by the appearance of vaulted stone architecture, monumental inscriptions, and polychrome pottery; as we have noted above, all three of these traits are now known to have appeared at differing times during the Terminal Preclassic in various sites, and the "official" beginning of the Classic has been pushed back to A.D. 250 (from A.D. 300) to accommodate the newly discovered stelae dating to the third century.

Although recent work has shown that much earlier Maya inscriptions exist in the highland zone, for example at Abaj Takalik, and may also be present in the lowlands (as at Polol), it is still true that monumental inscriptions in the lowland zone did not become widespread until the fourth century. Numerical notation on seals is known to have occurred earlier, and the utilization of bark or deerskin books for keeping official records and almanacs during the Late Preclassic era must be reckoned probable. What happened at the beginning of the Classic period was the codification of the numerical system and writing for lapidary use on public monuments, the purpose of which was to reinforce the power and glory of the ruling dynasty: writing progressed, in the Maya civilization as in those of the Mediterranean, from private record keeping to public propaganda.

At present the earliest dated monument in the lowlands (apart from the incompletely deciphered altar at Polol) is Stela 29 at Tikal, A.D. 292 (Figure 4.14); but there is, of course, no reason to suppose that this was the first such monument to be carved and erected. The monuments of Abaj Takalik (Figure 4.15) on the Pacific slope have yielded one Long Count date of A.D. 126, and another monument there seems to be at least as early as the first century B.C. and possibly as early as the third century B.C. Early monuments at El Baul, also on the Pacific slope south of Guatemala City, and Chiapa de Corzo in Chiapas show that Abaj Takalik is not a unique site, and the prospect of still earlier monuments and inscriptions is a very real one. The origin of monumental inscriptions in Mesoamerica is still debated, although those of Oaxaca are generally accepted as being the earliest so far known. There is no evidence that the Olmec had either writing or a calendar prior to 500 B.C., and on the present balance of proof either a single or a dual origin for numeracy and writing, in an area between the valley of Oaxaca and eastern Guatemala, seems equally plausible in the period 600–300 B.C.

Although a plain stela, dated by its stratigraphic context to about A.D. 100, is known from the site of Cuello in Be-

4.14. The earliest dated Maya stela, Stela 29 at Tikal. At least one plain stela some 200 years earlier is known, and the stela cult may have antedated the use of stelae as dynastic monuments with public inscriptions in the Maya lowlands.

lize, the first Maya lowland stelae to have carving and dated inscriptions occur in northeast Petén, at Tikal and its dependency Uolantun, at Uaxactun—a few hours' journey north—and at Balakbal still further north. This region, in the heart of the lowlands, has been characterized by William Rathje as a core zone, surrounded by a ring of buffer zones. Rathje suggested in a notable *American Antiquity* article that the core lacked natural resources, specifically hard stone for *metates*, obsidian for cutting tools, and salt; that the need for these materials stimulated the development of long-distance trade routes; and that the managerial organization necessary to conduct such trade arose as a direct response. The monuments and elaborate architecture of core sites such as Tikal were a concrete expression of the power of this managerial elite.

The buffer zones, on the other hand, had easier access to these vital resources, did not need such managerial expertise, and did not develop such a social mechanism capable of organizing commercial and political power; the practice of stela erection and the political control it betokened were exported from the core to the buffer zone. In Rathje's

Classic period from A.D. 400 to 700, the second a Terminal Classic from A.D. 800 to 900. If both were adopted (and acceptance has been only partial so far), then Classic Maya chronology would appear thus:

Early Classic A.D. 250–400
Middle Classic A.D. 400–700
Late Classic A.D. 700–800
Terminal Classic A.D. 800–900.

The Middle Classic division was originally proposed by Lee Parsons as being the period during which the influence of the great city of Teotihuacan, in the central basin of Mexico, spread throughout southern Mesoamerica. Parsons suggested two phases, the first from A.D. 400 to 550, during which Teotihuacan made economic and cultural contact with a number of centers in the Maya Area, including Tikal, Copan, and Kaminaljuyu; at these places Teotihuacan influence is recognizable in sculpture, architecture, ceramics, and iconography generally, and some scholars have postulated an actual Teotihuacan takeover at heavily influenced sites such as Kaminaljuyu. The second phase of the Middle Classic is described by Parsons as Teotihuacanoid, with some weakening of ties to the metropolis and increasing autonomy in art and iconography, terminating in the destruction of Teotihuacan and the cessation of its influence in the eighth century.

The impact of Teotihuacan, already a city of more than 125,000 and perhaps 200,000 people by the beginning of the Middle Classic period, is an aspect of Maya civilization that has become fully apparent only in the past two decades as the result of both excavation and epigraphic work. Teotihuacanoid warriors flank the figure of Stormy Sky, ruler of Tikal, on Stela 31 at that site (Figure 4.16), and the goggle eyes of Tlaloc, the Teotihuacano version of the Maya rain god Chaac, appear on pottery vessels decorated in exotic style. They also appear on a building known prosaically as Structure 5D–43, which is built in a hybrid Maya-Teotihuacan architectural style, and which lies just behind Temple 1 in a strategic location at the heart of Tikal. Sometimes jocularly called "the Teotihuacan embassy," the building is well placed to monitor all ceremonial activity

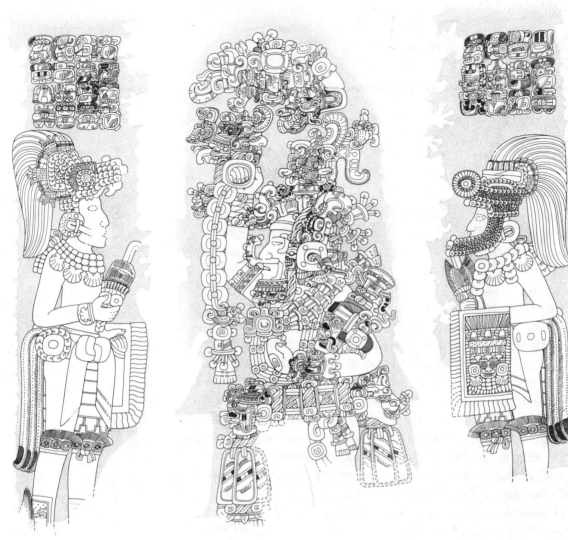

4.16. Stela 31 at Tikal, erected probably in A.D. 445, shows the ruler Stormy Sky, who came to the throne there in about A.D. 426, in Maya costume, but flanked by two shield-bearing warriors in Teotihuacan style. In the sky above the ruler is his predecessor, Curl Nose.

and much of the commercial and political life of the great Maya center. It has been suggested that the ruler Curl Nose was an outsider who married into an old, established Tikal family and legitimated his claim to the throne, but how, why, and whence he came are matters of debate. Given the great Teotihuacan impact on the highland site of Kaminaljuyu, and the fact that highland-lowland trade and interaction were well established (with Kaminaljuyu probably controlling the great El Chayal obsidian source that supplied Tikal), it seems more likely that Curl Nose came from there than that he was a metropolitan Teotihuacano,

but the latter possibility cannot be ruled out. Similarly, the
warriors on Stela 31 at Tikal suggest a possible military in-
tervention to put Curl Nose on the throne. In that Tikal's
rise to prominence as a major Early (or Middle) Classic
center coincides with the rule of the Sky Dynasty, the impact of Teotihuacan or a Teotihuacanized Kaminaljuyu
may well have been a vital catalyst.

Far to the north, a short episode of Teotihuacan intrusion
has been documented at Dzibilchaltun, where a building in
pure *talud-tablero* style (see the following paragraphs) was
constructed in an area with few inhabitants. It was a late
intrusion, dating to ca. A.D. 600, and E. Wyllys Andrews V
suggests that its builders may have been concerned with
monitoring the coastal salt beds a short distance to the
north and perhaps controlling distribution of the product,
as they may have done with the obsidian and cacao produced around Kaminaljuyu.

Teotihuacan influence has been detected at several other
lowland sites also, with similarly obscure implications. At
the small Belizean coastal plain site of Altun Ha a tomb was
found containing a cache of obsidian. The obsidian itself
was the green variety from a source near Teotihuacan, and
the layout of the cache was reminiscent of offerings of the
Miccaotli phase at Teotihuacan itself. Both physical contact
with central Mexico and the presence of an individual
knowledgeable in the ritual of Teotihuacan are attested.
The date given to this burial, at the very beginning of
the Early Classic period, has been challenged by Duncan
Pring, who places it substantially later and probably within
the main Middle Classic phase of Teotihuacan influence;
this challenge, if correct, removes one of the most fascinat-
ing implications of the Altun Ha find—that Teotihuacan
influence was present in the Maya lowlands at just the moment when Classic civilization emerged, butterflylike,
from the chrysalis of the Late Preclassic.

At Becan a similar conjunction of Teotihuacan physical
contact and ritual knowledge has been reported, in the discovery of a pottery vessel containing a set of small human
figurines; green obsidian has also been found at Becan.
Several other sites have yielded only green obsidian, indicating contact with an exchange network that included
central Mexican sources, and the overall Teotihuacanoid

presence in the Maya lowlands seems to be directly restricted to only a few sites; this is, however, no guide to the underlying importance that inclusion in the southern Mesoamerican interaction sphere, dominated by Teotihuacan, may have had for the development of Maya civilization.

In the highlands, by contrast, there is overwhelming evidence of Teotihuacan's cultural presence: the C.I.W. excavation of Mounds A and B at Kaminaljuyu in 1936–1942 revealed buildings with the *talud-tablero* architecture characteristic of Teotihuacan (a sloping panel with a framed vertical panel above it), and the major mound group called the "Acropolis," excavated by Gustavo Espinosa, proved to consist of a massive succession of such Teotihuacanoid buildings. The burials in Mounds A and B yielded pottery either imported from Teotihuacan or copying the style assiduously; they also contained Maya-lowland vessels of Early Classic date (and the synchronism thus established between the valley of Mexico, the valley of Guatemala, and the Petén showed clearly that Classic Maya civilization was later in its beginnings than the urban expansion of Teotihuacan, a discovery that greatly altered interpretations of Mesoamerican cultural development).

The most recent work at Kaminaljuyu between 1968 and 1971 by William Sanders and Joseph Michels has led to an interpretation of the site as the seat of a chiefdom, divided into five subchiefdoms, each split into moieties. One of the subchiefdoms is seen as having been paramount and another to have acted as host to the Teotihuacan community. That community has itself been envisioned by various archaeologists as a conquering-warrior aristocracy or as a settlement of economically powerful merchants. The location of Kaminaljuyu on the continental divide and its proximity to valuable resources, including obsidian at El Chayal and good cacao-growing country on the Pacific piedmont, lend credence to this economic interpretation of both its prosperity and its attraction to Teotihuacan, and Kenneth Brown has recently suggested that both the site and the valley around it should be interpreted as a "port of trade." Certainly, Teotihuacan cultural influence reached out into the rich agricultural countryside of Escuintla, to the south of Kaminaljuyu on the Pacific slope: looting on a massive scale in recent years has yielded thousands of elaborate incensarios and other funerary vessels in pure metropolitan Teotihuacan style.

It has been suggested that a hiatus in the erection of stelae between 9.5.0.0.0. and 9.8.0.0.0. (A.D. 534–593) in the central part of the lowlands was the result of withdrawal of direct contact with Teotihuacan—an economic jolt with political repercussions—and that the final destruction of Teotihuacan in the eighth century had an even more disastrous, though slower-acting, effect that resulted in the collapse of Late Classic Maya civilization and the

Page 137, para. 1, change last sentence to read: Both theories have factors in their favor, but neither is so far proven, and regional warfare and conquest may have been a more proximate and potent cause.

After the hiatus the stela cult recovers its vigor, and with the beginning of the Late Classic phase the civilization of the Maya enters its most spectacular period. At Tikal in particular, with the advent of a new dynasty, there began a colossal program of construction which resulted in the six major temples and the numerous twin-pyramid groups that, together with the North Acropolis temples and the Central Acropolis palaces, form the spectacular ceremonial precinct we see today, more than a thousand years later (Figure 4.17).

The stela cult reached its apogee at the end of the eighth century: in 9.18.0.0.0. more sites dedicated monuments

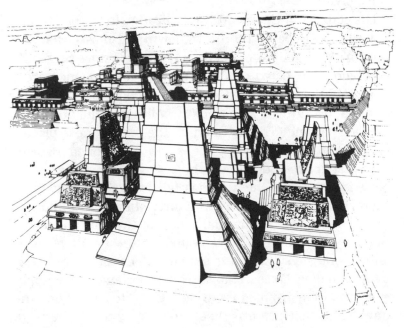

4.17. A major Classic period ceremonial precinct: the great plaza of Tikal.

4.18. The latest known Initial
Series date: a stela from
Tonina, Chiapas, dated to
10.4.0.0.0 (A.D. 909).

than ever before, and between 9.15.0.0.0. (A.D. 731) and
9.18.0.0.0. (A.D. 790) more stelae were erected than in any
other comparable length of time. In the ninth century, however, the cult fell into rapid decline (Figure 4.18), and at
the same time the great ceremonial precincts began to be
abandoned to the rain forest. Archaeological evidence is not
precise enough to say whether abandonment occurred immediately after the latest monuments, but at a few sites
there is evidence indicating that the ceremonial precinct
and settlement continued to function for decades after the
erection of the last stela. Pusilha, in southern Belize, is a
case in point; the last firmly dated stela is at 9.15.0.0.0., but
the site continued to be occupied and to support the makers of fine pottery for perhaps another century. Pusilha also
imported pottery figurines from the neighboring center of
Lubaantun, which flourished for about one hundred and
fifty years from A.D. 700 to 850 without erecting a single
stela. Although the depopulation and abandonment of the
rain-forest sites resulted in the end of stela erection, the
converse is not necessarily true.

The characteristics of the Classic period have been only
sketched in this chapter, for much of the rest of the book
deals with them: the Classic, and in particular the Late and
Terminal Classic, are our major sources of information on
Maya civilization.

The collapse of Classic Maya civilization in the ninth century A.D. is probably the best-known and most-discussed
topic in the whole history of the Maya. Ever since Stephens
at Palenque reflected on "the spectacle of this once great
and lovely city, overturned, desolate, and lost, discovered by
accident, overgrown with trees for miles around, and without even a name to distinguish it," the reason these places,
once so prosperous and alive, were abandoned has intrigued scholars and laymen alike.

A wide range of theories has been advanced, invoking
the malign operation of both natural phenomena and human actions. One influential group of theories suggested
that the environment deteriorated as the result of over-
cultivation: the soil became exhausted, erosion removed it
to fill in shallow lakes, removing an important water supply,
or competition from grass weeds grew too great for the
Maya with their primitive tools to be able to till the land.

Extensions of these ecological theories suggest variously that the environment was basically unsuited to support an advanced society, so that its failure was predestined, that population outran resources, or that epidemic disease swept through the Maya lands.

A second major group of theories are social rather than ecological, and suggest weakness in the structure of Maya society leading to internal dissolution, or tempting invasion from without—in either case stimulating warfare and the collapse of the Maya elite. One of the most influential social models has been that propounded by Eric Thompson, who suggested that the peasantry became disaffected by increasing burdens of tribute and an increasingly exotic and irrelevant group of cults that they were compelled to support; a gap opened between rulers and ruled that led to bloody revolution, the destruction of the elite and their temples and palaces, and a return to a less organized type of agricultural society. Thompson's model thus linked economic stress to moral dismemberment, and in later versions of his model he incorporated the influence of malnutrition and disease as explanations for the massive depopulation of the rain-forest zone that accompanied the collapse of the social order.

A number of scholars have suggested military intrusion from Yucatan or from the Gulf Coast as a significant factor in the collapse, while admitting that such intrusions could have been into a power vacuum resulting from an internally generated collapse, rather than themselves being its cause. Their evidence comes from new pottery types and art motifs found in particular at Seibal, where leaders with non-Classic Maya standards in iconography appear on ninth-century monuments during a late florescence of the site.

These ecological and social explanations can be argued as having been either internally or externally generated, with environmental degradation, disease, and revolution as essentially internal causes, and invasion and economic collapse due to changes elsewhere in Mesoamerica as external ones. The whole topic of the collapse has been exhaustively examined by the authors of *The Classic Maya Collapse* (edited by T. Patrick Culbert), and a much more complex model of the dissolution of Maya civilization has emerged. In this, the withdrawal of Teotihuacan influence led to increased independent control by the local Maya elites, who expressed their power vis-à-vis their subjects and their neighbors and rivals in the construction of more elaborate temples than had yet been seen. The social distance between elite and commoners increased, the elite became hereditary, and greater burdens were placed on the commoners. Population size, density, and pressure increased, putting a strain on food resources and forcing the adoption of intensive and collective methods of agriculture. The hunger for land led to increasing friction between neighboring communities, and between the Maya and adjacent societies. A decrease in nutritional standards, detected in the skeletons of Late Classic burials, increased susceptibility to endemic diseases, which may have become epidemic. The level of managerial organization of Maya civilization was inadequate to cope with these unprecedented stresses, and the buildup of strain resulted in a swift and catastrophic collapse accompanied by widespread depopulation through warfare, malnutrition, and disease, until those who survived were again able to achieve a stable agricultural society at a much lower level of population density and social organization.

In a way this multiple-cause model of the collapse can be likened to a great descending spiral with the speed of descent forever increasing. The stress on food resources —already being distributed by an administrative system stretched to the utmost to ensure that supplies reached the semiurban populations concentrated around the great ceremonial precincts—would have needed to increase only slightly for the ensuing malnutrition to lead to a substantial decrease in the efficiency with which work was done. The first people to suffer would not have been the elite, with preferential access to and guaranteed supplies of food (reflected, again, in their excavated skeletons), nor the rural farmers who could always supplement their diet in the forest. The initial impact of malnutrition would have been on the lower members of the administrative and artisan classes in the semiurban settlements, the clerks and porters on whom depended the whole tightly geared machinery of food distribution and social organization. Disruption in this sector could have led to widespread food shortage even while production was still just adequate, and the disruption would have been both cumulative and spreading. Such conditions could have produced Eric Thompson's revolt of the commoners against their rulers, even if the burdens of work and the isolation of the gods had not done so, and also opened up the Maya lands to neighbors made aggressive by similar stresses.

After the collapse, which on archaeological evidence certainly combined widespread depopulation with a·decay of the artistic, political, and intellectual superstructure of society, people still continued to live in many parts of the rain-forest zone, especially around the lakes and along the coasts. Northern Yucatan continued to function at a much higher level of population and organization, and there is archaeological evidence that people from the north moved southward into the vacuum left by the southern collapse, perhaps relieving pressure on the northern centers.

The Postclassic Period

The period following the abandonment of the rain-forest centers is known as the Postclassic, and terminates with the far greater disaster of the Spanish conquest in the mid-sixteenth century. The Long Count method of dating was not used, and monumental inscriptions were no longer carved, although the cyclical Calendar Round remained. Dating events within the Postclassic period is thus a problem, and radiocarbon dating, even with its margin of error, again becomes useful.

The Postclassic era is formally divided into an Early and a Late component by some scholars, although a triple division including a Middle Postclassic is probably more useful. In this the Early period would last from about A.D. 900 to 1250, the Middle from 1250 to 1450, and the Late from 1450 to the conquest.

The Early Postclassic is in some places difficult to separate from the Terminal Classic, marked as the latter is in some sites by irruptions of non-Classic Maya influence, and the precise chronology of the major site of this period, Chichén Itzá, has in turn been shifted back and forth over a span of some three centuries. In this book I take the view that the Toltec buildings in the north sector of the Chichén Itzá ceremonial precinct are not later in date than all the Puuc-

style buildings of the southern sector, and that they represent a northward extension of a functioning Late Classic
precinct, built by the same labor with the same materials
and thus with an inevitable structural and stylistic continuity. The Puuc style itself I take to be the northern equivalent of the grandiose Late Classic styles of Petén, beginning by A.D. 700 and persisting beyond A.D. 900. The exact
nature of the Toltec intrusion—whether it was, as legend
has it, a group of highland Mexicans who left the plateau
and established a new state in Yucatan, or whether the
Mexican influence was actually exerted by coastal Putun
Maya from Tabasco expanding their commercial and political sway—remains uncertain. What is certain is that non-
Maya ideas dominate the architecture and art of the north
sector of Chichén Itzá, and that many of them have close
parallels in Toltec Tula, north of the basin of Mexico. The
four stairways of the Castillo (Figure 4.19), the forest of
square piers in the Mercado and around the Temple of the
Warriors, the grisly platform of the *tzompantli* decorated
with severed heads, and the emphasis on bloody sacrifice
in the ball-court carvings all show a new and alien influence at work (Figure 9.27). The beginning of this influence may be as early as the ninth century, on the basis of
radiocarbon dates, and it has been suggested (though not
widely accepted) that the beginning was even earlier and
that the direction of cultural impact was from Chichén to
Tula rather than the reverse.

The most likely

Page 142, add to end of para. 1: Recent excavations of Isla Cerritos, an islet off the north coast of
Yucatan identified as a port for Chichén Itzá, showed that 85 percent of the obsidian came from sources
in the region of Tula.

...ship at Chichén allied to a new po-
litical rulership. No comparable sites exist in Yucatan,
however, and so we must choose between Chichén flourishing parallel with the latter florescence of the Puuc sites,
or surviving alone after their abandonment. The former
seems the more likely, but since we have little evidence for
the date of abandonment of sites such as Uxmal, its precise
placement in time remains debatable.

One episode of northern expansion does have some
chronological firmness, and that is the southward movement of Yucatec peoples in the period immediately following the southern collapse, in about the tenth century. At
the site of Nohmul, in northern Belize, stone-walled build-

4.19. The Castillo at Chichén Itzá: the major temple pyramid of the "Toltec" northern sector of the site dating to ca. A.D. 900, showing a fusion of Maya and central Mexican traits.

ings of northern form directly overlie the clean plaster floors of Late Classic houses of the eighth and ninth centuries, and graves containing pottery of northern inspiration are associated with both styles of building. The ceremonial precinct of Nohmul contained new buildings, placed in some cases in front of the stairs of abandoned Classic buildings, which included a circular structure related in type to the Casa Redonda at Chichén Itzá and a hollow-square building recalling the gallery-courtyard structures common at Chichén (Figure 5.15). The evidence from this site, although so far little excavation has been done, is of continued habitation right through the collapse period, with an incursion of a new elite group from the north; how long the Classic houses remained occupied, and how much of the Classic ceremonial precinct remained in use are questions that only extensive future excavation can answer.

A similar continuity of occupation into the Early Postclassic has been documented at Barton Ramie, in the Belize River valley, where the density of population diminished very little in the century following the collapse, although the site was then abandoned. Barton Ramie lies within one of the few areas of the southern lowlands in which extensive Postclassic occupation has been archaeologically documented, an area that reaches east from Lake Petén Itzá toward the Caribbean. A continuous pottery sequence covering the half millennium between the collapse and the conquest has been elucidated by William Bullard,

George Cowgill, and others, and a number of impressive sites have been explored; probably the most spectacular is Topoxte (Figure 4.20), on a series of islands in Lake Yaxha, with a tightly planned ceremonial precinct and dense areas of habitation. The layout of Topoxte resembles the coeval fortified towns of the highland zone more than it does the expansive Classic period ceremonial precincts of its own region—such as Yaxha, which faces Topoxte from the north shore of the lake. It has been suggested that the Maya town of Tayasal, visited by Hernan Cortes in 1525 and conquered by the Spanish only in 1697, may have been Topoxte and not the island site in Lake Petén Itzá now occupied by Flores, the modern capital of Petén. Wherever Tayasal lay, the account of Cortes's march makes it clear that the central Petén lake region was densely occupied by Maya villages and in this region, at least, there had been a recovery from the Classic collapse to a level of organized, if not civilized, life.

In about A.D. 1250 major changes occurred in northern Yucatan: if Chichén Itzá had not already been abandoned

4.20. Two of the islands of Topoxte in Lake Yaxha, Petén, with densely packed buildings of the later Postclassic period. The overall plan resembles the fortified sites of the highlands, but some of the building groups show close parallels to the late capital of Mayapan in northern Yucatan.

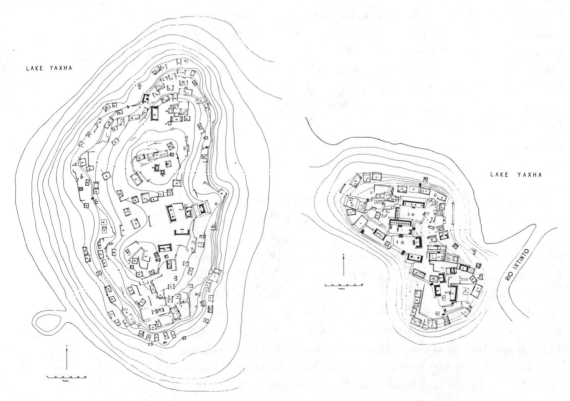

4.21. Mayapan, the last lowland Maya capital; the Castillo
is a smaller copy of the Castillo
at Chichén Itzá.

as a center of power it was now, and a new Maya capital
was founded at Mayapan, southeast of Mérida. Maya documentary evidence indicates that the settlement served to
concentrate political power, the local nobility being brought
to live there in comfortable confinement under the suzer-
ainty of the Cocom clan. Although the principal temple at
Mayapan was a deliberate, smaller-scale, copy of the Castillo at Chichén Itzá (Figure 4.21) (the center also had a
circular *caracol* and other structures of clear Chichén inspiration), the plan of the settlement was innovative and
unique in the Maya Area. It was a densely packed town,
with houses jammed together and separated by low boundary walls, encircled by a masonry defensive wall. An inner
circuit of walls separated the ceremonial precinct from the
residential area. In some ways Mayapan was a conscious
harking back to the earlier Maya past—the stela cult was
revived, and buildings set around an enclosed patio were
common—but the use of serpent columns and colonnaded
halls reflects the architectural influence of Toltec Chichén
Itzá. Several other walled towns were built, along the east
coast of Yucatan: at both Tulum and Ichpaatun the sea
formed the eastern perimeter and the defensive wall was
rectangular in plan. Both sites also erected stelae, but they
seem to have reused ancient monuments from elsewhere,
since the hieroglyphic dates are much earlier and the material of the Ichpaatun stela is foreign to the area. A third

instance of such recycling was found recently at a small site in northern Belize called Chan Chen; it may be that the monuments were brought down the Rio Hondo from an abandoned site in Petén as a way of linking Postclassic Maya culture to the lost Classic past. Similar behavior has been noted in the construction of small, crude, stone plat-forms on and against abandoned Classic temples, and on some sites in southern Quintana Roo the covering of an-cient buildings with quite substantial, but still crude, con-structions. A third example of such atavism can be seen in the common use of abandoned Classic sites as pilgrimage centers, with effigy incense burners deposited in fragments on the ruined mounds of the Classic temples: in a survey of northern Belize almost every major Classic pyramid had fragments (but never complete examples) of such *incen-sarios* in provincial variants of those found at Mayapan.

A major center during the Postclassic period was the is-land of Cozumel, off the northeast corner of the Yucatan Peninsula. At the time of the conquest it was the principal shrine of the goddess Ix Chel, a pilgrimage center, and also, not coincidentally, an important trading port. A survey of the island by Jeremy Sabloff and William Rathje showed that there was a principal center in the middle of the is-land, called San Gervasio, together with more than thirty other sites, of which many were small coastal shrines that probably doubled as lookouts or beacons. Much of the is-land was covered by a grid of boundary walls on a common orientation of 20°, showing that the land had been parceled out according to some overall plan—a large-scale version of the house lots at Mayapan. Some of the sites near the coast consisted of massive open platforms, which seem likely to have been storage areas for goods in the course of ship-ment: exactly what one would expect in a trading commu-nity, but in their scale showing huge investment of labor and materials, and supporting the contention of Sabloff and Rathje that this period of the Postclassic era saw "the triumph of a new merchant elite who rapidly rose to a posi-tion of economic and political ascendancy from Tabasco to the East Coast." Eric Thompson thought that this elite were the Putun, the Chontal Maya of the swampy Tabasco lowlands around the estuaries of the Usumacinta and Gri-jalva, and that their rise had begun in the eighth century.

Certainly it is around this time that new forms of pottery vessel adapted to stacking and therefore to mass marketing appeared. It may be that the circumpeninsular canoe route was instituted by the Putun, but that Cozumel developed as a pivotal point on that route only in the thirteenth century.

Occupation at this period reached down the coast of Quintana Roo into Belize, and in the period after the fall of Mayapan in the mid-fifteenth century the peninsula and its eastern coast became divided into a number of small and often antagonistic states, not unlike those of the Holy Roman Empire or medieval Italy on the other side of the Atlantic. In spite of this political fission, Maya culture remained unified, and there is evidence of continued external contact, presumably along the long-distance trade routes. At the Belizean site of Santa Rita, which may have been the capital of the state of Chetumal and itself borne that name, a building was decorated with murals in a style that derived partly from the central highlands of Mexico, and similar murals are found further up the coast at Tulum. The Mexica (Aztec) of central Mexico were in commercial contact with the west coast of the peninsula, and were reportedly planning to add the Maya to their empire at the time of the Spanish invasion. In the other direction, great canoes traveled as far southeast as Costa Rica and Panama, and from the tenth century onward metal objects of copper and gold became increasingly familiar to the Maya.

Contact with the highland Maya zone continued throughout the Postclassic period, but culturally the highlands had been, from the Classic period on, a separate sphere of development and one in much closer touch with central Mexico to the west. Part of this contact had come in the form of migrations eastward into the Maya highlands by people speaking languages allied to the dominant Nahua group of Mexico (Nahuatl was the language of the Mexica empire), who penetrated as far as El Salvador. These immigrants must have contributed to the political fragmentation of the highland zone, which became as great as its linguistic diversity and resulted in a number of mutually antagonistic kingdoms.

Archaeologically these are reflected by the hilltop defended towns of the highland Postclassic period, charac-

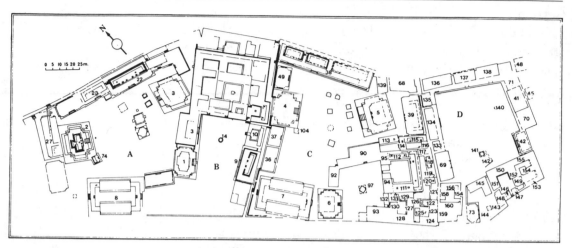

4.22. Iximche, a highland Maya town of the Late Postclassic period and the capital of the Cakchiquel. It became the first capital of colonial Guatemala in 1524. The twin plazas and palaces towards the east end of the site are thought to reflect a dual monarchy.

teristically set on a ridge surrounded by deep ravines and approached by a single narrow causeway. Stephens had visited one of these, the ancient Quiché capital of Utatlan, in 1840, and Maudslay had mapped several others four decades later. A typical site is Iximche (Figure 4.22), the capital of the Cakchiquel until it was stormed by the Spaniards under Alvarado in 1524, when it became the first colonial capital of Guatemala. A series of small plazas is bordered by squat, pyramidal temples and long, galleried buildings, while the palaces of the rulers are set at one end, each around a courtyard. Several of these highland capitals have been excavated, including Iximche, Utatlan, and Zaculeu, capital of the Mam; they, and their culture, are more an eastern extension of the Mexican highlands than they are descendents of the Classic Maya tradition, however, and in this brief book they must perforce receive less attention than is their due: the succeeding chapters will concentrate on the emergence, florescence, and qualities of Classic Maya civilization in the lowlands.

In 1513 Ponce de Leon was the first European to sight Yucatan; on March 1, 1517, some thirty Maya were entertained on board Hernández de Córdoba's flagship lying off Cape Catoche, the northeastern tip of Yucatan. In 1542 the Adelantado Don Francisco de Montejo founded Mérida as the Spanish capital of Yucatan, and with his son began the reduction of the northern Maya. In 1697 the Maya of Tayasal in the heart of Petén surrendered to Martin de Ursua.

The conquest of the Maya had taken 180 years, and even then those living in eastern Quintana Roo and parts of Belize remained effectively beyond the control of the Spanish crown. The last battle between the Maya and the British (who had gradually established control over what is now Belize from the mid-eighteenth century onward) occurred at Orange Walk in 1872, and the War of the Castes, in which the Maya took on and nearly defeated the Mexican federal army, ended officially in 1855 but left the Cruzob Maya effectively independent for almost half a century. Thus the colonial or historic period in the Maya lowlands is a curious one, during which nominal European sovereignty often overlay cultural independence: at Lamanai on the New River Lagoon in northern Belize a large Classic Maya site continued to be occupied into the Postclassic period, and then became the seat of a Spanish *visita* church (Figure 4.23). When the friars withdrew in 1644, the Maya continued to bury their dead within the church, with pottery vessels identical with those used before the Spanish penetration; apart from the remains of the church, which still survive, it was as though the conquest had never occurred.

Today almost all of the two million Maya have been integrated to some extent into the modern states in which they live, although in the highlands their communities retain internal integrity and make contact with the outside world mainly through *ladino* officials and merchants. In Yucatan and Belize, there has been much greater participation in the political and economic processes of the modern world, and Nash's "machine-age Maya" are flourishing, not crumbling, with the contact.

4.23. The ruins of the Spanish *visita* church at Lamanai, Belize, abandoned in 1644; the church was excavated in 1974 by the Royal Ontario Museum.

5

Subsistence and Settlement

THE historic Maya shared one major problem with their prehistoric forebears, and that was feeding themselves. Skeletons of Preclassic Maya indicate a people taller than those of the Classic period or than the modern Maya, and the analysis of nutritional deficiencies in the skeletons of the prehistoric populations of Tikal and Altar de Sacrificios show that at least part of this overall decline in stature is the result of a worsening diet.

Neither the tropical forest soils of Petén nor the scrublands of Yucatan are optimally suited to agriculture, but the archaeological evidence of population density and semiurban settlement shows that arable productivity must have been quite high, especially at the Late Preclassic and Late Classic population maxima. It has been estimated that the population of Tikal reached 70,000 persons at the latter time, in the eighth century A.D.

civilization seemed to its students to deny such simple ecological possibility, in that the type of agriculture possible on tropical forest soils will support only a low level of population density. This type of farming, still practiced in many parts of the world, is known variously as swidden, shifting cultivation, slash-and-burn, *roza*, and *milpa*, the last being the term used in Mesoamerica for a field cultivated by this method; recent consensus has agreed to use *swidden* for the method and *milpa* for the field itself.

Swidden farming consists, first, of cutting down the trees and undergrowth over the area to be cultivated; in the Maya Area this is done during the first part of the dry season, between December and March. Steel machetes are now used, but in pre-Hispanic times axes of chert or hard igneous rock mounted in wooden hafts served, efficient at cutting but about three times slower in clearing a given

5.1. A chert axe, made by flaking, with a cutting edge shattered by use. Such axes were used to clear land, dig ditches, and perform other heavy tasks. This example was made and found at Colha, Belize.

area. Thousands of chert axes have been found on lowland Maya sites (Figure 5.1), often with the blade crushed and blunted by use, and sometimes resharpened. These axes were up to 30 centimeters (12 inches) long and weighed 500–1,000 grams (1–2 pounds), so that a fair amount of force could be put behind the blow. At Colha, a site in northern Belize where there are vast outcrops of chert, workshops for making these axes have been found over an area of several square miles, and one workshop studied in detail yielded more than two hundred unfinished and discarded axes, abandoned at all stages in the manufacturing process whenever some fault in the material or the knapping technique became apparent. The smaller volcanic stone axes of the highlands were made by grinding and polishing the roughout, rather than by chipping and pressure flaking.

The large trees in the forest may have been killed by ringbarking to make them easier to fell, the smaller simply chopped down. All of the felled brush was left to dry for the remainder of the dry season, forming a tangle of roots and branches almost impossible to penetrate. Then, when the rains appeared imminent, the dried brush was burned, the outer margin of the field probably being fired first to clear a firebreak and prevent the flames from spreading into the forest. It was important not to burn the brush too long before the rains, or fresh weed growth would appear, and not to leave it too late, or the brush would get wet and be difficult to burn; many of the prognostications in the surviving Maya codices are concerned with just this sort of regulation of the farming year.

For planting a long pointed stick was used, with which a hole was made and a few corn or bean seeds dropped in and covered over (Figure 5.2). Landa describes the practice of planting corn in the sixteenth century thus: "In cultivating the land they do nothing except collect together the refuse and burn it in order to sow it afterwards. They cultivate the land from the middle of January to April, and they sow in the rainy season. They do this by carrying a little bag on their shoulders and with a pointed stick they make a hole in the ground, and they drop these five or six grains, which they cover over with the same stick. It is a wonder how things grow, when it rains." The first corn shoots appeared, in fact, soon after the rains germinated the seeds and grew during the summer. Weeding was carried out at intervals, and late in the summer the stalk was bent to prevent rain from running into the husk and rotting the corn. Then in fall came the harvest, maize followed by beans, and after a brief pause the whole cycle began again.

After two years or so weed competition became so intense that yields fell to an unacceptable level, and the old *milpa* was abandoned for years (seven to ten in modern Yucatan) to grow over with secondary forest, the canopy of which would gradually shut light out from the weeds and reduce their growth. The forest plants would restore the humic content of the soil, and eventually the plot would again be ready to farm. Meanwhile, a new *milpa* would be cut and cultivated.

Swidden farming is not quite as simple as the model I have outlined above, which takes no account of possible early and late plantings of corn as insurance, nor of con-

5.2. Planting maize with a digging stick: a modern farmer sows his *milpa*, and God B from the Madrid Codex drops seeds that sprout from the calendar-day sign *Kan*, itself a symbol of the maize seed.

tinued use of the *milpa* after abandonment for the extraction of other crops, such as roots, less afflicted by weed
competition. This model, which has been until very recently the standard interpretation of ancient Maya subsistence, also assumes the primacy of maize in the diet and of
swidden as an agricultural technique, with a dispersed
rural population adapted to this economic strategy, spread
across the countryside between the ceremonial centers.
The practical and theoretical basis of the model was a study
of farming in Yucatan in the 1920s, where maize formed
85% of the diet. The conservatism of Maya culture was assumed to include their economy, so that this model could
be projected back in time to explain the way of life of the
Classic Maya.

Until about twenty years ago Mayanists were quite hap-
py with this interlinked model of settlement and subsistence—the rural population coming periodically to the
basically empty ceremonial center for festivals, but otherwise living out among their *milpas* cultivating corn, beans,
and squashes, and to a lesser extent root crops such as
sweet potato. This model forms the basis of Morley's *The
Ancient Maya* and Eric Thompson's *Rise and Fall of Maya
Civilization*, the two best general studies of the Maya.
These two men were also the most influential scholars of
their time, so that from the 1920s their model was accepted
as gospel, and the contrasting views of Oliver Ricketson,
favoring more densely populated centers and a more diverse and intensive economic base, received scant attention. Too little was known of settlement patterns and agriculture of the Classic period for the Thompson-Morley
hypothesis to be seriously challenged on the basis of fact.
The power of the model can be seen in the 1950s, when
Gordon Willey's Belize Valley survey demonstrated the existence of dense settlement along the river terraces. It was
assumed that they had used the hills behind the river for
milpa, and so no survey of the hills was ever carried out
to determine whether the dense populations did in fact
spread back there.

The first serious doubts about the Thompson-Morley
model arose in the late 1950s, when the area around the
Tikal ceremonial precinct was mapped in detail (Figure
5.13), and it was discovered that dense suburbs spread out

from the center for several miles. The clusters of residential platforms were too close together for *milpas* to have existed in the vicinity of the settlement, or for sufficient corn to have been grown if they had existed. This meant that the fields had to lie elsewhere, out beyond the suburbs. An additional problem arose, however: other major centers lay close by, such as Uaxactun only 18 kilometers (11 miles) away, and these must also have had substantial populations. The wide-open spaces between the Maya centers, with their scattered bucolic farmers, suddenly became filled with closely packed and hungry suburbanites.

The Tikal study was given regional perspective by a survey in northeastern Petén carried out by William R. Bullard, Jr., a member of the Belize Valley team; he showed that around the major centers were smaller, minor ones, all set into a background of rural settlement of varying density. Some of the clusters of house platforms were large and close-packed, repeating in endless microcosm the pattern of incipient urbanism seen at Tikal.

This radical change in the known range, size, and concentration of Classic Maya settlements provoked a reassessment of their economic base: no longer could unlimited areas of land for swiddening be assumed to have existed in the Classic period. In 1966 Bennet Bronson examined the importance of root crops, demonstrating their great productivity and the undervalued colonial documentary evidence for such crops as *yuca* (manioc), *camote* (sweet potato), and *jícama* (yam bean). Root crops could be grown below ground in the same *milpa* as maize and beans, so the basic model of agricultural production was unchallenged—merely the relative importance of different crops.

Dennis Puleston then suggested that the Maya had obtained a large proportion of their sustenance not from *milpa* crops at all but from the tending and harvesting of the *ramón* (breadnut) tree, which grows in vast numbers throughout Petén. Cyrus Lundell had noted in the 1930s that *ramón* trees tended to cluster around ancient Maya ruins; Puleston confirmed this with a survey at Tikal, and pointed out that a single tree could yield nearly 1,000 kilograms (2,200 pounds) of edible and nutritious seeds annually. He then experimented with *chultunob*—underground chambers with narrow bottlenecks, scooped from the limestone, which had long been assumed to be storage chambers of some kind—and showed that they could be used to store *ramón* nuts for a long period.

The only problem with Puleston's ingenious theory was that Maya documentary sources indicated that *ramón* was thought of as a famine food rather than a preferred staple, at least in Postclassic Yucatan. Nevertheless, the theory brought into prominence the possibility of silviculture, by deliberate planting or selective culling, as a factor in the ancient Maya economy; and recent calculations by Bruce Dickson suggest that a suitable mixture of *ramón* and root crop cultivation combined with kitchen gardens, but without maize, could have supported between 70,000 and 77,000 people at Tikal. Dennis Puleston made a good case for the potential importance of *ramón*, which may well have served as a critical resource during the population maximum of the Late Classic period, but its widespread normal use in ancient Maya diet has not been proved.

Corn, root crops, and *ramón* are all starch carbohydrate sources with some protein content; beans, especially black beans, have a higher proportion of protein, but some animal protein was still considered necessary by the Maya. Frederick Lange has suggested that marine resources were used to supply concentrated animal protein to balance the carbohydrate-dominant vegetable diet, but while some marine mollusc shells and fish bones have been found even at sites in the heart of Petén, it seems unlikely that marine products made a major contribution more than a short distance inland. There would have been problems in transporting perishable fresh fish over long distances in a tropical climate, although filleting and drying, perhaps salting also, would have been solutions. Similarly, the marine mollusc shells have not been found in quantity and many are decorative: they could have been exchanged as shells, devoid of their original occupants, and shellfish meat needs to be consumed in prodigious quantities to be of any real dietary use. Even at a coastal plain site such as Lubaantun, 25 kilometers (16 miles) from the coast in southern Belize, the numerous marine molluscan species were represented by only a few examples of each, and the one species of Pacific coast origin was clearly imported for its decorative value and not its meat content.

Evidence from Lubaantun and other sites does, however, indicate a heavy exploitation of freshwater Mollusca for food: the Rio Columbia at Lubaantun is inhabited by the spiral-shelled *Pachychilus pyramidalis*, known locally as *juté*, and thousands of shells were found in trash heaps at the site, the tips of the spires broken off to facilitate extraction of the animal. Some large shells were deposited as offerings, but only after they had been emptied. The *juté* seem to have been progressively overexploited during the Late Classic period, since the average size at which they were gathered diminished steadily during the occupation of Lubaantun. A second kind of edible mollusc, the swamp and freshwater snail *Pomacea flagellata*, was exploited to a minor extent at Lubaantun in the Late Classic period. In the Preclassic period in northern Belize, however, it was heavily utilized—some trash heaps yielding thousands of shells in a single layer—and the uniformity of shell size suggests that *Pomacea* may actually have been farmed in local swamps or river margins. Eric Thompson has proposed that freshwater fish were farmed also, using the artificial canals between raised fields (see p. 161, below).

The bulk of animal protein would seem to have come from hunting, and the species most exploited, both in terms of meat yield and in the number of animals killed, was the white-tailed deer (*Odocoileus virginianus*). Other cervids such as the little brocket deer were also hunted, together with the two species of wild pig, the white-lipped and the collared peccary. A study of animal exploitation in one region of the Maya lowlands, northern Belize, has enabled Elizabeth S. Wing to conclude that the pattern of hunting and the species utilized remained the same from the Preclassic period through the Classic and into the Postclassic. Evidence from two sites in the area, Cuello and Nohmul, occupied from 1000 B.C. to after A.D. 1000, showed that deer were the most commonly hunted animal, followed by two species of turtle. The third source of meat was dog, domesticated rather than hunted and perhaps similar to the Mexican hairless dog of historic times. The turkey, known to have been domesticated at the time of the con-

5.3. A hunter killing a deer with a stone knife, perhaps after wounding it with the spear he carries: a Late Classic figurine from Lubaantun, Belize.

quest, does not appear in the Preclassic-Classic archaeological record in northern Belize, nor at Lubaantun, and both the date and the geographical range of its domestication remain at present uncertain.

There has been debate as to the precise relationship between the Maya and the animals they hunted. Were they simply stalked in the bush as they are today, were they trapped, or did man in some way encourage or compel the animals to stay in his vicinity so that he might more easily use them? There are hints in colonial sources that deer may have been at least partly controlled, and it has been suggested that the burning of the cut brush in the *milpa* provided a source of salts that would attract them. Some of the noted pottery figurines of Lubaantun (Figure 5.3) show a crouching deer being killed with a stone knife; it has been assumed that the deer was shown as having been injured by the spear the man carries, but it is possible that the dispatch of a tamed animal could have been carried out in the way the modern Lapps kill reindeer and Upper Paleolithic peoples seem to have done in northern Europe, with a stabbing thrust from a short spear at close quarters, neither the victim nor its companions expressing alarm. The proportion of deer to other wild species (which included also armadillo, agouti, pisote, and *tepezcuintle*—a large rodent) is so high as to suggest some difference in the procurement pattern, but the study of hunting and butchering activities in the Maya pursuit of protein has only just begun.

After canvassing these varied ways of enhancing the ancient Maya diet it was still evident to scholars that population densities in parts of the lowlands had clearly exceeded any capability of a swidden system to support them. While one avenue of research was to seek out further plant and animal resources that might have been used, another was to examine ways in which production of the known crops could have been intensified. An initial conclusion was that even the swidden system as it has operated since colonial times is capable of intensification, with more crops being taken per year, more years of cropping being obtainable from a *milpa* by intensive weeding, and soils of less than optimum quality being used to enlarge the potential area of *milpa* within the territory exploited by a single community.

It was also realized that the dooryard garden, the area immediately around the house, which could be constantly tended by women and children and manured with household trash, was capable of high productivity, although not usually of staples such as maize. Many of the *ramón* trees recorded by Lundell and Puleston must have stood in such gardens, and the range of fruits, flavorings, delicacies, medicinal herbs, and purely decorative plants grown in modern examples is very wide.

Intensive ways of producing more staple crops include not only a gearing-up of the swidden system but also the utilization of fields artificially constructed and maintained, which enabled ecological niches unproductive under swidden to yield economic crops. The first of these "artificial econiches" to be noted by archaeologists was that of hill terracing, where stone walls were built across a sloping hillside or a valley to act as erosion controls and silt traps, collecting a deep soil in the space behind the walls (Figure 5.4). Although it had been noted in the 1920s, terracing was thought to have been marginal in location and economic potential until recently, when the work of B. L. Tur-

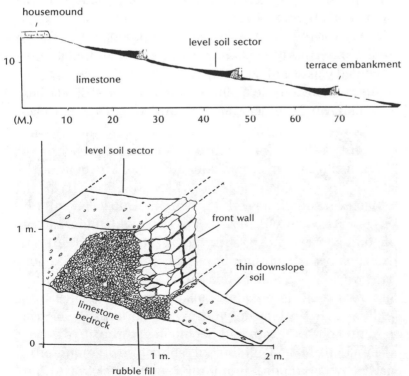

5.4. Hillside terracing for land allotment, erosion control, and silt entrapment, from examples recorded in the Rio Bec region of the central lowlands.

ner II around Becan demonstrated that terraces occurred over very large areas in the lowlands, on moderate slopes as well as the steep hillsides where they had hitherto been recorded. The planned field-wall networks plotted by Turner east of Becan, with walkways and farmsteads included in the system, documented a kind of land use in which cultivation for a year or two followed by abandonment for a decade seemed unlikely, and the organization and energy invested in the construction of the terracing suggested a more than casual policy of land allocation and cultivation. In the Maya Mountains around the sites of Tzimin Kax and Caracol such terracing has been shown to date to the early part of the Classic period.

A similar conclusion arises, even more dramatically, from the creation of a second form of artificial econiche, that of raised fields in swampy areas. These are similar in function to the *chinampas* of the valley of Mexico, which supplied the Aztec capital of Tenochtitlan with much of its food, but instead of being built out into open lakes, they are created by draining marshy river margins or basins. A series of drainage ditches is dug, parallel or in grids (Figure 5.5), the upcast from which is piled up on either side to create an area of land above the level of the water table. Periodic cleaning of the ditches results in additional elevation as well as refertilization of the raised plots, and the latter are rendered capable of continuous production.

Apart from the Mexican *chinampas*, raised fields have been known in other parts of the Americas, especially

5.5. Raised fields in the Rio Hondo valley, northern Belize, April 1973. The canals between the fields still hold water at the height of the dry season. A freshly burned *milpa* lies on the limestone ridge in the background.

northwestern South America, for some years; they were
first identified in the Maya Area only in 1972, on the Rio
Candelaria (Figure 3.3) in southern Campeche, by Alfred
Siemens and Dennis Puleston. Eric Thompson suggested
that the "canals" between the fields were the most important feature, and that they had been used to raise fish as an
intensive method of protein production. This idea extended
Lange's thesis of the importance of fish as food by removing the practical difficulty of getting the perishable meat to
inland sites—any community with river access could grow
its own protein supply.

It seems most likely, however, that a people as ecologi-
cally astute as the ancient Maya would have utilized both
canals and raised plots: the former for keeping fish (and
perhaps turtles) and as access routes by canoe, the latter
for growing crops intensively on a year-round schedule. A
survey of the canal system surrounding the site of Edzna,
not far north of the Candelaria, showed that each length of
canal had a raised sill at the entrance, which could have
acted as a silt trap, or kept fish from escaping, or both.

The identity of the crops grown on the raised fields is
known to some extent. Puleston mapped large areas of
such fields along the Rio Hondo in northern Belize and
took pollen cores from the silts in the canals between them,
from which the pollen of maize and cotton have been firm-

5.6. Prehistoric raised field,
cleared and restored by Dennis
F. Puleston for experimental
crop planting, at San Antonio
on the Rio Hondo, northern
Belize.

ly identified. He also restored an ancient raised field (Figure 5.6) and planted experimental crops on it; cotton flourished, but everything else was eaten by the local pigs.

It seems likely that maize as a subsistence crop and cotton as a cash crop were among the products of the raised-field areas, but a second important cash crop seems likely to have been grown also—cacao. At the time of the conquest the state of Chetumal, which includes northern Belize, was famed for its cacao, and the crop was doubly important because the beans served as currency—money literally grew on trees. Of the local econiches, only the areas provided by the raised fields are really suited to cacao production. An economic symbiosis is also made possible by growing cacao on raised fields: the cacao plant is pollinated by a species of midge that breeds on the surface of open water, the midge eggs form food for the fish breeding in the canals, and the fish feces enrich the muck at the bottom of the canal, which is periodically dredged up to mulch the roots of the cacao trees. The economic importance of cacao in Postclassic times (a formal exchange rate between the beans and the Spanish *real* persisted for long after the conquest, and beans were "forged" by being emptied of their meat and refilled with earth), and the high social status of cacao, mixed liberally with pepper, as a beverage, both suggest not only that the initial investment in raised-field construction would have been economically wise but also that such construction and cultivation might well have been under official control.

In the past five years huge areas of raised fields have been found in southern Quintana Roo, over most of northern Belize, and in Petén around Tikal and other sites. The use of Side-Looking Airborne Radar (SLAR) in a project led jointly by Richard E. W. Adams and T. Patrick Culbert and by Walter F. Brown of the Jet Propulsion Laboratory has revealed dense networks of canals linking grids of fields in several of these areas (Figure 5.7), and the entire economic landscape of the Maya lowlands now looks completely different from the picture that we had even at the beginning of the 1970s.

The construction of raised fields is the earliest mean intensive Maya agriculture for which we have evidence. It may go as far back in time as the end of the Early Pre-

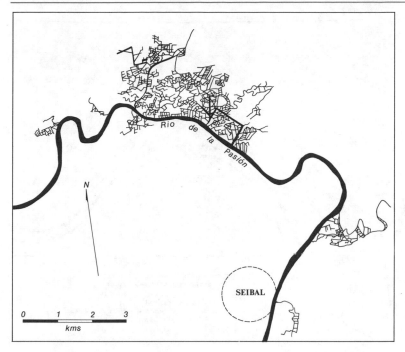

5.7. Large-scale pattern of prehistoric canals and other features, traced from SLAR (Side-Looking Airborne Radar) imagery, in the Seibal region of Petén.

classic period, since one radiocarbon date for a sharpened post thrust into a canal bank on the Rio Hondo in northern Belize is equivalent to about 1400 B.C. in calendar years (although the post could belong to some earlier and non-agricultural feature such as a fish trap, and the association with the canal cut may be fortuitous). It is possible, although unproven and probably unprovable, that intensive agriculture in small areas close to the rivers was the initial economic adaptation of the Maya, with swiddening on the higher ridges being a response to additional pressure on the agricultural system as the result of an expanding population, and a supplementary means of production rather than the basis of the economy. What is certain is that raised fields are so widespread in the lowlands that their contribution to the economy was a fundamental one, and that from at least Late Preclassic times onward their existence and distribution was an important factor in Maya subsistence and settlement patterns.

The changed perception of Maya subsistence outlined above came about as the result of a reassessment of settlement patterns as detailed maps of sites such as Tikal became available in the late 1950s. Further progress in locating and mapping sites has led to a similar general change

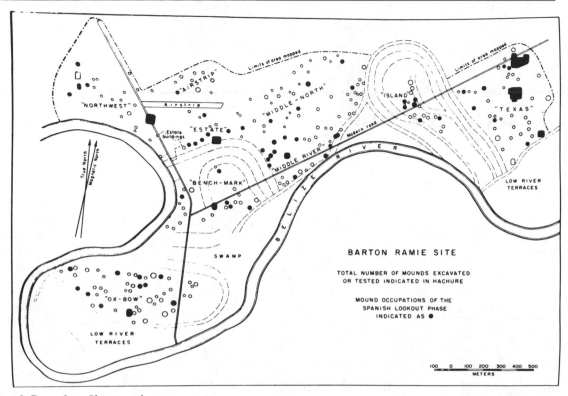

5.8. Dense Late Classic settlement recorded in a 25% sample
of house mounds excavated at
Barton Ramie, central Belize,
in 1953–1956. This was the
first project explicitly to study
ancient Maya rural settlement
patterns.

in the traditional model of ancient Maya settlement and its
relationship to landscape and natural resources.

The development of Maya settlement archaeology owes
much to Gordon R. Willey, who in 1953 brought to the
Maya Area the techniques of field recording and analysis
that had been developed in the survey of the Virú Valley on
the coast of Peru. Willey instituted a project at Barton Ramie in the Belize Valley that was the first deliberate study of
a nonceremonial site. Of some 240 mounds mapped a large
sample, more than 60, were excavated wholly or partially
so that the changing overall pattern of occupation could be
elucidated. The site was found to have been first settled in
the early Middle Formative period, dated at the time by
guesswork to the mid-first millennium B.C. and now known
to be several centuries earlier; it was then continuously occupied for more than two thousand years, until it was abandoned around A.D. 1000. The size and density of the population increased gradually, up to the Late Preclassic period
when there was a sudden increase, an occurrence that has
been noted at many other lowland sites. A further increase
took place during the Protoclassic occupation at Barton

Ramie, and it has been suggested that immigration from El Salvador was the cause (see Chapter 4, p. 125). The period of maximum occupation, when every structure excavated was shown to have been in use, was the Late Classic period, A.D. 600–900 (Figure 5.8), with only a slight drop in the Postclassic.

The Barton Ramie excavations, set in the regional context of a more general survey of the middle Belize River valley, showed what a vast, untapped reservoir of archaeological information lay outside the spectacular ceremonial centers that had occupied the attention of Mayanists for the preceding century. Nevertheless, research projects focusing on the study of single, major ceremonial centers continued through the 1960s at Seibal and Altar de Sacrificios (both directed by Willey) and for part of the decade at Tikal and Dzibilchaltun; but at each of these sites the research design included the mapping and excavation of substantial areas of the settlement around the ceremonial nucleus. Several smaller sites were also investigated, among them Altun Ha and Lubaantun, with integral mapping and study of the settlement, and serious attention was paid to Postclassic settlement. Study of Postclassic sites had begun in the late 1950s with the work at Mayapan, the swan song of the C.I.W.'s Division of Historical Research, and continued in the early 1970s with the island-wide survey of Cozumel.

The present range of approaches in Maya settlement studies has three main emphases: single-site mapping, as at Tikal or Seibal, in which the structure of a community and its relationship to a ceremonial center is examined; intersite or regional projects like that in the Belize Valley, or more recently in northern Belize and on Cozumel, where the interrelationships between communities and their common relation to the landscape are investigated; and quasi-historical studies in which the data emerging from the decipherment of monumental inscriptions are used to infer political relationships between communities. By combining the information from all three approaches we can obtain a fair understanding of the way in which the ancient Maya fitted into their environment.

Single-site studies indicate that residence was normally in houses of perishable material, probably very close in design to those of the modern Maya (Figures 3.15, 5.9, also

5.9. A Maya house of the fifth century A.D. at Cerén, El Salvador, overwhelmed by ash from a volcanic eruption nearby. The walls are standing, but the roof has collapsed. Pottery vessels containing food, including beans, were found in the house, and the furrows of a cornfield were discovered nearby, still with traces of the maize plants in position. The thickness of the cornstalks showed that the eruption probably occurred in early June.

9.1), set upon low basal platforms for drainage and ventilation and to keep out some crawling insects. Such houses might occur singly or in pairs, but are most usually found in groups of three or more around a courtyard or patio. A small structure, interpreted as a dynastic or household shrine and sometimes containing a burial—perhaps a venerated ancestor—is often found on one side or in the center of the courtyard (Figure 5.11). It has been suggested that

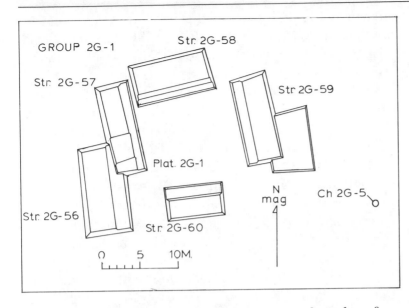

5.10. A characteristic Classic Maya courtyard of houses, Group 2G-1 at Tikal (after William Haviland). Figure 6.1 shows Haviland's reconstruction of the pattern of occupation of this group over several generations.

the single and double houses were those of nuclear families, parents and children, and that the courtyard groups held an extended family of three generations, including the spouses of some children brought to live in the parental home for a period. One such group at Tikal has been analyzed in great detail by William Haviland, who has suggested a model of six generations of occupancy during the Late Classic period (Figures 5.10, 6.1), and there is no reason to suppose that this is at all an unusual or complex pattern of use. The major problem is, as always, obtaining the archaeological information to match such hypotheses.

What is and always has been beyond doubt is that the numerous low platforms scattered in clusters across the Maya landscape *were* in fact dwellings. There have been suggestions, however, that not all houses were placed on platforms, so that a proportion would escape even a careful survey (as has been confirmed by excavation at both Tikal and Seibal). The single or grouped house platforms are often found in clusters, each group in the cluster being perhaps 100 meters (325 feet) from the next, and such clusters might be interpreted as the dwellings of related families, as has been found in the ethnographic study of highland Maya at Zinacantan (see Chapter 3). The space between dwellings is not much less than 100 meters even where it would have been possible: at Nohmul, on the flat, limestone ridges of northern Belize, this spacing is main-

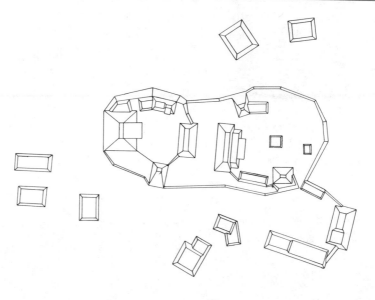

5.11. A minor ceremonial center: Chowacol, in the settlement area surrounding the larger center of San Estevan, northern Belize, has two plazas. A public space is dominated by the small pyramid, and a more enclosed residential plaza has a long palace substructure and a small pyramidal private shrine.

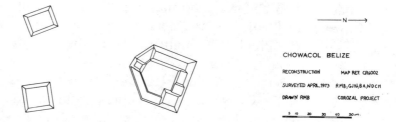

tained, presumably for privacy and in order to have room for a dooryard garden.

At more widely spaced intervals there occur groups of more elaborate buildings that have been called "minor ceremonial centers" and interpreted as local elite residences and seats of government. Such a site characteristically included a small pyramid set on a formal plaza, and structures interpreted as elite residences—long, relatively low substructures not unlike oversized house platforms (Figure 5.11). In some sites the pyramid and long structures bore stone-walled buildings with vaulted roofs, evidence that specialist masons had been employed. Many of these minor ceremonial centers lie within the large settled areas around major sites, and Haviland has argued that they were not used for government at all, but were simply the dwellings of the social elite. It seems more likely, in view of the wide distribution and fairly regular spacing of these complexes (Bullard estimated that they occurred at intervals of about 1 kilometer (0.625 mile) in northeast Petén), even beyond the limits of the major sites, that they combined the functions of elite residence with those of social control as residences of local rulers or officials. The medieval English complex of church and manor house as the core of religious and social life and the seat of the magistracy may be an apposite parallel.

Haviland, however, has made out a good case for at least one exception to this assessment: in the suburbs of Tikal is one such minor center with an inscribed stela, which he has argued was the "dower house" of a former ruling family, founded by a deposed ruler and used while the dynasty was out of power; and other exceptions may exist. The trouble lies in the poverty of our analytical vocabulary—so that we subsume functionally distinct groups of buildings under the umbrella label of minor ceremonial center—and in the evidence available to make such distinctions with any certainty.

5.12. A small major ceremonial center: San Estevan on the New River in northern Belize has three public plazas with pyramids and a ball court and three private, elite residence plazas with private, although substantial, shrines. Chowacol (Figure 5.11) lies 1.75 kilometers (1.1 miles) to the southeast.

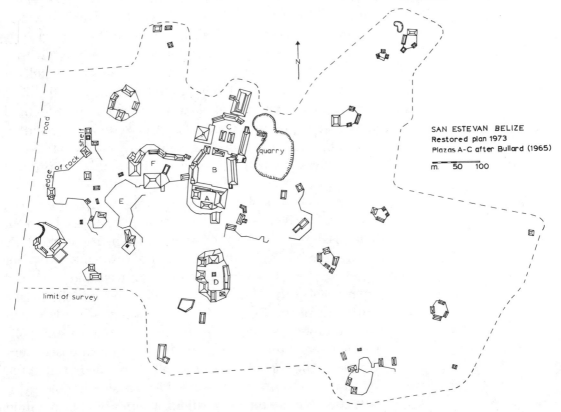

SAN ESTEVAN BELIZE
Restored plan 1973
Plazas A-C after Bullard (1965)

m.   50   100

The formal plaza with public buildings lining its margins is the major feature of the largest Maya sites, known as major ceremonial centers; here again poverty of vocabulary is a problem, since sites with this description range from modest concentrations of ceremonial architecture such as San Estevan, Belize (Figure 5.12) to the massive precincts of Calakmul and Tikal (Figure 5.13). San Estevan has one major plaza, divided by a ball court, on which stand four temple pyramids. At its northern end is a secluded court surrounded by long, low substructures, probably an elite residence/administrative building, and to the west are two more plazas that appear to be residential, one of them with a pyramid that seems to be a private shrine. Another detached residential plaza lies to the south of the main group, and surrounding the ceremonial precinct are a number of discrete residential compounds set on elevated platforms, again arguably the residences of the local elite. Beyond these, smaller compounds and single platforms are more widely scattered, with some clustering to the south around the minor ceremonial precinct of Chowacol, which is effectively within the settlement of San Estevan. Chowacol (Figure 5.11) has two small plazas, one dominated by a pyramid some 8 meters (26 feet) high, the other with a miniature pyramid shrine and a long, range-type building; here we see the separation of functions of these minor sites into the public ceremonial plaza and the private residential plaza, a separation that occurs in every ceremonial center, though often obscured by the complexity of the plan.

By contrast with San Estevan, Tikal has a ceremonial core that would by itself cover the entire distance from San Estevan to Chowacol, with several large groups of temples linked by broad causeways, sacbeob—("white roads," from their plastered surfaces). The original heart of the site, around the Great Plaza where the towering bulks of Temples I and II face each other from east and west and the temples of the North Acropolis look south to the palace courtyards of the Central Acropolis, was first settled soon after 1000 B.C.; a trench cut through the North Acropolis revealed more than a millennium of superimposed construction. The core of Tikal gradually expanded until in the eighth century A.D. there were five massive temple pyramids covering the tombs of rulers, a series of twin-pyramid groups erected at *katun* intervals, numerous palaces, smaller temples, ball courts, and other ceremonial and religious structures. It was a Maya metropolis, and recent work on the stelae has begun to give us an idea of its political influence. Beyond the ceremonial core lay the spreading suburbs, and although there is dispute as to the exact size of the population, there is no doubt that it was in the tens of thousands, and that in size and function Tikal was a preindustrial city comparable with those of the Old World.

The study of ancient Maya settlement is at present one of the most active areas of research. In advancing our knowl-

5.13. A metropolitan center: the central precinct of Tikal and some of its surrounding settlement, from a single sheet of the University of Pennsylvania's map. The mapping project in the late 1950s changed many ideas about ancient Maya settlement patterns and population density.

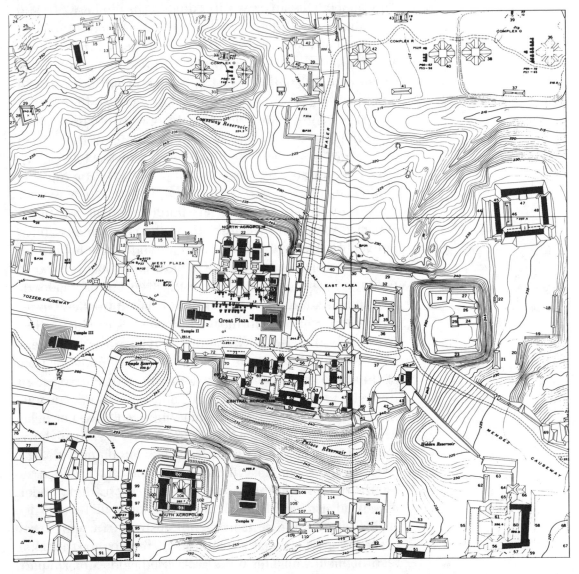

edge there are four main problems: the collection of information, its analysis, the theoretical models put forward to explain our observations, and the overall goals of the research.

The problem of acquiring information breaks down into the smaller practical problems of locating, identifying, and recording settlement, and determining the extent to which the sample acquired is representative of a site, a region, or of the Maya Area as a whole. It is clear that over the past quarter-century there has been a move from the study of ceremonial precincts and their monuments to that of rural and domestic populations; the smaller sites in between and the minor ceremonial centers have so far received little attention. The move to study settlement has, apart from Barton Ramie, resulted in mapping of the settlement around major centers such as Tikal or Seibal, or smaller but still focal points in the cultural landscape such as Edzna, Cerros, Lubaantun, and Nohmul. In only two cases has it been thought worthwhile to study a transect of the terrain and settlement along the entire way between two neighboring major centers—from Tikal north to Uaxactun and southeast to Yaxha.

In studying location there are initial practical questions. What are we looking for? Are all dwellings assumed to have left visible remains? We know from work at Seibal, Tikal, and Cerros that houses were built directly on the ground from the Late Preclassic through the Terminal Classic periods, so that a few centuries of humus accumulation would hide all trace of their former existence; this is a factor that we must acknowledge in our studies, realizing that only extensive sampling will give us a true picture. Another aspect of the same problem is that the degree of visibility varies from site to site and region to region: in northern Yucatan even low foundations are easily visible and have not been disturbed by root action, while in Petén trees may have ripped house platforms apart and covered them with leaf mold. In the Motagua Valley flood deposits have buried all but the most prominent house platforms at Quirigua under a thick layer of silt.

The term "settlement pattern" does not, of course, embrace only residential structures: defensive earthworks, *sacbeob*, field walls, terraces, and raised fields all form part

of man's division of the landscape, and residence and economy are so intertwined that the pattern of settlement can
be understood only as an entity and as a dynamic system
now fossilized in disuse.

The crucial process in translating the archaeology on or
in the ground into analytical results is that of *recording*: we
need to know how far the patterns reported have been recorded by comparable methods. Some sites may have been
mapped under thick undergrowth by estimating distances
by pacing and taking directions with a Brunton compass,
others in cleared *milpa* with a theodolite; the observations
may then have been plotted as a contour map of what is
there now (Figure 5.14) or translated immediately into the
standard convention used for Mesoamerican sites (Figure
5.15). The latter process is uncheckable, and since it assumes a basically rectangular structure beneath an ovoid
mound of debris, the truly circular building will be conventionalized out of existence. In Figure 5.14, the main precinct of Nohmul, the contour plan of Structure 9 shows it to
be subcircular; in Figure 5.15 it has been rectified to a
cular square. Excavation of Structure 9 in 1979 showed it to be
subci circular *caracol* resembling those at Chichén Itzá and
Mayapan, and a building of considerable significance. This
is one particular peril; but in this vital process of recording
perhaps the most important thing is for Mayanists to establish explicit rather than general conventions, so that results from one site can be reliably compared with those
from another.

The second major problem, that of analyzing the results
of survey and excavation, again turns on questions of definition and consistency: there are few agreed units of comparison, so that "structure," "group," "site," "minor ceremonial
center," and "major center" are terms employed with gay
abandon. Individual buildings are labeled "houses," "elite
residences," "temples," "palaces," and so forth with a sub-
jectivity that is implicit rather than stated—a "feeling of
definition is in the air." Obviously, the form of a building or
collocation of buildings should be explicitly defined before
a function is ascribed, and concrete distinctions made to
explain *why* a site is termed an "informal cluster," a "minimal ceremonial center," or a "regional ceremonial center"
(all terms from an attempt that I made some years ago to

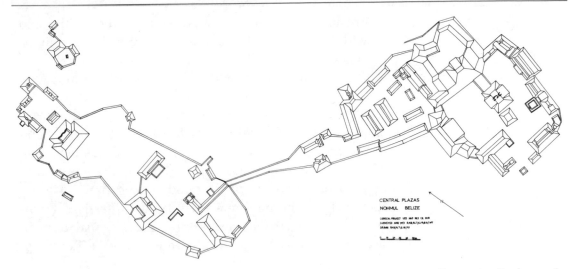

CENTRAL PLAZAS
NOHMUL   BELIZE

5.15. Conventionalized map of Nohmul made from the contour map in Figure 5.14. ~~Note that the subcircular Structure 9 has been squared off; subsequent excavations showed it to have been a circular building.~~

5.6, and this figure has been used by archaeologists, in some cases uncritically, to generate population estimates for prehistoric Maya sites, based on the number of house platforms recorded in survey. Such estimates range from a simple multiplication of 5.6 × number of platforms, to more subtle calculations in which the use of some platforms for storage and kitchen buildings is allowed (Haviland, for instance, allowing 16% at Tikal), and in which the possibility of some platforms being vacant at any one time is also considered.

The range of theoretical models currently in use includes such direct ethnographic comparisons, and moves through the development of functional models such as that used for Cozumel to imposed formal models derived from locational analysis, which examine the geometry of the cultural landscape and the ways in which human adaptation to it can be predicted. All are equally valid, if not equally valuable, ways of studying Maya prehistory; what is important is that their practitioners be explicit about what they are doing.

Our final problem is one of goals: why do we study ancient Maya settlement, and what can a knowledge of the distribution in space and time of their facilities for residence, religion, trade, and other activities tell us? The major goal of the immediate past has been to establish the size and density of settlements, and to relate these to the capacity of the agricultural system to maintain the population.

The imbalance between recorded population densities and the swidden model of the economy, and the changed interpretations that resulted, has been discussed earlier.

A second and still debated question is that of Maya urbanism. Can we truly say that the Maya lived in cities comparable with those of the Old World? The notion that ceremonial precincts were deserted for most of the year and that the population was scattered and rural has been discarded, and it has been recognized that populations around the major precincts were larger and denser than those at a distance. The argument now turns on the question of density—is the suburban pattern seen at Tikal, Seibal, or Nohmul comparable with the crammed compounds of Teotihuacan? The question is perhaps missing the point: instead of engaging in endless debate about urban *forms*, the aspect of the city most visibly affected by the local environment, we should be examining the range of urban *functions* that the Maya centers shared with the acknowledged preindustrial cities of Eurasia and highland Mesoamerica.

There are, I think, four levels at which we can pursue the future study of Maya settlement, and the goals at each level are different. At the *minimal* level a single feature or group of features forming a locus of activity is studied: the dwelling house is one such locus, the base of a nuclear social unit within which the activities of different individuals and sexes can be discerned. The relationships examined here are essentially those between individuals.

The *micro* level of study is that of several linked loci and their ambient space, together forming an economic unit. The compound of several houses with the enclosed patio and enclosing dooryard garden would fit into this category (Figure 5.10), and at this level we are looking at the relationships between indoor and outdoor space, at the tactical relations between settlement and topography and between people and their environment.

At the *meso* level we study a number of economic units linked in an economic network. The realm ruled by a single political power would be a case in point, with the tactical relationships of internal structure contrasting with the strategic external relationships with other realms. An example of this level would be the realm of Lubaantun, a small Classic center in southern Belize. The realm (Figure

5.16) is estimated to have covered about 1,600 square kilometers (625 square miles) and to have embraced ten environmental zones ranging from a high plateau to offshore coral islands. Each zone had its own lures and bars to settlement, and each offered its own range of exploitable animal, vegetable, and mineral resources. Products from all the zones reached the ceremonial center, which lay in the middle of its realm and in the most densely populated part of it, while exotic goods brought in from other realms were found in decreasing quantity from the ceremonial center out to small rural settlements.

The fourth, *macro*, level of study, with the widest perspective, is that at which we examine the relationships between realms in terms of economy and diplomacy: the tracing of trade routes and the elucidation of conquest and marriage alliance are major avenues of approach. Problems at this level relate to the entire Maya lowland polity, and only tangentially to the internal patterns of settlement and economy within its constituent realms. An example would

5.16. The realm of Lubaantun, a small Late Classic polity in southern Belize. The ceremonial center, the largest site in the realm, lies at the heart of a region of some 1,600 square kilometers (625 square miles) that embraces ten contrasting environmental zones ranging from mountain plateau to the Caribbean coast. A regional trade system (Figure 8.1) would integrate the products of these zones, with a principal market probably at the Lubaantun ceremonial precinct (compare Figure 3.13).

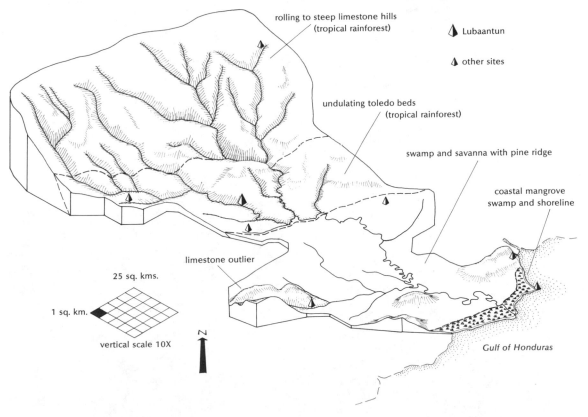

rolling to steep limestone hills
(tropical rainforest)

Lubaantun

other sites

undulating toledo beds
(tropical rainforest)

swamp and savanna with pine ridge

coastal mangrove
swamp and shoreline

limestone outlier

25 sq. kms.

1 sq. km.

vertical scale 10X

N

Gulf of Honduras

be the widespread abandonment or semiabandonment of a number of well-sited and prosperous centers (such as Seibal, Dzibilchaltun, and Cerros) at the beginning of the Early Classic period; another would be the extent to which the location of major centers was influenced by the overall political geography of the lowlands rather than by local environmental factors.

At all four levels of study there is still far more work to be done than has yet been accomplished. With understanding of the economic base and the political superstructure of Maya society already advancing, an increased consciousness of the structure and importance of Maya settlement systems is, however, likely to be one of the proximate developments in our investigation of the civilization.

6

The Structure of Society

THE mode of agricultural production and the pattern of settlement determined the relationship between the Maya and their environment; they also formed the foundation upon which Maya society developed, and as our knowledge of subsistence and residence patterns has changed, so has our understanding of the way in which that society worked.

For many years understanding of ancient Maya social structure was based on a model put forward in popular works by the late Eric Thompson. Known as the "priest-peasant model," it suggested that the Maya in Classic times had a theocratic aristocracy that ruled by divine right and popular consent in the ceremonial centers, interpreting the events of the heavens and the complexities of the calendar to the rest of the population. This population was made up of peasant farmers who lived in small rural villages or hamlets among their *milpas*, making festal visits to the ceremonial center which functioned as a focus of political, religious, and economic activity and thus of social control. The long growing season of maize, and the period of inactivity during the dry season while the felled brush in the *milpas* was drying, provided a pool of labor that could be used to build the great temples, palaces, and other structures in the ceremonial precinct; the labor was freely and joyously given in the service of the gods and, being seasonal, did not disrupt the swidden economy.

Thompson's model was based at least partially on ethnographic reality, the empty towns of highland Chiapas such as Zinacantan. These have a ceremonial center consisting of the church and a few houses, including the *cabildo*, the town hall, grouped around the plaza. In this center the reigning officials chosen by the *cargo* system resided during their term of office, before returning to their farms to earn the money for another *cargo* office. The rest of the population lived in hamlets and waterhole groups, in which social activity was concentrated, and came into the center for periodic fiestas and market days.

Sylvanus Morley saw enough similarity between Thompson's model and the way of life of early twentieth-century Yucatan to adopt the model, and the conjoint views of these two influential scholars molded those of the rest of the academic community. That a change occurred was due partly to a new view of the relationship between man and environment in the Maya lowlands, and partly to the first decipherment of the subject matter of the Maya monuments of the Classic period. We now have abundant evidence that Classic Maya society was divided into a number of layers, with rulers at the top and common people, some of them peasants, at the base of the social pyramid. It has become clear that this complex and many-layered society must have had a great many specialists and that any one layer in the pyramid could have embraced a range of occupations, many pursued as full-time economic specialties. Evidence for the existence of such specialists occurs, explicitly or implicitly, in the archaeological record, while at the peak of the social pyramid some individuals can now be named and are moving slowly out into the light of history from the anonymity that has heretofore shrouded them.

The basic unit of Maya society, as of almost all others in the history of mankind, was the family: the settlements that we study reflect the former residential patterns and social relationships of families, so that we can make a certain number of informed guesses about family life. The major problem is one of sample size: at only three sites (Tikal, Seibal, and Dzibilchaltun) has mapping been carried out on a large enough—but also delicate enough—scale and linked to extensive excavation, so that both the interrelationships of structures within a group and of groups to their environment and to each other can be understood. None of the sites has yet been completely published, but enough has been made public to enable us to offer some tentative assertions. In all three cases, the investigators point out, a major limitation is the coarseness of the time scale: without dated inscriptions, the most sensitive indicators of the passing of time are changes in ceramic style and radiocarbon dating, and in the Maya lowlands neither of these can be fixed within an amplitude of much less than a century. Since human society runs through three generations during that period it is easier to detect trends than to isolate the activities of individuals.

Nevertheless, William Haviland at Tikal has made a valiant attempt to detect individual activities, correlating the small-scale changes detected by excavation in a single residential group (known from its location on the map grid as 2G–1), lying some 1.8 kilometers (1.1 miles) northeast of the ceremonial core of Tikal, with the actions of several generations of Late Classic Maya who lived there.

Group 2G–1 (Figure 5.10) consists of five low, roughly rectangular platforms set around a courtyard about 13 meters (42 feet) square and oriented approximately to the four cardinal directions. The structures are labelled 2G–56 through 2G–60, clockwise from the southwest corner of the courtyard, and are all set on a common basal platform, 2G–1, the top of which forms the surface of the patio. Structures 56 and 57 lie one behind the other on the western side. Structure 2G–59 on the east side is known to be the earliest building, which Haviland interprets as the dwelling of the founder of the family that lived in this group, and after his death successively the home of his son, grandson, oldest great-grandson, and eventually his youngest great-great-grandson (Figure 6.1). Structure 2G–59 had six successive periods of architectural modification, and Haviland has proposed that each of these was the result of the death of the previous occupant and the use of the building by his successor. Structure 2G–58 had only three phases of construction and Structure 2G–57, two: Haviland suggests that both were first constructed in the fourth generation, when there were three great-grandsons of the founder to be accommodated. At this period the group would have consisted of three platforms around the patio, which lay open to the south; in the succeeding generation the south side was closed by the addition of Structure 60, occupied by the founder's great-great-grandson, and Structure 56 was added to the back and side of 57 for use by another great-great-grandson. According to Haviland, the occupants of the joined buildings may have been brothers rather than cousins. A generation later the surviv-

6.1. Hypothetical genealogy of the occupants of Group 2G-1 at Tikal (see Figure 5.10) over four generations in the Late Classic. The shifting occupancy accounts for successive periods of alteration in the architecture detected by excavation (after Haviland).

ing great-great-grandson lived in the senior residence, 59, while the other four houses were occupied by great-great-great-grandchildren and their families.

Although Haviland's model is hypothetical, it fits well with the information obtained from excavation. Events such as the remodeling of several structures at the same time can be seen as a series of moves, like musical chairs, triggered off by the death of the senior member of the group and the availability of his house. The fit between hypothesis and evidence does demonstrate, says Haviland, "that an extended family model is realistic as a device for understanding the unit of social organization" that occupied this characteristic Maya residential group, and "lends powerful support to the oft-made assertion that the usual Classic Maya household was an extended family," one in which more than the nuclear group of parents and children was present.

In offering this suggestion, Haviland made a number of assumptions: that residence was patrilocal—a man brought his wife to live with his parents; that the senior nuclear family of parents and children at any one time occupied the most prominent structure in the group, 2G–59; and that this seniority was based on primogeniture and generation, so that an older brother had precedence over a younger and a father over his sons. Granted these assumptions, and also the imperfections of archaeological evidence and the incomplete nature of the excavation of the 2G–1 group, "the 'fit' is surprisingly good, and ages can be assigned to the various 'actors' in this reconstructed 'drama' which allow for the births of sons at reasonable stages in their fathers' life spans and which do not require men to live to unbelievable old ages," according to Haviland.

The fact that most residential platforms occur in groups of three or more supports Haviland's argument that the Classic Maya family (and by extension, on more limited evidence, the Preclassic family also) was extended rather than nuclear in its residential pattern; the mapping of such groups from Copan in the south northward through Petén and Belize to Yucatan indicates that this was the general state of affairs. The extended family probably consisted of two or more related nuclear families spanning two or more generations with a common ancestor; the foundation of the family must itself have occurred as the result of a nuclear family splitting off from its own parent group and establishing a new residence, as the founder of 2G–1 did when he built Structure 2G–59.

One governing assumption has been that residence was patrilocal, not matrilocal, and that the common ancestor was male; this assumption is supported by colonial documentary evidence, and Haviland argues that the archaeological evidence for increasing political complexity and the predominance of men in monumental art both fit with the widespread ethnographic observation that male preeminence is normally associated with patrilocal residence. The burials of men at Tikal are more richly furnished than those of women, and the burials in important buildings were preponderantly those of men. Finally, the partial decipherment of monumental inscriptions from Tikal and elsewhere indicates patrilineal succession to rulership, from father to son, implying patrilineal descent: such patterns of descent develop out of residence patterns. Since patrilineal succession at Tikal dates back to at least the fourth century A.D., and perhaps as early as the first century B.C., the associated pattern of patrilocal residence may also be projected back at least as far. There is some evidence, from greater parity of grave goods, that women at Tikal were closer to equal status in the Late Preclassic period, but Haviland suggests that with the emergence of a complex society the position of men became progressively more prominent.

6.2. Woman grinding corn on a *metate*, with a swaddled baby slung on her back; a Late Classic figurine from Lubaantun. The *metate* has legs, like numerous grey basaltic lava examples found at Lubaantun and imported there from the highlands of Guatemala; most Maya lowland *metates* lacked legs.

The size of the family, both the extended unit occupying the courtyard group of houses and the individual nuclear units of which it was composed, is a matter of dispute. Some scholars have used the Chan Kom average of 5.6 persons per house, but this has been criticized as atypical. Raoul Naroll has proposed a universal standard of 10 square meters (11.8 square yards) of interior living space per head, based on cross-cultural ethnographic comparisons, which would reduce the putative capacity of many ancient Maya dwellings well below that figure; if the platforms in group 2G–1 at Tikal were *completely* utilized as interior space the maximum number of people in the five dwellings would be 22, against 28 on the Chan Kom model. Others, including myself, have felt that even this number in a circumscribed space might be too large: for the residential groups at Lubaantun I proposed an arbitrary population of 10 persons, although I now think this is probably too low by 50%.

It has been suggested that not all structures in a group need have been simultaneously or continuously occupied, and that even entire courtyard groups might have been left uninhabited from time to time, as after the death of a senior inhabitant. Both proposals are based on ethnohistoric and ethnographic evidence that even desirable residential locations are not necessarily fully utilized. Some structures in a group would also undoubtedly have been granaries, kitchens, and other domestic appurtenances, as well as shrines, so that no simple ratio of structures to people will probably be correct.

In spite of the many courtyard groups that have been mapped and excavated, in only a few instances has the internal layout of an ancient Maya house been recovered in sufficient detail to suggest the range of activities carried out there. This is mainly because the postabandonment growth of tropical vegetation has disturbed anything left *in situ*, partly because the Maya kept their houses clean, dumping broken vessels and domestic trash outside; thus we have nothing comparable to the Preclassic houses excavated in Oaxaca, where the debris left on the floors could be used to identify male and female work areas within the house. It is also probable that many Maya domestic activities took place outside the house, in the courtyard, and were communal among the members of the extended family.

We can, nevertheless, gain some idea of the range of activities from the artifacts and trash that have survived, and of the sexual division of labor both from depictions in sculpture and painting of the Classic period and from later documentary sources. An activity attested by both artifacts and depictions is the processing of maize: after being steeped in limewater (to soften the husk and liberate useful amino acids—not that the latter were known to the Maya), the corn was ground on a *metate* with a *mano*, and then often formed into a round tortilla and baked on a flat pottery *comal* set on the three stones of the fireplace. *Manos*, *metates*, *comales*, and even a few undisturbed fireplaces have been found in excavations, sometimes on the floors of abandoned houses, while on both a polychrome vase and on several mold-made figurines from Lubaantun a woman is shown grinding corn, a baby slung across her back in a shawl (Figure 6.2). That processing corn was woman's work is well attested by documentary sources also. Landa notes that "the Indian women put the maize to soak. . . . They next grind it on stones. . . . They prepare many kinds of bread . . . not good to eat when cold, so that the Indian women are kept busy making it twice a day."

Hunting, on the other hand, was an exclusively male activity; some of the Lubaantun figurines (Figure 5.3) show a deer being killed. Musicianship was also exclusively male, either in solo performance like that of the rattling drummer on another Lubaantun figurine (Figure 6.3) or in an ensemble like that shown in the Bonampak murals (Figure 9.23). The sexes are usually unambiguously differentiated in Maya art, less by physique than by dress and hairstyle, although a woman's breasts may be indicated. Women are usually shown with a long skirt (Figure 6.4) and a loose, blouselike *huipil* which may be elaborately decorated, like those of modern Maya women. Men wear the **"ex."** a long loincloth with the ends hanging down back and front (Figure 6.3). Both the *maxtli* and the woman's skirt were sometimes decorated, but not enough research has been done on the patterns depicted on figurines, vase paintings, murals, and sculpture to determine whether designs were sex-, class-, or community-specific; in present-day Chiapas both male and female costume convey community and status information to the initiate observer (Figure 3.12).

6.3. Male musician with elaborate hairstyle and wearing a pendant in the shape of a cacao pod and a long loincloth (*ex*), depicted on one of the Lubaantun figurines. He has a small drum tucked under his right arm and holds a rattle in his right hand, while beating the drum with the left hand. A similar musician is seen on the Bonampak mural (Figure 9.23) at the left-hand end of the group.

6.4. Woman in *huipil* and skirt. The head of this Lubaantun figurine is missing.

Page 185, Fig. 6.4 caption, add: Note the depiction of elaborate embroidery (cf. Figures. 3.12, 8.3, and 10.8).

Such information as we can extract from the archaeological evidence about sex roles in the pre-Hispanic period suggests that in this aspect of life, as in so many others, Maya society was a conserving one and it would be more legitimate to assume a similar division of activities in historic and prehistoric times than it would be to suppose that there had been significant change.

One aspect of Maya society in which there has been definite and radical change since the end of the Classic period is that of its class structure—the number, content, and relationship of the layers in the social pyramid. Modern Maya society consists essentially of a single class, with agriculture the major occupation, and a certain amount of part- or full-time specialization in such crafts as potting, basketry, and carpentry; within this class are a number of distinct roles, which may be individual-oriented and sometimes hereditary, such as divination and healing, or codified into a structure such as that of the Zinacanteco *cargo* system into which any man can enter and through which he can progress by performing the prescribed activities. What stratification there is, however, is linked to age: no young man will occupy a high status.

The evidence from the Classic period shows an entirely different situation, in which society consisted of a number of strata, membership in which was obtained by birth, or perhaps by occupation—which may have been hereditary. The most obvious division is between rulers and ruled; the governing dynasty was self-perpetuating, apparently by patrilineal primogeniture, and entry into it from below impossible except by absorption through marriage. Even among the majority, those who were ruled, distinctions are discernible, and one recent source of evidence has again been the mapping of settlement of Tikal and Seibal. Groups of house platforms vary greatly in size, not only in number of platforms (which is likely to be a function of family size) but also in the size and impressiveness of the platforms themselves: some may be only a single layer of stone high, of rough boulders, and just large enough to hold a small house with a floor area of 25–30 square meters (30–35 square yards), while others may have an elaborate elevated platform two meters (6.5 feet) or more in height, approached by a stone stairway and large enough to accommodate both a house and a generous front terrace. Some groups may incorporate a structure too small to be a dwelling, which was probably a shrine. Although we have no precise social correlates for these variations in residence type, it seems likely that the more grandiose, absorbing more labor and materials in their erection, were the dwellings of families toward the upper end of the social scale. One such group, excavated in 1977 by Gordon Willey and Richard Leventhal at Copan, possessed a bench set with a carved hieroglyphic inscription in the most prominent structure, and was approached from the ceremonial precinct by a raised *sacbe*; here, if anywhere in a dwelling, are status and privilege exemplified (Figures 6.5, 6.6).

It has long been assumed that the rulers of the Maya realms lived in the long, vaulted buildings dubbed "palaces" by archaeologists (although other functions including seminaries and administrative activity have also been suggested for them), examples of which are found at most major sites. One of the best known is the complex lying south of the Great Plaza at Tikal, known as the Central Acropolis, where Peter Harrison has analyzed the layout

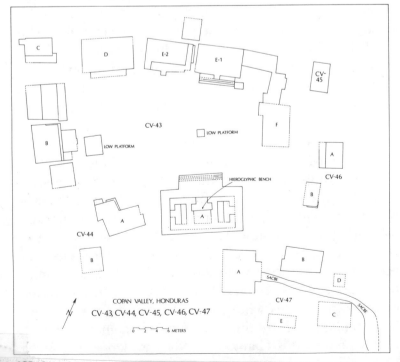

6.5. Plan of an upper-class residential group on the outskirts of the ceremonial precinct of Copan. The main structure had an internal bench decorated with a hieroglyphic inscription carved on stone blocks (Figure 6.6).

Page 187, Fig. 6.5 caption, add: The main structure had an internal bench decorated with a hieroglyphic inscription carved on stone blocks recording honors paid by the ruler of Copan (Figure 6.6). A similar group nearby, the residence of a scribe of elite status, also had a hieroglyphic bench.

6.6. The main structure in Group CV-43 at Copan, as excavated in 1977, showing the interior hieroglyphic bench.

and possible functions of the linked courtyards (Figure 6.7). It is also possible, however, that the rulers lived in, or used as alternative residences, elaborate courtyard groups such as the one at Copan mentioned earlier.

William Haviland has suggested that one very elaborate group, known as 7F−1, in the suburbs of Tikal, was a "dower house" for the deposed ruling family; if true, this would suggest that apart from the ruling dynasty itself the existence of an aristocracy was recognized, of families who by birth or former tenure of high office maintained a high status and the economic ability to support it in style. Progressive decipherment of the monumental inscriptions may yield further evidence on this putative aristocracy and its relationship to the ruling group.

That such an aristocracy came into existence during the Classic period is suggested by the work of William Rathje, who has studied the distribution of grave goods in burials in both ceremonial precincts and house platforms, at sites ranging from the major center of Uaxactun to the rural settlement of Barton Ramie. He found that in the Early Classic period access to scarce imported goods such as jade was open to all sections of society, but that by Late Classic times these goods were becoming concentrated in the possession of a few individuals who had as their burial places grandiose buildings in the heart of the ceremonial precincts. Rathje sees in this changing pattern evidence that Maya

society was becoming more strictly stratified, so that movement of sumptuary goods down the social scale and of individuals up it became progressively more restricted. The
jades that had served as the jewelry of those who could afford them in the Early Classic period became the regalia of
those entitled to wear them in the centuries that followed.

The bulk of our evidence on the existence of classes in
ancient Maya society comes from the Late Classic period
(apart from documentary evidence of the conquest period),
partly because more sites of this age exist and partly because earlier evidence is buried at most sites beneath as yet
unexcavated Late Classic remains. At present we can detect the existence, from archaeological evidence, of at least
seven levels in Late Classic society, with some individuals
doubtless spanning more than one level; to what extent
this division was explicitly recognized in the Late Classic
period is unknown.

The topmost level was that of the ruler, or the ruling family, whose marital and military exploits are commemorated
on the stelae, lintels, and altars of sites such as Tikal and

6.7. The Central Acropolis at
Tikal, showing a hypothetical
division between various public
and private functions suggested by Peter Harrison, who
directed the excavations in this
complex structure. The acropolis is, in effect, an agglomera-
tion of courtyard groups, with
the superstructures rendered
permanent in stone and extended to several stories in
height. One building in the
complex stands five stories
high, the roof of each level
forming a front terrace for the
rooms above.

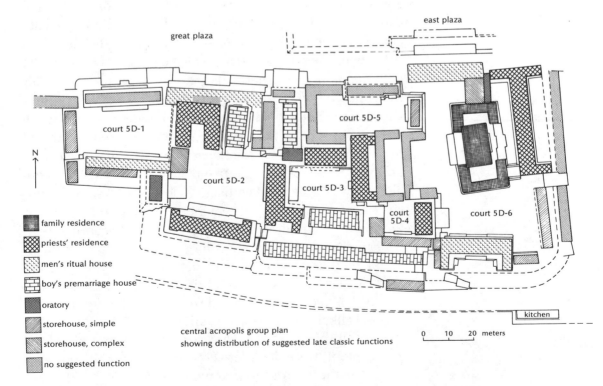

central acropolis group plan
showing distribution of suggested late classic functions

family residence
priests' residence
men's ritual house
boy's premarriage house
oratory
storehouse, simple
storehouse, complex
no suggested function

Yaxchilan. The ruler himself acted as chief executive of the complex organization that maintained the superstructure and administered the infrastructure of civilization, and was probably a religious as well as secular head of state. The decipherment of some of the monumental inscriptions has given us more information about a handful of Classic Maya rulers as individuals than we have about any other pre-Hispanic American Indians, and these data are discussed in Chapter 7.

The ruler of a realm containing perhaps 50,000 people would clearly be able to exert control only through an administrative class, and the existence of such a class may therefore be postulated from the mere existence and florescence of Classic Maya culture. The function of its members would have been to translate the ruler's directives into appropriate administrative action: decisions as to which resources of men or materials were to be allocated to a particular task, and the dissemination of necessary information about its performance.

This higher bureaucracy would have been within constant reach of the ruler, and below it we may propose a lower, executive bureaucracy responsible for the actual execution of directives on the spot, beyond the immediate control of the central administration. Such officials would be responsible for the assembly of the labor force, specialist craftsmen, and raw materials for a building project, or for the conscription, arming, and supply of a raiding or defensive force. They would necessarily operate at a local level, and some of the minor ceremonial centers probably would have acted as their bases of operation. Whether their position was purely administrative or whether, as seems more likely, it was associated with a high local social status (similar to that of the lord of the manor in medieval England or the district commissioner in the nineteenth-century British Empire), we cannot know for certain. Similarly we cannot know the extent to which a population was obligated to its local overlords as well as to the ruler, although Richard Adams has recently suggested that a feudal system of obligation is likely to have existed among the Classic Maya.

Many of the directives, whether from the central or local government, were doubtless concerned with the construction, decoration, and maintenance of public buildings—

temples, ball courts, and all the other nonresidential structures clustered in the ceremonial precinct—and these activities in themselves would, as elsewhere in the preindustrial world, have been carried out by specialist artisans, working under a system of public patronage but also doubtless capable of undertaking private commissions. The kind of life described by Benvenuto Cellini in his *Autobiography* may not have been so very different from that of a topflight Maya craftsman.

The range of such activities can be seen by envisaging the construction of a single public building—for instance, Temple 1 at Tikal (Figure 6.8). The design of the building is coherent, subtle, and structurally sound, the marks of a good architect. It contains a prodigious quantity of quarried and cut stone, hauled to the spot; the calculation of what was needed, how many men would be required, and when delivery would have to be made could have been calculated by the architect, or by the Maya equivalent of a quantity surveyor. The stone had to be dressed by masons, and hauled into place by laborers. Some of it, on the roof comb, was set into a huge architectural sculpture, the detail of which would have been carved by sculptors perhaps more usually employed on modest monuments such as stelae. The whole structure had a coating of glistening white stucco, made, mixed, and applied by specialist plasterers, who would also be capable, if required, of producing the kind of delicate three-dimensional stucco sculpture seen at Palenque (Figure 9.21) and in some parts of Tikal. Some or all of the stucco might have been painted, and certainly some Maya buildings were ornamented with murals in a *secco* technique, as at Bonampak (Figure 9.23), Uaxactun, and in the Postclassic period at Tulum and Santa Rita. The doorways of Temple 1 were spanned by wooden lintels, carved in low relief with complex scenes and hieroglyphic inscriptions as detailed and delicate as any stone or stucco carvings known, and from occasional wooden figures that have survived, we know that the Maya used this medium in the round as freely and competently as they did others.

A building such as Temple 1 expresses in its form as well as its ornament a system of belief rendered as iconography. Much of Maya iconography remains obscure to us, in the

6.8. Temple 1 at Tikal, built in about A.D. 700 as the tomb of Ruler A (see Chapter 7), epitomized the range of specialist designers and craftsmen at the service of a Maya ruler, including architect, masons, sculptors, stucco workers, wood carvers, painters, and ritual specialists.

same way that the structure of a Christian church would to someone with no knowledge of the beliefs that inspired it—the cruciform plan, the baptistry at one end and the altar at the other, the divided choir of a monastic church contrasting with the aisleless nave of a Jesuit preaching hall. We may confidently assume that in the construction and adornment of Temple 1 the architect and sculptors were closely guided by a concerned priesthood, ensuring that this royal funerary temple was ritually correct.

For all of these specialists the evidence is palpable, as it is for the unspecialized labor force they must have controlled. Similar evidence exists for other specialist artisans, working on a private rather than a public scale and for a private clientele rather than under corporate patronage: two activities for which archaeological evidence is especially abundant are the making of pottery vessels and stone tools.

Potting is probably the most widespread skill for which we have evidence among settled preindustrial societies: the evidence survives because although a pot is a fragile object, the sherds into which it breaks are virtually indestructible. The average Maya excavation yields hundreds of thousands of sherds, and the relatively rapid manner in which pottery has changed in style and technique through time has made the comparative study of ceramic sequences the best method of relative dating between Maya sites—of far wider utility than the restricted, though more exact, evidence of dated stelae. Some aspects of pottery as evidence for trade and as a fine art are discussed in Chapters 8 and 9; here it is necessary to note only that in preindustrial societies generally (including the modern Maya of Chiapas and Yucatan), potting is a skill practiced by only a few individuals in the community, and often in only a few settlements in a region, who supply a wide local or regional market with domestic and ceremonial ceramics. Maya Classic period pottery ranges from competently made large jars for the storage of liquid or grain, through single-color, slipped bowls used for serving food, to highly decorated polychrome vessels which are most usually found in graves (Figure 7.14). Even in the Early Preclassic sites there is a range of vessel types and decorative techniques that seem to distinguish kitchen pottery from that used in the house, but the finest figure painting does not appear until the Late Classic period. Then, perhaps, as in ancient Athens, potter and painter were different individuals, cooperating from time to time on a specific commission; from what we know of Maya crafts it would not be surprising if the potter were a woman and the painter a man.

Stone tools in the Classic period, as in the rest of the pre-Hispanic period, are of two main kinds: those of ground stone and those of chipped stone. The former class includes such implements as axes of hard stone, usually brought into the lowlands from the volcanic regions of the highlands, and *manos* and *metates* for grinding corn; they were often imported from the highlands, however, where they were made from gray basaltic lava. A major manufacturing center also existed in the Maya Mountains of central Belize where suitable granites and quartzites outcropped. All such ground-stone tools were made by pecking a boulder or quarry block roughly into shape with a heavy maul, then gradually smoothing out the lines and if necessary grinding the working surface smooth. Because of weight the objects were probably finished as close to the source of raw material as possible, and workshop sites undoubtedly exist in the Maya Mountains and in highland Guatemala. The necessity of working at an often remote location, as well as the techniques involved, suggest that this was a specialized occupation.

The major kinds of chipped stone used in the Maya Area are chert in the lowlands and obsidian in the highlands; the latter was also exported to the lowlands. Although the working of these easily fractured rocks into tools is not difficult (man has been using them for over a million years in the Old World), there is evidence that many of the tools in the Maya Area were made by specialist artisans. This evidence consists of workshops, at which large quantities of chipping debris have been found, and a corresponding lack of waste material in most domestic sites: tools were made in certain places, and sent out from them to a wide consumer market.

Obsidian workshops in the lowlands tend to be fairly small in scale, corresponding with the relatively small quantities of obsidian imported; two well-documented ones have been excavated at Tikal and at El Pozito, Belize, and the recovery from several sites of partly used prismatic cores suggests that obsidian came from the highlands in the form of roughed-out cores. These would be broken down into hundreds of thin sharp blades, either in the market by a traveling craftsman, or at a workshop from which they would be distributed in retail packages, carefully wrapped in corn husks or leaves to preserve the razor edge. Not all obsidian or chert was for practical use: elaborate objects such as the "eccentric" chert with multiple human profiles from El Palmar or the incised obsidian flakes with deities portrayed on

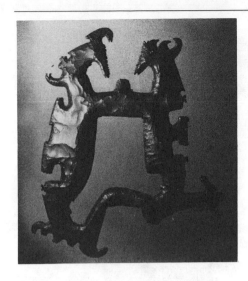

6.9. Craftsmanship in stone: a finely chipped and pressure-flaked "eccentric chert" showing several Maya profile heads; from El Palmar, Quintana Roo.

them, found in caches at Tikal and Uaxactun, show the skilled hands of specialist workers.

Although obsidian is relatively rare in the lowlands, chert is overwhelmingly abundant, being a flintlike material formed naturally in the limestone (Figure 6.9). For tool-making some varieties of chert were more suitable than others, and outcrops of good-quality stone were heavily exploited. Tikal is located on a fine outcrop of chert, while in northern Belize the site of Colha has an estimated 7.5 square kilometers (2.8 square miles) of chert workshops. A detailed study of one of these, Structure 100, by Richard Wilk documented some two hundred and fifty discarded implements in all stages of manufacture on the surface of the mound, together with hammerstones for initial working of the chert. The mound itself was built up by the accumulations of millions of waste flakes. Although the study of this industrial center has only just begun, it is clear that the Maya there had as good a repertoire of chert-working techniques at their fingertips as any of the master flint-workers of prehistoric Europe or the Middle East, and one of the most accomplished modern flintworkers, Donald Crabtree, has declared Colha to be "one of the most important sites in the New World for the study of stone-working techniques."

Other specialist occupations can be inferred from archaeological evidence. The working of jade, for example, both as low-relief and in-the-round sculptures and as mosaic work,

6.10. Craft specialization: The "Gann Jade," a superbly worked low-relief jade plaque of Late Classic date, probably made in the lowlands or in the northern highlands of Guatemala, but allegedly found at Teotihuacan in central Mexico.

must have required the skill of specialist lapidaries who could work the hard and refractory rock without damaging it; the quality of Maya jades can be seen from figures 6.10 and 9.29. Some other occupations were likely to have been specialized but part-time, musicianship being one and curing the sick another. Individuals may well have risen from a lower class to a higher when exercising these skills, although the elite and the commoners may have maintained separate specialists in these fields.

The two lowest levels in Maya society can be inferred: unskilled labor and subsistence farmers. The former supplied the muscle needed to carry out the construction projects in the ceremonial precinct, and performed the innumerable menial tasks that spring up in any socially stratified semiurban settlement, while the latter were responsible for producing the surplus of foodstuffs needed to support rulers, bureaucracy, and specialists. The surplus was presumably exacted from the farmers as a feudal due, as a secular tax, or as religious tribute. It is possible that some individuals were both farmers and laborers, as Thompson and Morley argued, spending part of the year in the fields and part, especially the January–April dry season after the cutting of the *milpa*, in voluntary or compulsory labor in their capital or in the service of a local lord; but there must have been substantial numbers of nonfarming, nonspecialist residents in the suburbs of large sites such as

Tikal, who would be more continuously and immediately available as laborers than the rural peasant. To be an unskilled or semiskilled laborer, providing a service to fulfill public and private needs, would surely have been an economically viable occupation in Classic Maya times.

We may thus propose the existence of the following levels in Classic Maya society, without assessing any possible mobility or status differences among them: (1) ruling individual or family; (2) administrative bureaucracy; (3) executive bureaucracy; (4) intellectual specialists—architects, priests, scribes, and the like; (5) craft specialists—potters, sculptors, lapidaries, painters, and so forth; (6) common laborers; (7) peasant farmers.

Such a functional division accords with what we know of early civilizations in the Old World, such as Sumer and Egypt, and suggests that the emergence of a complex society generates its own needs: the establishment of a ruling class necessitates both a bureaucracy to administer decisions and panoply to distance the rulers from the rest of society. The provision of such panoply begets a patronage system, which in turn supports those specialists whose output, intellectual or artistic, is reinforcing the regime. The basic economic supplies—labor and food—that support this superstructure are extracted from the ruled population voluntarily or otherwise by the application of a carrot-and-stick system of inducements, material or notional, and sanctions, spiritual or physical. Although we do not know precisely how this system worked in the governance of Classic Maya society, nor when and how it developed, its existence is demonstrated to us by the tangible remains of Classic civilization.

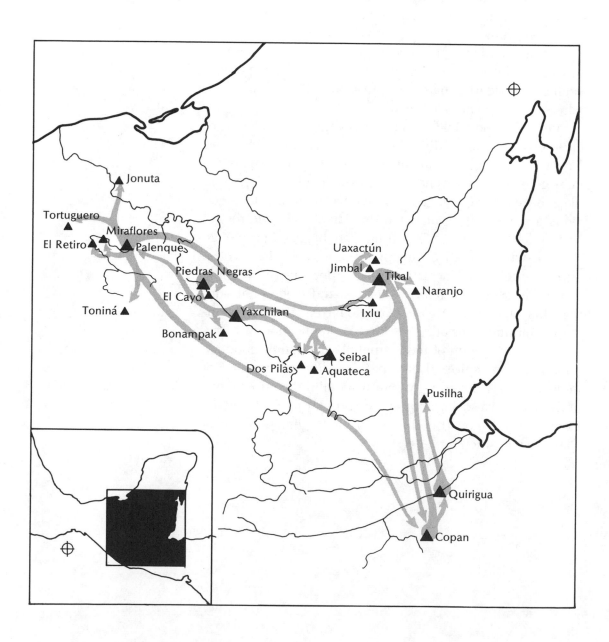

7

Politics and Kingship

 IN the last chapter we noted the existence of a Maya ruling elite, although how large a group of a ruler's kin it included we are unable to say. Of the rulers themselves, however, we know far more than we do about any other section of ancient Maya society, for the simple reason that, like rulers everywhere, they erected images of themselves and inscriptions listing their conquests

7.1. Emblem glyphs which may be place names or the names of tribes or dynasties, for the polities centered on Copan, Yaxchilan, Palenque (two variants), Piedras Negras, and Tikal (one of two variants). Recognition of these signs, which share the water-group prefix of a skein of dots, and the *ahpo* prefix (above the main part of the glyph, which varies from center to center), was a major step in showing that Maya hiero-glyphic inscriptions are histor-ical in nature (after Berlin).

Page 199, Fig. 7.1 caption should read: Emblem glyphs, probably the names of polities and perhaps also of their capitals, for Copan, Yaxchilan, Palenque (two variants), Piedras Negras, and Tikal (one of two variants). Recognition of these signs, which share the "bloodline" (or "water-group") prefix of a skein of dots, and the *ahpo* or *ahau* "lord" prefix (above the main part of the glyph, which is polity-specific), was a major step in showing that Maya hieroglyphic inscriptions were historical in nature (after Berlin).

his knowledge of Old World civilization,
Copan portrayed rulers and that their inscriptions were historical in content, he and his successors were unable to decipher them. Even after the chronology of the Maya monuments had been elucidated, their meaning remained hidden, and for forty years in this century Morley and Thompson persuaded the majority of Mayanists that the inscriptions were esoterica and the figures hierophants; any kind of historical understanding of Maya civilization seemed unattainable.

The picture changed with dramatic suddenness in 1958–1960, when first of all Heinrich Berlin demonstrated that a certain glyphic prefix recurred consistently in combination with a range of main glyphic signs, and that each of these signs had a concentrated and restricted geographical distribution focused on a single site (Figures 7.1, 7.2). The term *glyph* is employed in discussing Maya writing as a short form of "hieroglyph," denoting any one of the signs.

Opposite:
7.2. The distribution of some emblem glyphs in the Maya lowlands: apart from a few foreign occurrences, such as the presence of the Tikal glyph at Copan and Seibal, the distribution is within the region of the parent site and may well delineate the limits of that center's political influence. The foreign occurrences demonstrate definite, although spasmodic and unexplained, contact between the elites of several major centers (data from Marcus and others).

Page 199, Fig. 7.2 caption should read: The distribution of some emblem glyphs in the southern Maya lowlands: arrows show where a site's emblem is mentioned at another center. These occurrences accompany statements about royal marriages, warfare, and visits between rulers. Most occurrences of a center's emblem glyph are in the region surrounding it, and may well delineate the limits of the polity. Some long-distance citations of other polities' glyphs may be more rhetorical than substantive in meaning.

Berlin suggested that each sign denoted the place name or the identity of the ruling dynasty at that site, and this ambiguity of interpretation of what are called "emblem glyphs" remains. Emblem glyphs were identified by Berlin for Tikal, Palenque, Yaxchilan, and Piedras Negras, and since then they have been recognized for Seibal, Quirigua, and other sites. Several variant forms exist for some sites, such as Tikal and Palenque, the reason for which remains unknown. The existence of these signs and their geographical concentration suggested immediately that the inscriptions containing them must deal, at least in part, with mundane and terrestrial matters and not just with the arcane and celestial topics suggested by Morley and Thompson.

Concurrently with Berlin's work, Tatiana Proskouriakoff of the C.I.W. noticed that the stelae recorded at Piedras Negras on the Usumacinta fell into an unusual and yet consistent pattern. In each chronological group of stelae, the earliest showed a seated figure in a niche at the top of a ladder; footprints on a mat up the ladder indicated that the figure had just climbed to his seat (Figure 7.3). Proskouriakoff called this the "ascension motif," and the date on the monument that referred to this event she called the "inaugural date." Each of these stelae also bore an earlier date, referring back to some event years or even decades before the inaugural date, which she termed the "initial date." The period of time between any two initial or inaugural dates is such, she says, "that no single series exceeds the span of a reasonable lifetime"; consequently it is plausible to suggest "that the initial date represents something in the nature of a birth or name day of a ruler who accedes to power on the inaugural date, and that each set of monuments records the history of a reign." The richly dressed figures on the stelae can then be interpreted not as priests, but as portraits of secular rulers and their families, and the content of the inscriptions not as purely calendric and astronomical calculation but at least partly as recorded history and genealogy.

Proskouriakoff recorded seven successive groups of monuments at Piedras Negras (one of them doubtful, having only a single stela), spanning the period from 9.9.0.0.0. to 9.18.5.0.0. (A.D. 613–795). The reigns of the six best-documented rulers were, respectively, 35, 47, 42, 28, 5, and

Opposite:
7.3. Two accession stelae of rulers at Piedras Negras: the rulers sit in niches framed by celestial bands representing the great god Itzam Na (Chapter 10); their ascensions are marked by the ladders and footprints leading up to the niche. A woman, perhaps a wife or mother, stands beside the ladder at right. At least six rulers at Piedras Negras erected such accession monuments, and one exists also at Quirigua. These date from A.D. 731 and 761 (Stelae 11 and 14); the photographs are by Teobert Maler.

17 years, averaging nearly 30 years; their ages at accession ranged from 12 to 31 years, and their lifetimes from 56 to 60 years or slightly longer. Reigns and life-spans were longer than might be expected on the basis of colonial and modern documentary evidence, and Proskouriakoff suggested that perhaps a younger brother might have continued a reign in the name of a deceased sibling, and also that succession might not have been by primogeniture but simply from among the eligible men in the ruling group. I think that these qualifications are unnecessary (without necessarily being incorrect), in that the privileged position of the ruler may well have ensured a longer and healthier life and also that colonial Maya had to contend with a whole new range of diseases. Among the figures on the monuments were some in robes and skirts, identified as women, and subsequent genealogical work at a number of sites, including Tikal, has indicated the importance of female descent in legitimate succession.

It seems clear that at Piedras Negras each incoming ruler erected an accession monument on the *hotun* (five-year) anniversary following his elevation to the throne, referring back to the precise date of his accession and also to the earlier initial date—that of his birth or some other notable moment in early life. The fact that he knew that date several decades later shows how carefully records were kept, among the elite if not for the population at large. Further monuments were erected at *hotun* intervals, without the ascension scene, until that individual's reign ended —in view of the known ages, probably at his death. Then another ruler took over and erected his own accession monument.

Proskouriakoff followed up this paper, which more than any other single publication established the historicity of the Maya monuments and their inscriptions, with a study of the inscriptions of the great site of Yaxchilan, which lies up the Usumacinta from Piedras Negras on the opposite bank and which seems to have had some dynastic ties with Piedras Negras. Yaxchilan did not have monuments as conveniently placed and dated in groups as those at Piedras Negras, but nevertheless several rulers could be identified and some of their exploits described. The actual forms of Maya rulers' personal names are beginning to be understood, as we shall see, but direct transcription of apparent glyph forms may not always be correct. Two of these rulers were dubbed "Shield-Jaguar" and "Bird-Jaguar," so named from the forms of their name glyphs—a small, round shield with a profile jaguar head, and a bird resting on a jaguar head—but these are not necessarily their Maya names. The former in Maya might have been Pacal Balam (literally, "Shield Jaguar"), but the name could have meant something like "fierce protector."

Bird-Jaguar was a notable warrior: Lintel 8 and Lintel 41 at Yaxchilan, carved slabs placed over doorways in the ceremonial precinct, show him and another lord capturing two individuals, or perhaps eponymous figures representing tribes or places. Bird-Jaguar's captive has a name written on his thigh, a skull in a circle of beads, which has been rendered "Jewelled Skull" (Figure 7.4). The capture of important individuals (or places, perhaps) was commemorated by the taking of titles, rather as the Roman emperors added the names of conquered provinces to their own (Trajan's *Dacicus*—"conqueror of Dacia" [modern Romania]—is an example), so that Shield-Jaguar of Yaxchilan is called "captor of Death, captor of Ahau." Shield-Jaguar was a remarkable man: he was born about 9.10.15.0.0. (A.D. 647) and became lord of Yaxchilan by 9.12.10.0.0. (A.D. 682), living eventually to more than 90 years of age. Proskouria-

7.4. Lintel 8 at Yaxchilan, depicting the ruler Bird-Jaguar

...emy whose ...welled Skull," ...high (after

Page 203, Fig. 7.4 caption, add: The number of captives taken, and their identities, added to a ruler's status and were often cited in inscriptions. Other rulers were rarely captured, and most raiding was probably on the borders of neighboring polities.

military exploits on its carved lintels (although they were
probably taken there from an earlier building and reused,
she feels). They indicate "a battle of some political importance, perhaps even one in which Shield-Jaguar won the
lordship of Yaxchilan," since he thereafter takes the title of
Captor of Ahau. The date of the battle is given precisely as
9.12.8.14.1., 12 Imix 4 Pop, the equivalent of February 23,
A.D. 681; since there is no accession monument for Shield-
Jaguar, although he is known to have been ruler by the time
the 10-year (half-*katun*) monument for 9.12.10.0.0. was
carved a few years after the battle, it does seem likely that
he took the throne of Yaxchilan by force and not by birth-
right. He may have died on 9.15.10.17.14., 6 Ix 12 Yaxkin,
June 17, A.D. 742, although this is not certain; but Bird-
Jaguar did not accede until 11 years later, suggesting that
there may have been dispute over the succession. Bird-
Jaguar's use of Shield-Jaguar's name in his inscriptions
may have been an attempt to achieve respectability by invoking the memory of his great predecessor.

The important general point about the lintels of Yaxchilan is that they illustrate *history*—they are not set up as
regular calendric markers but are carved to commemorate specific events of personal and political importance in
the lives of the rulers of Yaxchilan. So we know that two
kinds of public monument exist: those set up to mark specific events, and those set up as markers of the passage of
time, which nevertheless embody dynastic and historical
information.

Proskouriakoff's breakthrough was followed up by other
scholars. The first was David H. Kelley, who proposed a series of three rulers and perhaps two more for the site of
Quirigua in the Motagua Valley. Quirigua is famous for its
tall, slender, sandstone stelae, one of which, Stela E (Monument 5 in the recent reclassification) is nearly 11 meters
(35 feet) tall, the highest Maya monument known; the site
is also noted for the three-dimensional boulder carvings
known as zoomorphs because of the monstrous animals
they portray. Renewed work on the Quirigua monuments
by Christopher Jones and Robert Sharer has resulted in
additional inferences about the site's rulers. The first, designated Cauac Sky from a free rendering (but not either a
literal or phonetic reading) of his name glyph, was respon-

7.5. Stela E (Monument 5) at Quirigua, showing the ruler Cauac Sky in full regalia. The stela was erected in A.D. 771, and at 10.75 meters (35 feet) is the tallest known in the Maya Area. The photograph is by Alfred Maudslay. A stela of 9.5 meters (31 feet) was discovered at Nim li punit in southern Belize in 1976.

sible for the Late Classic florescence of Quirigua, and some of the most splendid monuments commemorate his reign (Figure 7.5). He came to the throne in A.D. 724, from an unknown origin that might be local, or that might be southern Belize; the sites there at Pusilha and Nim li punit, and farther away at Caracol, seem to have links of some kind with Quirigua and to have been already established centers of elite culture at the time of the rise of Quirigua.

The precise relationship of Quirigua to the major center of Copan, a short journey to the south in an upland valley, has not yet been established, but it seems that in A.D. 737

the forces of Cauac Sky won a great victory over Copan and even captured the Copanec ruler, known from his name glyph as "XVIII Jog." (The Roman numeral shows that a Maya number *18*, three bars and three dots, formed the first part of his glyph, while a "Jog" is a conflation of "Jaguar" and "Dog" invented by Eric Thompson to describe the animal form that is the second part of the glyph. Linda Schele has recently identified the Jog as a rabbit, but one representation at Copan with a large claw suggests that a kinkajou is possibly the creature intended, and a pocket gopher has also been suggested.) Quirigua became, if it was not already, fully independent and in control of the strategic trade route of the Motagua Valley and perhaps of its jade sources.

As long-distance canoe routes around the Yucatan Peninsula, reaching eventually to Panama, became increasingly important, Quirigua's stranglehold on the Motagua increasingly benefited her rulers. Cauac Sky used some of his new power and wealth to transform Quirigua into a monumental expression of his rulership, at a time when other Maya centers such as Palenque were already falling into desuetude. The original courtyard of the royal residence, with an adjacent ball court in Copanec style, was buried under a series of high platforms and linking walls that made this "acropolis" defensible, if not actually defen-

7.6. Zoomorph P (Monument 16) at Quirigua was carved to commemorate Cauac Sky's successor, Sky Xul, and was set up in A.D. 795. The huge boulder sculpture shows the ruler in the embrace of a celestial/earth monster.

sive in function. To the north Cauac Sky laid out a great plaza, and in the final years of his long reign erected seven imposing monuments there, including five tall stelae with portraits of himself. This plaza, 300 by 150 meters (975 by 488 feet), is the largest known in the Maya Area, emulating the Great Plaza of Copan laid out by Cauac Sky's defeated rival, XVIII Jog.

Cauac Sky died in A.D. 784 after a reign of three *katunob*, leaving on the axis of the plaza the massive theriomorphic boulder carving called Zoomorph G as his funeral monument. He was succeeded by Sky Xul, probably his son, who was already middle-aged and reigned for only 11 years. His death may be marked by the magnificent Zoomorph P and its altar, set up in A.D. 795 (Figure 7.6). Two further rulers are poorly documented, but the final lord of Quirigua, Jade Sky, came to power in A.D. 805 for a reign that saw the final architectural expansion of the site. The recent work by Sharer and Jones has linked the reigns of Quirigua's rulers to four phases of construction in and around the site, but the sought-for tombs of Cauac Sky and his successors have not come to light, and may lie outside the ceremonial precinct in some ancestral necropolis. A significant discovery in the final season at Quirigua in 1979 was an Early Classic stela, found some distance from the main precinct. (An early stela has also been found recently at Copan, and the obscurity of these two sites before their Late Classic florescence was clearly not as marked as had been thought.)

At Tikal burials in several of the pyramids including Temple 1 have been linked to the documented rulers of the site over a period of centuries. The decade of excavation by the University of Pennsylvania has provided Mayanists with the largest body of data on a single site that has ever been obtained, or probably ever will be (although most of it is as yet unpublished). Work on the ruling dynasties of Tikal has proceeded by analysis of iconography combined with epigraphic study, linked to the excavation of rich burials and their content and location; a dynastic succession covering nearly four centuries, from the late fourth to the late eighth century A.D., has been elucidated by the work of Clemency Coggins, Tatiana Proskouriakoff, Christopher Jones, and others, based on William Coe's excavations, and

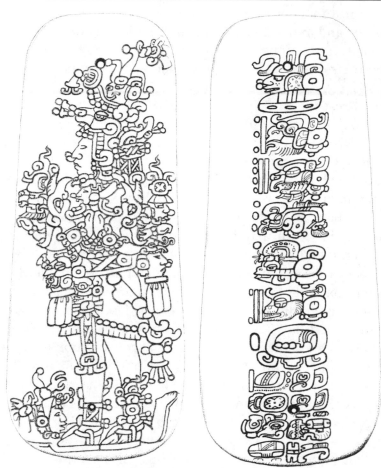

7.7. The Leyden Plate, a jade plaque incised on both sides and including a very early Long Count date of A.D. 320. The figure is thought to be Jaguar Paw, a ruler of Tikal who died in A.D. 376, and the jade is similar in style to early monuments at Tikal such as Stela 31 (Figure 4.16).

the monuments, name glyphs, and in many cases the tombs of eleven generations of Tikal's rulers have been identified.

The first identified ruler, "Jaguar Paw," died in A.D. 376 and is thought to be the person portrayed on the Leyden Plate (Figure 7.7), a jade found on the southeast coast of Guatemala but probably carved at Tikal, which bears one of the earliest known Long Count dates. His daughter, Clemency Coggins argues, married "Curl Nose," who is portrayed on two of the stelae at Tikal (No. 4 and No. 18); their son "Stormy Sky" erected the famous Stela 31 (Figure 4.16), on which he stands between two warriors accoutred in the style of Teotihuacan, with his father looking down from the sky above. On Stela 31 Stormy Sky refers to both his father, Curl Nose, and his maternal grandfather, Jaguar Paw, and his tomb is thought to lie, together with his grandfather's, in the building behind Stela 31, in the heart of Tikal.

The next ruler, "Kan Boar," is thought to be the son of Stormy Sky, and is notable as the father of a prominent daughter, at present known only as "Woman of Tikal," the first Tikal woman to appear in monumental art. Stela 23 was dedicated to her, and on Stela 25 she stands in honor at her husband's right (Figure 7.8). Her probable tomb is associated with his, one of the few elaborate burials of Maya women known, and contained such unusual items as the skeleton of a spider monkey and shells of the spiny oyster *Spondylus*, a valued import from the Caribbean coast. *Spondylus* shells are usually found only with the burials of elite men, emphasizing the Woman of Tikal's high status, but Coggins feels that her husband rather than she herself was the ruler of Tikal. It seems that succession could pass through a woman, but that she could not hold office: her husband became a son to her father in every way except biologically, and thus succeeded as ruler; the couple's son, in turn, had the right of succession. William Haviland has argued for patrilineal descent in ancient Maya society, and for succession to title and office in the same pattern: the polite fiction of "adopting" a daughter's husband enabled this pattern to be maintained and prevented power passing to another lineage.

Following the reign of the Woman of Tikal's son—a second Jaguar Paw—three generations of the dynasty remain somewhat obscure, although there are links with the rulers of Dos Pilas, a site to the southwest on Laguna Petexbatun. It has been suggested that a different lineage ruled at Tikal following the death or deposition of the second Jaguar Paw's son, and that the original dynasty was later restored, in A.D. 682.

This restored ruler, known at present only as Ruler A (although Jones has suggested that his name might be something like "producer of chocolate") seems to have sparked off a cultural renaissance at Tikal, which may have been associated with a spiritual revitalization movement. He carefully chose as his accession date the 260-year anniversary of the accession of his great predecessor and ancestor, Stormy Sky, and this deliberate selection of the end of a cycle of 13 *katunob* symbolized, in the words of Coggins, "the end of the preceding 260-year cycle of history," with himself "the inaugurator of the new cycle." Since the

7.8. Stela 25 at Tikal, showing the "Woman of Tikal," daughter of the ruler Kan Boar, on a monument of his successor, her husband. She was one of the first women to appear in Maya official art; her presence here indicates her importance in legitimating her husband's rule.

Maya had a concept of history repeating itself in such 13-*katunob* cycles, Ruler A, as an augury for his coming reign, was making very explicit reference and appeal to what was perceived as a time of past greatness. (Dennis Puleston has recently suggested that the Classic collapse may be related to a similar 13-*katunob* anniversary of the unlucky Katun 11 Ahau, 260 years after the *katun* marking the late Early Classic hiatus in stela erection, and a further 260 years after the previous Katun 11 Ahau which occurred about the time of the eruption of Ilopango and the early Early Classic depopulation of such sites as Seibal.)

Ruler A began the cultural revival at Tikal by building his own funerary pyramid, Temple 1 on the east side of the Great Plaza, and also beginning the sequence of "twin-pyramid groups" (Figure 7.9) that marked the close of every *katun* throughout the eighth century. Each of these groups consisted of a large platform supporting two flat-topped pyramids, each with four stairways, a long, range building with one room and nine doorways, and a stela enclosure containing a carved stela with the ruler's portrait and an altar, often with a bound captive on it. The enclosure lay on the north side of the platform, the nine-

7.9. A reconstruction (by Norman Johnson) of the twin-pyramid group Q at Tikal, erected in A.D. 771 by Ruler C to commemorate the *katun* ending 9.17.0.0.0. Seven such groups were built at Tikal through the eighth century, and another is known at the nearby center of Yaxha. The drawing shows the stela enclosure on the north side of the central plaza, the nine-doored building on the south, and the two flat-topped pyramids, each with four stairs and numerous plain stelae set in front. The stela in the enclosure bore a portrait of the ruler, the altar in front of it a bound captive.

7.10. Incised bone from the tomb of Ruler A beneath Temple I at Tikal, showing a man (perhaps the ruler) in a canoe with animal deities. The seven occupants probably give a fair idea of the size and capacity of Classic Maya river and lake canoes; seagoing craft may have been larger.

doored building on the south, and it has been suggested that the group is a cosmic diagram, with the enclosure representing the sky, the nine doorways the nine lords of the underworld and night, and the twin pyramids the passage of the sun god across the sky from east to west. Jorge Guillemin pointed out that the number of terraces on the pyramids could also be used to symbolize the thirteen layers of the heavens and the nine layers of the nether world; the complexes clearly embody arcane ritual statements, in which the ruler seems to be equated with the sun god in the glory of his reign as a passage through time.

Ruler A's revitalization of Tikal seems to have worked: his reign and those of his son and grandson (Rulers B and C) cover the century of Tikal's greatest growth and prosperity, and resulted in the tremendous group of ceremonial, religious, and secular buildings we see there today. Ruler A was over 60 when he died—just how old we do not know—and he had reigned for 52 years. He was buried below Temple 1 with a rich assortment of grave goods including jades, pottery vessels (perhaps containing food), and a pile of carved bones. This pile included a pair of well-used tweezers with his "monogram" and a delicately incised scene of a canoe-load of animal gods bearing away a man—perhaps Ruler A being borne after death to join the gods, or going on a mystic journey in life (Figure 7.10).

Ruler A died not long before A.D. 731 (9.15.0.0.0.), and Ruler B was inaugurated in A.D. 734. He ruled for 34 years and like his father lived to more than 60 years of age. He was anxious to make his mark when he came to the throne, and erected Stela 21 at the first quarter-*katun* interval, the only such *hotun* marker at Tikal. At his first *katun*, ending in 9.16.0.0.0., he built another twin-pyramid group, continuing his father's practice, and not long afterward he built the colossal Temple IV, nearly 70 meters (212 feet) high, the tallest building in the Maya world. Temple IV lies west of the main precinct of Tikal, marking the limits of monumental architecture in that direction, and looking east from it the roof combs of Temples I, II, III, and V can be seen exploding through the forest canopy. Temple IV was approached by two *sacbeob*, one running west from Temple III and the other southwest from Ruler B's twin-pyramid group, and the network of *sacbeob* that enmesh the center of Tikal seem to date from his reign. Another leads southeast from the center of the site to the last dated monumental building of the reign, the Temple of the Inscriptions (sometimes called Temple VI), which has a roof comb covered entirely with gigantic glyphs detailing historical and mythological events.

Three dates on the roof comb go back beyond the Classic period, the earliest of them, from 1139 B.C., dating to the end of the Early Preclassic, when Tikal may not have even been occupied, although areas to the east in the Belize Valley certainly were. Since the date, 5.0.0.0.0., 12 Ahau 3 Zac, was the ending of a *baktun* it seems more likely to be a formal announcement of the founding of Tikal than a precise record maintained for nearly nineteen hundred years. The second date, however, 6.14.16.9.16., 11 Cib 4 Zac, falling in 457 B.C., seems specific enough to record some actual event, and by that time Tikal was certainly a substantial settlement that may have included the keeping of the calendar among its activities.

By A.D. 768 Ruler B was dead; his tomb may lie beneath Temple IV, but it is unlikely that archaeologists will have enough funds to excavate it (although looters may penetrate, as in so many sites, and destroy the evidence to stock museums and satisfy collectors). Ruler B was succeeded by Ruler C, the last lord of Tikal who can be identified in the texts on the monuments. His reign is marked by the construction of two very large twin-pyramid groups, the last to be built, but the length of his reign, the date of his death, and the place of his burial remain unknown.

Another site from which much dynastic information has been obtained in the past few years is Palenque, lying far down the Usumacinta basin on the edge of the Tabasco plain, looking out toward the Gulf of Mexico. Palenque has been known and explored for longer than any other Maya site, but the most dramatic moment in its investigation came in 1952 when the Mexican archaeologist Alberto Ruz

7.11. The Temple of the Inscriptions at Palenque: the tablets inside the temple contain
the longest known Maya texts,
which have been interpreted as
dynastic records, and from the
floor of the temple, a stair descends through the pyramid to
a rock-cut tomb with vaulted
roof in which Pacal, the first
great ruler of Palenque, was
buried in A.D. 684.

7.12. The burial chamber of
Pacal, with the carved lid of the
sarcophagus in the foreground.
The design on the lid is illustrated in Figure 2.8.

L. finished the clearing of a stairway descending through
the pyramid of the Temple of the Inscriptions (Figure 7.11).
The stair led to a chamber cut into the bedrock, inside which
was a great sarcophagus with an elaborately carved lid (Figure 7.12); the coffin contained the skeleton of an elderly
man smothered in jade jewelry. Around the edge of the lid
ran a long inscription that included a number of dates and
personal names. In 1974 this inscription, along with a
number of others at Palenque, was interpreted by Peter
Mathews and Linda Schele, who proposed a dynastic sequence for Palenque covering almost the whole of the seventh and eighth centuries A.D.

Mathews and Schele propose that the man buried in
the vault was named Pacal ("shield," probably in the form
"Lord Shield Pacal"), and that he was born in A.D. 603 on
March 24, came to rule at Palenque on July 27, A.D. 615,
and died on September 29, A.D. 684 at the age of 81. It is

only fair to note that Ruz disputed this on the ground that the skeleton was that of a man of about 40, and felt that Mathews and Schele had misread the inscription: "taking the first date on the south side as his birth and the last one on the west side where the glyphic text ends as that of his death, gives us an age of 39 years, 9 months and a few days." Schele replied forthrightly, "If Pacal and his dates are thrown out, we must also discard Shield Jaguar of Yaxchilan, who was between 92 and 96, Bird-Jaguar, Cauac Sky of Quirigua, who was over 80 and Rulers A and B at Tikal who were over 60, as well as all other historic dates." It seems that a reexamination of the skeleton of Pacal is needed to try to resolve the dispute, in which the views of Mathews and Schele seem so far to be obtaining greater acceptance.

The results that Mathews and Schele, working with Floyd Lounsbury, have obtained seem to be both internally consistent and externally comparable with material from other sites; the Palenque inscriptions include the longest intact Classic texts from any site, and the dynasty of Pacal is therefore a good case study to help us in understanding the nature of Maya succession and the advances that have been made in the field so far. According to Linda Schele, "in the century following A.D. 600 Palenque grew from a site of minor importance to become one of the principal Late Classic centers. The texts of this period record one ruler between A.D. 615 and 684, whose culminating work seems to have been his funerary monument, the Temple of the Inscriptions. Texts in the temple record his birth date as 9.13.8.9.0., 8 Ahau 13 Pop, in A.D. 603, his accession as 9.9.2.4.8., 5 Lamat 1 Mol, in A.D. 615, and his death at 9.12.11.5.18., 6 Etz'nab 11 Yax in A.D. 684. His name is recorded with a glyph easily identifiable as a small, round shield like those worn by rulers on stelae throughout the Maya lowlands (Figure 7.13). A second group of glyphs accompany this—three glyphs with the phonetic values of *pa*, *ca*, *la*; these phonetic values are derived from contexts independent of each other, but when put together they give *pa-ca-l(a)*.

"It is a magnificent coincidence that 16th century dictionaries of Yucatec, Tzeltal and Tzotzil have entries which list *pacal* as 'shield' or 'small round shield.' Apparently this great ruler was named Pacal, and his name could be written with an ideographic glyph of a shield and also spelled syllabically as *pacal*, the word for shield.

"The texts which Pacal commissioned to celebrate the events of his life include a history of the rulers who preceded him in office; the sarcophagus text records the death dates for each of them, and the east panel in the temple above records their accessions. This list begins shortly before A.D. 514 and concludes with the accession of Pacal's eldest son, Chan-Bahlum, 132 days after his father's death. Seven persons are named, including two women, who held the throne before Pacal." (If these women were actual rulers, then a different system of descent from that in force at Tikal would seem to have obtained at Palenque.)

7.13. The name glyph of Pacal, ruler of Palenque from A.D. 615 to 684.

"Chan-Bahlum built the temples in the Cross Group, those of the Sun, the Cross, the Foliated Cross and Temple XIV [Figures 1.7, 9.20, 10.1]. He also records an ancestor list with the same people as in Pacal's lists, but stops short at the name of the ancestor for whom he himself was named, an earlier Chan-Bahlum. The accession dates match those in the Temple of the Inscriptions, and here we are given the birth dates as well; there are also at least two, perhaps four, generations preceding the earliest ruler on Pacal's list, and a mythical origin for the dynasty which is detailed on the three main carved tablets from the Group of the Cross.

"Chan-Bahlum died in A.D. 702 and was succeeded 53 days later by his younger brother Kan-Xul or Hok, who spent much of his reign enlarging and elaborating the Palace, where House C, the accession monument of Pacal, was made the focal point of an architectural complex including the north building and the four-storeyed tower; the tower would have provided a view over the roofs to see the sun sink at the winter solstice, the day on which it appears to enter the underworld through the Temple of the Inscriptions over Pacal's tomb.

"During Kan-Xul's reign Palenque reached its greatest degree of expansion. We don't have his death date, but he was succeeded for a short time by a ruler called Xoc, who we think was his younger brother, and then his son Chaacal III acceded in A.D. 721. We know little about him, but think that he built two temples at Palenque. He was in

turn succeeded by Chac-Zutz' in A.D. 722, a man who was
aged 52 at the time. He reigned for at least eight years, and
the Tablet of the Slaves records his 60th birthday (three-
katuns) in A.D. 729.

"After this there is a gap in the records for 35 years, until
Kuk, son of Chaacal III, comes to the throne in A.D. 764
and reigns for at least one *katun*, since that anniversary is
celebrated on the Tablet of the 96 Glyphs [which together
with the Tablet of the Slaves is in the site museum at Palen-
que]. Kuk followed the practice of his grandfather Kan-Xul,
of associating important events in his life to important
events in the life of their ancestor Pacal, carefully establishing genealogical descent from Pacal. This practice has given
us a detailed record in which the same events are restated in
a variety of ways and related both to Early Classic and to
later events in this history of Palenque. The repetition, inter-
locking and symmetry of the patterns of dates, events and
names of Palenque's dynastic history is remarkable.

"The latest dated text from Palenque is found on an inscribed pot, recording the accession of a ruler in A.D. 799;
the ruler has a calendric name, 6 Cimi, the only such name
in a Classic Maya inscription and one which suggests non-
Maya influence at Palenque by the end of the 8th century."
Similar intrusion half a century later has been documented
on the stelae of Seibal, far up the Usumacinta basin, and
has been linked by Eric Thompson to the expansion of the
Mexicanized Putun Maya, who lived on the Tabasco plain;
others, however, have suggested a movement south to Seibal from Yucatan, pointing out northern correspondences
in the art and inscriptions of the late monuments at Seibal
from 10.1.0.0.0. (A.D. 851) onward.

The florescence of Palenque was a century earlier than
that of Seibal, from A.D. 600 to 800; the first of these two
centuries, from the accession of Pacal in 615 to the death of
Chan-Bahlum in 702, saw a rapid and remarkable growth
in the size, influence, and wealth of Palenque, while the
succeeding reigns of Kan-Xul, Chaacal, and Chac-Zutz'
saw slower growth and consolidation, and that of Kuk the
beginning of decline.

"Although the veracity of the Early Classic dynastic history as recorded by Late Classic rulers cannot be fully
tested," says Linda Schele, "we are fairly sure that the dy-

nasty list from about A.D. 500 records real history, even
though the importance of the rulers was probably exag-
gerated, judging by the archaeological evidence. Chan-
Bahlum's list of rulers, however, goes back to *Baktun* 8
and we cannot be sure if these were historical persons, or
manufactured to extend the dynasty back to the beginning
of what the Late Classic rulers saw as 'recorded history' [as,
perhaps on the roof comb of Temple VI at Tikal]; we cannot
know how much of the information left to us was altered in
order to reinforce the positions of the rulers who had the
tablets carved."

In spite of these reservations, and in spite of the likeli-
hood of astute political modification of fact in a way familiar
from, for instance, our knowledge of Roman imperial inscriptions, the dynastic sequence at Palenque and the series of magnificent buildings and sculptures with which it
is associated give us a good idea of the way in which a small
Classic Maya center rose to political and cultural prominence. Palenque gives us better historical evidence than
any other site because of the length of its texts, which were
on wall panels rather than stelae, giving a large surface
area. This expanded space, Schele explains, "enabled the
scribes to incorporate not only the kinds of information included in the monumental texts of other sites but also the
historical or mythological contexts within which contemporary events were seen."

We can see from the examples so far an essential consistency from site to site in the nature of rulership and descent, the latter from father to son whenever possible; we
have seen that relationships between dynasties could be
unfriendly, as when Cauac Sky of Quirigua vanquished
XVIII Jog of Copan, but there is increasing evidence for
more normal and peaceful contacts also. One means of
contact and of maintaining friendly relations was the dynastic marriage, as important to the Maya as to the Haps-
burgs. John Molloy and William Rathje suggested that
old, established centers such as Tikal were able to extend
their political and economic influence by marrying out the
daughters of the elite into the more recent dynasties of
other sites, so that the next succeeding ruler would have
strong maternal-kin ties to Tikal. The rulers of Tikal seem
to have been the Sky dynasty, and this name, together with

mention of the Tikal emblem glyph, occurs at Copan and Yaxchilan. The site of Naranjo, a short journey east of Tikal on the headwaters of the Rio Hondo, received two elite brides from Tikal, the first of whom had a son named Scroll Squirrel; when he was 23 years old he married another woman from Tikal, cementing the alliance. His mother is mentioned also, as Joyce Marcus has pointed out, on Stela 1 at Coba, far to the north in Quintana Roo but notable for the Petén-like style of its buildings and monuments. (A "corridor" of such Petén-style sites is now known to have existed down the Rio Hondo and north through Quintana Roo, but we do not know what events these reflect.)

Occasionally a vignette of an individual event comes to light. The excavations at Altar de Sacrificios revealed a double burial, that of a middle-aged woman accompanied by a younger one, the latter perhaps being a sacrifice. The pottery vessels accompanying the burials included imports from the Tikal and Yaxchilan regions and from the Alta Verapaz. One vessel, made probably at Yaxchilan, depicted a ceremony involving six people (Figure 7.14). Although Linda Schele and others have recently claimed a conventional underworld mythic significance for the scene, Richard Adams has interpreted it as an actual portrayal of the funeral, with one figure being the young woman killing herself with a chert knife like that found beside her in the grave. Among the other figures in Adams's interpretation are a Bird-Jaguar of Yaxchilan, dancing in jaguar-skin trousers and a mask, and a member of the Sky dynasty from Tikal, also in jaguar costume, whom Clemency Coggins thinks may be the younger brother of Ruler B. The middle-aged woman must have been of high birth to have had such illustrious mourners at her funeral, and Adams suggests a relationship to Bird-Jaguar or to Cauac Sky of Quirigua; since Altar de Sacrificios is a relatively small site, she may have been a partner in a dynastic marriage deal like those proposed by Molloy and Rathje. The distance of her possible family links is demonstrated by the sources of the funerary vessels: both Tikal and Alta Verapaz are more than 125 kilometers (80 miles) away in air line, much farther by trail or canoe.

The distribution of emblem glyphs has been suggested as an index of the political sway of a center. Heinrich Berlin

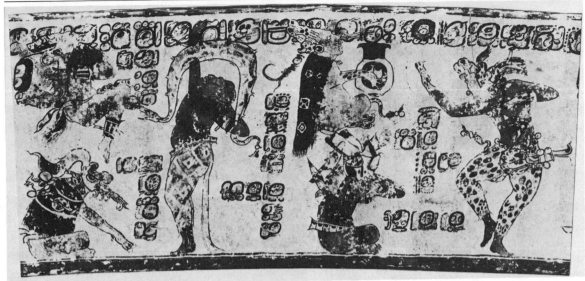

noted that "the presence of the emblem of one center in the inscriptions of another indicates a relationship between them . . . [and] in this way the emblems can be used to initiate a study of the geographical relationships at least." Joyce Marcus suggested that a subordinate center would mention the emblem glyph of its superordinate capital more often than the reverse, and this is a useful method of ranking sites, as far as the evidence goes, although there are problems due to poor preservation of some inscriptions, and others of interpretation, as when Pusilha uses Quirigua's emblem glyph some forty years before it is first found at Quirigua itself.

More generally, it seems likely that the overall reach of any site's political influence, whether by rule or alliance, can be estimated from the distribution of the emblem glyph. Unfortunately only a few of the hundreds of Maya centers, and a small proportion of the scores that erected inscribed monuments, have identified emblem glyphs: those most intensively studied so far lie in the Usumacinta basin and northern Petén (Figure 7.2). Tikal has an emblem found commonly at the site itself, and with an external distribution north to Uaxactun, east to Naranjo, and a considerable distance southwest on the Usumacinta, where it occurs at several sites from Yaxchilan upstream to Seibal.

Yaxchilan's emblem appears at sites along the river, downstream as far as Palenque and upstream to Dos Pilas,

7.14. The "Altar Vase," a Late Classic polychrome cylinder vessel found in a double burial at Altar de Sacrificios on the Rio de la Pasión during the Peabody Museum (Harvard University) excavations of 1959–1963. It has been interpreted as depicting the funerary rites of the woman with whom it was buried, including the self-immolation of a young woman whose skeleton was also found in the burial. The figure in jaguar-skin trousers and a mask has been identified as Bird-Jaguar of Yaxchilan, the next major center down river, and one which may well have exercised some sort of control over the smaller center of Altar. Some of the figures are probably mythical, however, and an underworld interpretation for the scene has also been suggested.

and including Piedras Negras, which has its own emblem with a purely local distribution. Palenque has an emblem that appears at sites nearby in the hills and northwest into the Tabasco plain, and the work of Robert Rands suggests that this distribution may well define the area of Palenque's economic sway (see Chapter 8). The Palenque emblem also appears at two distant sites, Tikal and Copan, and Tikal's emblem is found at Copan also; the nature of these links, over distances of 250–425 kilometers (155–265 miles), is uncertain. Apart from dynastic ties through marriage, or trade, any alliance must have been notional rather than practical in function. Joyce Marcus has suggested that Thomas Barthel's model of four directional capitals in a quadripartite cosmogony might apply, with the unidentified fourth site being perhaps Calakmul; but if such an intellectual model did exist in the Classic period, it seems to have been confined to the Choloid-speaking area across the base of the peninsula, since none of the presumed capitals lies either in the highlands or in the Yucatec-speaking northern lowlands. Differences in calendrics and iconography between the rain-forest and scrub-forest zones also exist, hinting that intellectual divisions among the Classic Maya may have been greater than the overall uniformity of culture indicates.

At present, therefore, our knowledge of contact between Maya centers at the highest levels of diplomacy and alliance remains severely limited by the paucity and opacity of information, but some aspects are fairly certain. That dynastic succession within a polity was matched by dynastic marriage between polities has been demonstrated, albeit in few actual instances; our knowledge of specific battles and conquests is no broader. The limits are our current degree of understanding of the hieroglyphic inscriptions, and the limited range of information those inscriptions convey. There are, however, other means of studying contacts between centers and regions in the Maya world, using not the conscious and intellectual evidence of the inscriptions but the unconscious and material proof that careful analysis of objects traded from their place of manufacture or origin can provide. This evidence, and the role of trade in Maya civilization, are examined in the next chapter.

8

Trade and External Contacts

THE Maya were not isolationists: from the beginning of settlement in the Early Preclassic period, communities were reaching out, often to considerable distances, to obtain desired raw material or finished goods, and by the time of Spanish contact in the sixteenth century the Maya were participants in a widespread network of trade and exchange that reached south as far as Panama and north to central Mexico.

Columbus, on his fourth voyage in 1502, sailed down the Caribbean coast of Central America, and near the Bay Islands off Honduras encountered "an Indian canoe, as long as a galley and eight foot in breadth, laden with western commodities, which it is likely belonged to the province of Yucatan." There were twenty-five people aboard, "timid and proper people, because when one pulled their clothing they immediately covered themselves again, which gave great satisfaction in the Admiral and those with him. He treated them with great kindness, and presented them with some objects from Castile in exchange for some of their strange-looking things, to take with him in order to show what kind of a people he had discovered."

The "western commodities" included "much clothing of the kind they weave of cotton in this land . . . with many designs and colors, shorts which reach the knees and some square pieces of cloth which they use for cloaks; knives of flint, swords of very strong wood with knives of flint set along the edges, and foodstuff of the country." There were also copper axes and bells, and cacao beans, at that time the standard Mesoamerican unit of currency.

Eric Thompson analyzed this account and pointed out that although there was no direct evidence of the origin or destination of the canoe, the copper implements would point to a cargo from Central Mexico, the cotton textiles to one from Yucatan, and the cacao had probably been picked up on the way down the coast of Belize for shipment back to Yucatan on the return voyage. Thus the trip had probably begun in the Gulf of Mexico, perhaps at the great Aztec-Maya entrepôt of Xicalango on the Laguna de Terminos where land, river, and sea routes met, and was destined for the Gulf of Honduras where similar ports existed at Naco in the Ulua basin and Nito on the Rio Dulce. The merchants and crew Thompson guessed to be Putun, Chontal Maya from the Laguna de Terminos area whom he dubbed "the Phoenicians of Middle America." Some of the Putun knew the coastal settlements as far down the Caribbean coast as Costa Rica or Panama, and the presence in Maya sites of gold and gold-alloy metalwork from this isthmian area indicates a movement of goods that seems to have begun at least by the Early Classic period, at the same time as Maya influence began to be felt along the Pacific coast as far southeast as Costa Rica.

We can thus draw upon both archaeological and ethnohistoric evidence in studying the role of trade in ancient Maya culture, and can examine the materials that were traded, the means by which they were transmitted, and the motives underlying the existence of the exchange system. "Trade" is, in fact, a term loosely used by archaeologists, and may refer to the direct acquisition of something from its source, to exchange with the producer at the source, or to the activities of merchants either peripatetic or based in market centers. The precise mechanism by which a commodity leaves its source and reaches its destination is often not archaeologically detectable, but the varying implications that different modes of trade have for our understanding of ancient societies have, in recent years, stimulated much research in this field, not least on the ancient Maya.

It is clear that trade operates on a number of scales, in terms of distance traveled, bulk of goods carried, and the nature of the merchandise. The buying and selling of a current surplus of food—a few dozen eggs or a bag of corn—to a neighbor in the village market is trade on the local level (Figure 8.1); the availability of goods from a range of communities perhaps in different environmental zones or with different specialities constitutes regional trade; and the distribution through several regions of goods of restricted ori-

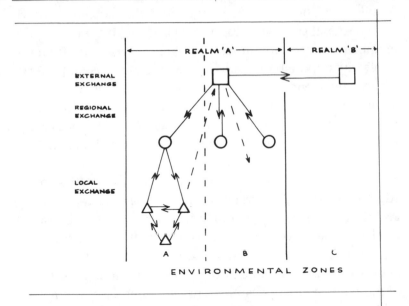

8.1. A simplified model of three levels of trade or exchange: the bulk of transactions occur at the local level in local produce including food. The produce of different environmental zones within one realm or polity is exchanged in a regional market (see Figures 3.13, 5.10), while external long distance trade exchanges commodities found or made only in certain areas but in general demand (see Figures 8.2 and 8.4).

gin but wide demand, such as obsidian in both the Middle East and Mesoamerica, constitutes long-distance trade. A finer division would be possible, but in general we may conclude that the greater the bulk of a commodity traded, and the more widespread its production, the less distance that commodity will travel; foodstuffs probably constitute the bulk of goods in any exchange system, and in a preindustrial society such as that of the ancient Maya, most would be locally grown and locally consumed.

There is a problem here for archaeologists: the detection of trade at the local level is difficult, because without documentary or ethnographic sources the extent to which goods are exchanged rather than consumed by their producers is unknown. In contrast, the mere presence of an exotic object or material gives evidence of trade reaching beyond the local level, although its volume and importance may be minimal in the economy. Most of the studies of ancient Maya trade that have so far been carried out have concentrated on the relatively easy identification of exotics.

A second problem is the perishability of much of the evidence. Food, textiles, leather, feathers, and salt, all known to have been used and traded by the pre-Hispanic Maya, just do not survive in a tropical soil. Thus for the Preclassic, Classic, and much of the Postclassic periods, our estimate of the significance of many goods in the economy must be based on analogy with the contact and colonial periods and on occasional survivals (Figure 8.2). The substantive study of ancient Maya trade must, however, be based on the relatively few imperishable substances that were used: pottery, stone, shell, bone, and occasionally metal. In these substances either the material itself or the style in which it is worked may indicate an origin far from the place of discovery, or may conversely suggest the operation of a local specialist working an exotic raw material.

We may obtain some idea of the present state of knowledge of ancient Maya trade by examining some case studies, at the local, regional, and long-distance levels. Those at the local level have been carried out mainly in the lowland region, and many have used pottery vessels as the subject of study because recent developments in analytical technique have made it possible to detect whether or not a vessel is made of local clay. Robert Rands has been working on the ceramics of Palenque for many years, and recently he and his colleagues have begun to analyze pottery fabrics from the surrounding region; the clay matrix was analyzed chemically, and the mineral inclusions derived from the soil or bedrock were identified under the microscope. The inclusions comprised mica, opal phytoliths from siliceous plant stems, volcanic dust originating in the Maya highlands and brought down by wind or in the Usumacinta drainage, and feldspars. Fifteen elements in the clay matrix were measured, and several chemical composition patterns emerged, which in some cases agreed precisely with differences in the mineral inclusions. Overall, the evidence showed that a number of different clay sources derived from different kinds of bedrock had been utilized to make an untempered "fine paste" ware. The pottery analyzed came from a number of sites on the lower Usumacinta, from Piedras Negras downstream and west across the Tabasco plain to Comalcalco. Palenque, Comalcalco, and Tortuguero all had pottery with distinctive compositions, and the latter site also had a unique combination of mineral inclusions; the conclusion was that stylistically and technically similar pottery was being made at a number of centers from the local clay. One group of sherds found at Palenque had a composition characteristic of the Trinidad region downstream to the northeast, however, showing

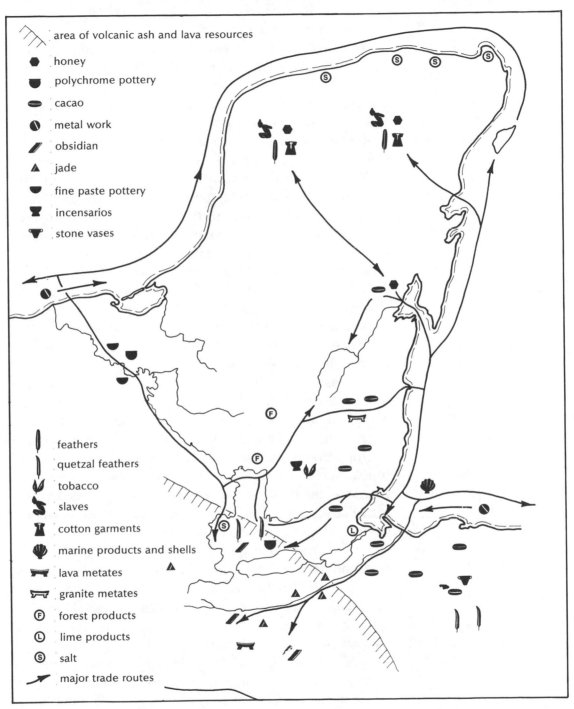

area of volcanic ash and lava resources
honey
polychrome pottery
cacao
metal work
obsidian
jade
fine paste pottery
incensarios
stone vases

feathers
quetzal feathers
tobacco
slaves
cotton garments
marine products and shells
lava metates
granite metates
F forest products
L lime products
S salt
major trade routes

8.2. Some Late Classic trade routes and commodities, based on both archaeological evidence and retrodiction from sixteenth-century documents.

"that a significant body of ceramics was imported to Palenque" between about A.D. 750 and 800.

Much of the pottery from Palenque itself had many opal phytoliths among the mineral inclusions; these derive from grasses and sedges probably growing in the plain, not in the hills on which Palenque stands. The implication is that Palenque obtained a substantial proportion of its pottery from makers living in the plain. Rands suggests that this is evidence of an inward-looking economic organization, in which the primary allegiance of potters (and presumably other traders) was to a single regional center, rather than an outward-looking organization in which potters hawked their wares around a number of markets. He calculates that the sustaining area, the products of which were channeled entirely into Palenque, covered some 300 square kilometers (112 square miles); it is interesting to note that the distribution of Palenque's emblem glyph at neighboring sites is mainly into the plain, the very region that on the evidence of the pottery was under Palenque's economic control. Beyond the sustaining area Rands suggests that there was a zone that supplied both Palenque and other major centers in the region, and some of the pottery imported into Palenque came from this greater distance.

Another, smaller-scale, study of pottery composition and its implications was carried out on material from Lubaantun, which lies on the far side of the Maya lowlands from Palenque, not far from the Caribbean coast to southern Belize. The site seems to have controlled the basin of the Rio Grande, from the crest of the Maya Mountains to the offshore cays in the Caribbean. Materials from many of the environmental zones within this realm have been found at Lubaantun, including marine shells and metamorphic mountain rocks; the evidence suggests that an inward-looking economic organization like that of Palenque is likely to have existed (Figure 5.16).

Some 13,500 sherds of pottery were recovered in the 1970 excavations at Lubaantun, from a wide range of vessel forms that served a variety of storage, cooking, serving, and ceremonial functions. Most of this pottery was of the same kind of clay, brownish with mineral inclusions that appeared to be from the local rocks, and the hypothesis at the beginning of the analysis was that this pottery had been made locally. There were, however, several hundred sherds of apparently different clays. Some were yellow in color and sandy in texture, with a tough, glossy, red slip on the surface, some were of a fine orange paste without mineral inclusions, and others, although fairly similar to the main body of the pottery with regard to the inclusions visible, seemed slightly different and also had different surface slips and decorations.

Clay samples were collected from the Lubaantun site and its vicinity, especially from clay pits used by modern Maya potters in the area. These samples, together with small sections drilled from about eighty sherds of different types, were subjected to neutron activation analysis at Brookhaven National Laboratory by Garman Harbottle. He established the proportions of some twenty trace elements, each present in only a few parts per million, in each of the samples; because each of the twenty elements could vary in its concentration independently of all of the others, two samples with closely similar compositions stood a very good chance of being made of clay from the same source.

The analyses largely confirmed the initial prediction: most of the storage, cooking, and service pottery had been made close to Lubaantun and of local clay. The most elaborate pottery, painted with polychrome designs, was also local and apparently made of clay from the ridge on which Lubaantun itself stood, suggesting a workshop actually within the ceremonial precinct. Among these products was a cylindrical vase depicting the sacred ball game *pok-ta-pok* being played in a stepped ball court (like the one at Lubaantun), giving proof that talented artists had been working at even such small and provincial centers as Lubaantun (although the very small quantity of such fine pottery raises the possibility that the artist was a traveling specialist, performing specific commissions on locally made vases).

The sandy yellow ware with the red slip proved to have a chemical composition completely different from that of the local clays, showing that it was an import, and both the appearance and the composition matched pottery of the same date from Barton Ramie in the Belize Valley, more than 100 kilometers (60 miles) to the north across the Maya Mountains (Figure 4.6). The form of the vessel, a flat dish with three rounded supports, is suitable for stacking in transit and may have been partly designed with trade in mind; certainly the dish and not any contents would have been the desired object, since it is a serving, not a storage vessel. More than a hundred such vessels were represented among the Lubaantun sample, the largest quantity of exotic pottery found at the site.

The fine-paste orange pottery, of which only about twenty-five sherds were found, proved to match closely the composition and appearance of Fine Orange wares from Seibal, over 150 kilometers (90 miles) to the west. Here again long-distance trade is indicated, probably up to the headwaters of the Pasión and then along the seaward slope of the Maya Mountains through Pusilha. That site, which lies 32 kilometers (20 miles) southwest of Lubaantun, proved to be the source of several unique sherds found at Lubaantun, each from a decorated vessel. Although Pusilha had stopped erecting dated stelae in A.D. 731 (9.15.0.0.0.), about the time that Lubaantun was founded, it nevertheless continued to support such specialists as high-quality ceramic artists for a century afterwards.

The overall result of the Lubaantun pottery analysis was to show that the bulk of the vessels used there were locally made, although local types were manufactured up to at least 6 kilometers (4 miles) from the actual site. There was exchange with neighboring Pusilha of single, highly decorated vessels, and this may have been a gift exchange, or prestation, rather than commercial trade. A few pieces of Fine Orange pottery arrived from the Pasión Valley, again perhaps as gifts, but the most curious import was the large number of tripod dishes from the Belize Valley: they did not supply any economic need at Lubaantun, but are too common to be high-status gifts. We cannot at present explain their presence, but they do offer valuable evidence of a contact for which no other archaeological indication has survived.

The question of perishable evidence was noted earlier. In some cases we can use the circumstantial evidence of archaeology to demonstrate the production of certain commodities, and thus to suggest what may have been exchanged for such imperishable goods as pottery, or for the obsidian, jade, and cinnabar of the highland zone. The case of cotton textiles is a good example. We have virtually no physical evidence for these in the Classic period, although in the sixteenth century they are known to have been widely traded out from Yucatan to both the eastern and the western extremities of the Maya Area; but we can link many disparate pieces of archaeological evidence to make a plausible case for their use in Classic times. Pierced pottery discs, trimmed down from broken potsherds or deliberately made in that form, are identical in shape to objects used as spindle-whorls in other parts of the world; these appear in the Maya archaeological record by the Late Preclassic period. The murals at Bonampak and Uaxactun, and the figurines of Lubaantun and Lagartero (Figure 8.3) show thin, easy-folding textiles that would seem to be cotton rather than barkcloth, with ornamentation resembling brocading or embroidery—brocading and feather ornamentation are known to have been used on cotton cloth in Postclassic Yucatan. Finally, cotton itself has been found from the Preclassic period onward in cores from the Rio Hondo raised fields, and Dennis Puleston's experimental raised field (see Chapter 5) showed that cotton could be grown there.

8.3. Figurine from Lagartero, a recently excavated site on the Chiapas-Guatemala border, depicting a woman clad in richly ornamental garments; the fine folds of the textile suggest a thin fabric, probably cotton, decorated by embroidery or brocading.

Another important crop, and a highly commercial one at that, for which direct archaeological evidence is difficult to obtain is cacao. Again, sixteenth-century sources tell us that the polity of Chetumal on the lower Rio Hondo, the Ulua valley in northwest Honduras, and several other areas, including the Pacific piedmont of Chiapas-Guatemala (the Aztec Soconusco) were prime areas of cacao production. In the Classic period cacao-pod effigies are known from Quirigua and other sites in the Motagua Valley, from Lubaantun, and from Pacific piedmont sculpture. Colonial sources describe the bringing of cacao from the Lubaantun area up into the Verapaz highlands around Cajabon, and the route is still in use today by *Cobanero* traders who bring back cacao among their other acquisitions. The use of cacao in the Preclassic period is still not well documented, but carbonized, putative cacao beans of the Late Preclassic period (around A.D. 100) and fragments of possible cacao-pod rind dating as far back as 1100 B.C. have been recovered from trash deposits at Cuello in northern Belize.

Salt is another product for which we have documentary evidence of trade in the colonial period, and the near certainty that this essential substance would have been equally widely distributed in the Classic and Preclassic periods; but more than almost anything else, salt is unlikely to be archaeologically detectable. Production centers with pans for evaporation or pots for boiling can be located, and evidence of this has been forthcoming from northern Yucatan, but detection of the salt at its destination remains impossible, since it was probably dispatched in nothing more substantial than a leaf wrapper.

The same problem applies to honey and beeswax, two important Postclassic products of the northern lowlands. The area of Chetumal supported thousands of hives of the native stingless bee, which produces a sweet, liquid honey, and Cozumel was also a noted center of apiculture. The bees were kept in log hives, and several of the stone or pottery discs with which the ends of the logs were stoppered have been found at Classic sites in Belize and elsewhere, but of the honey and wax at their destination there is again no trace.

These four examples—cotton, cacao, salt, and honey—from among the many perishable products of which we have evidence in colonial documents indicate how necessary it is to use this ethnohistoric evidence in trying to assess the range of pre-Hispanic Maya trade, but they also emphasize how limited the evidence is, both in its perishability and in the nonspecific nature of the goods if samples were miraculously to be preserved. It would be very difficult to establish the source of salt, honey, cotton, or cacao within their wide areas of production.

Some of the imperishable products traded by the Maya are closely identifiable as to source, however, so that we can trace them back from their eventual resting place to their origin, and suggest a route by which the transmission could economically have been carried out. The substance most easily characterized in this way, and one on which a relatively large amount of research has been done, is obsidian. This is a volcanic glass, usually gray-black in color (although Mexican highland sources produce green and gold obsidians also). It is found in many parts of the world, from New Zealand to eastern Europe, and because it fractures easily and can be made into tools with a sharp edge or point it has been exploited by man for thousands of years. In southwestern Asia it was traded over long distances over both land and water from about 6000 B.C. on.

Studies of Asian and American obsidians have shown that while most of the glass is made of silica, it also contains a number of trace elements, present in only a few parts per million (as in pottery clay). The particular combination of trace elements present and their relative proportions are often unique to a source, so that once a source has been located, sampled, and assayed, obsidians found in archaeological contexts can be correlated with it.

Numerous obsidian sources have been located in Mesoamerica, especially in the highland plateaus of central Mexico and the volcanic spine of Guatemala and El Salvador, and in Mexico the use of several sources from the Early Preclassic period onward has been demonstrated. In the Maya Area, apart from the very early use of obsidian from three sources at the Los Tapiales site, exploitation probably begins in the highland zone also in Early Preclassic times, with long-distance export of obsidian to the lowlands beginning before 1000 B.C. in the final part of the Early Preclassic period. The Ixtepeque volcano was used by the occupants of Chalchuapa, 40 kilometers (25 miles) away, from 1200 to 900 B.C. on, and the presence of waste flakes at Chalchuapa shows that the obsidian was collected as raw lumps and brought back to be worked: this is acquisition rather than trade. The first obsidian to appear in the lowlands comes from Cuello in northern Belize, where a single blade from late Early Preclassic levels of about 1300 B.C. is followed by increased (although still small) quantities early in the Middle Preclassic period; and coevally or shortly thereafter it was used at Barton Ramie, Seibal, and Edzna. The source used for all of this Middle Formative obsidian was at San Martín Jilotepeque, northwest of Guatemala City, and a trade route down into Petén and downstream on the Pasión-Usumacinta to the west, and down the Hondo to the northeast seems likely.

Most of the obsidian from Maya sites so far analyzed comes from Classic period contexts, and enough data now exist for an outline of trade routes to be suggested (Figure 8.4). Two major route networks seem to have existed, one

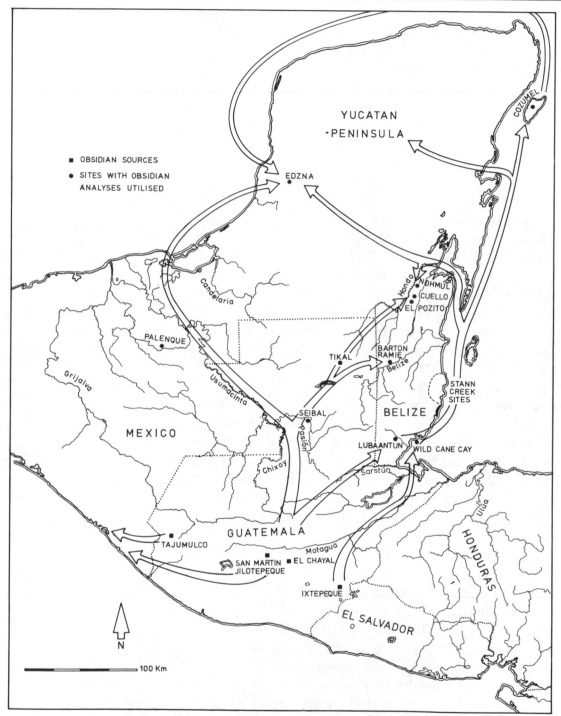

8.4. Obsidian trade routes in the Maya Area, based on the trace-element analysis of obsidian found in Preclassic, Classic, and early Postclassic sites. The San Martín Jilotepeque source was the principal supplier in the Middle Formative, and El Chayal from the late Formative through to the Terminal Classic using primarily an overland riverine route network.

Page 232, Fig. 8.4 caption, add: The Ixtepeque source exported obsidian to the lowlands from the Late Formative onwards, using primarily a network of canoe routes through the Motagua Valley and along the east coast. This network probably achieved a parity of importance with the Chayal network in the Late Classic; Ixtepeque was the dominant source from the Terminal Classic onwards. The map does not show imports of obsidian from central Mexico, which reached Tikal, Nohmul, and other southern sites in the Early Classic, and northern Yucatan in the Terminal Classic.

operating overland and down the rivers, the other running up the Caribbean coast around the Yucatan Peninsula and linking up with river or overland routes to the interior. The routes can be seen in outline from the archaeological distribution of obsidian originating in the two major sources of Ixtepeque, on the Guatemala-Salvador border, and El Chayal, 25 kilometers (16 miles) north of Guatemala City. The two sources can be easily distinguished from each other chemically by measuring the trace-element levels of any of ten elements: Chayal obsidian is higher in manganese, cesium, uranium, antimony, thorium, tantalum, and rubidium, while Ixtepeque is higher in iron, cobalt, and hafnium (Figure 8.5); both the pattern of difference and the actual levels of the elements remain constant over repeated analyses.

The distribution of Chayal obsidian follows the more sporadic one of San Martín Jilotepeque material, which indeed seems to have been driven from the market when major exploitation of Chayal began. The route runs north across the folded mountain ranges of the Verapaz and down into Petén, where canoe transport on the Pasión would have been the best means of travel. From around Seibal a route seems to have run overland to Tikal, which has a high proportion of Chayal obsidian, and from Tikal down the Rio Hondo as far as northern Belize, where El Pozito and Nohmul have substantial quantities also. From Seibal trade seems to have continued down the Pasión and Usuma-

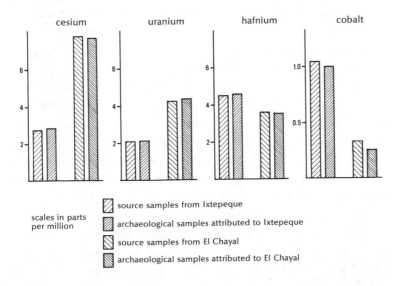

scales in parts per million

░ source samples from Ixtepeque
▨ archaeological samples attributed to Ixtepeque
░ source samples from El Chayal
▨ archaeological samples attributed to El Chayal

8.5. Differences in concentration of four trace elements, present in only a few parts per million (see vertical scales), enable obsidians from the Ixtepeque and El Chayal sources to be distinguished from each other. The archaeological samples all come from one site, Wild Cane Cay off the coast of southern Belize, which lay on the distribution networks of both sources in the Late Classic and into the Postclassic period. The four elements used here are among ten showing strong discrimination out of twenty-one in the original analyses.

cinta, since Palenque has a high percentage of Chayal obsidian, and linked up with the circumpeninsular sea route
on the Tabasco coast. Another inland route for Chayal obsidian seems to have run northeast, along the Maya Mountains to Lubaantun, where 95% of the obsidian was of
Chayal origin; this is the same route used to bring cacao up
to Cajabon, and reached beyond Lubaantun to link up with
the Caribbean coastal canoe route at Wild Cane Cay off the
southern Belize coast. The overall range of the Chayal network was about 350 kilometers (220 miles) in air line, and
perhaps two-thirds of the network was navigable by canoe.

Ixtepeque obsidian has a contrasting distribution, one
that suggests that the two sources were directly competing
for markets, extending far north of the Chayal network into
the Yucatan Peninsula. It is a pattern consonant with distribution down the Motagua Valley and north along the Caribbean coast, penetrating inland up rivers to reach important sites such as Tikal and Nohmul, and reaching the
Puuc sites by overland trails, the existence of which is documented in Postclassic times. Some Ixtepeque obsidian
went right around the peninsula to reach sites such as Palenque and Edzna in small quantities. The Chayal network
was more cost-efficient for the western sites, however, as it
was for Tikal and for the Rio Hondo sites as far north as El
Pozito.

On the tiny offshore island of Wild Cane Cay in southern
Belize obsidian from both sources was found, 80% being
from Ixtepeque and 20% from Chayal, suggesting a meeting of the two route networks (or a mixed cargo down the
Motagua, although other archaeological evidence suggests
this is not likely). Other goods found there include jade
beads, Tulum Red pottery from northern Yucatan, Plumbate pottery from Pacific Guatemala, Lubaantun pottery
figurines, and polychrome pottery. These demonstrate use
of the site from the Late Classic into the Postclassic period,
but the exotic nature of most of them also indicates that the
islet was an important point on the coastal canoe route. Another such islet with equally exotic goods, including a fragment of blue jade and part of a metalworker's tool kit, is
Moho Cay, off the mouth of the Belize River. It seems likely
that since the large seagoing canoes would have had difficulty in maneuvering up the rivers, and were in any case

on long-distance voyages, these small islands were used as transshipment points, and perhaps as neutral ports of trade where profit outweighed any current political enmities between seller and purchaser. Some goods got broken in transit and were left on the islands, while others were used on the spot: an Ixtepeque obsidian core weighing more than 500 grams (1.1 pounds) was collected on Wild Cane Cay, and had been partly used to make prismatic blades (Figure 8.6).

One exotic commodity brought into the Maya Area from the southeast was metal, although by the end of the Classic period there was some local metallurgy in the lowlands. The earliest piece of metalwork so far found in a Maya site is a claw-shaped pendant of *tumbaga*, a gold-copper alloy, made in Costa Rica or Panama and imported to the small Belizean site of Altun Ha before A.D. 550; the same cache contained Pacific shell and pearls that could have come from the Gulf of Nicoya on the Pacific coast of Costa Rica. *Tumbaga* objects were also found at Chalchuapa, on the Pacific piedmont of El Salvador, in a tomb of about A.D. 750.

These links with the isthmian region of lower Central America, which are confirmed by documentary accounts as persisting into the Postclassic period, include also a number of Maya objects that were traded in the opposite direction. They include a carved mirror back with a hieroglyphic inscription—perhaps from Tikal—a carved jade, and in the early Postclassic period examples of Plumbate pottery from Soconusco. All have been found in Costa Rica, which seems to have been a meeting place for goods, and presumably merchants, from as far apart as Mesoamerica in the northwest and Colombia in the south.

Metalworking in the Americas began in the Colombia-Panama region, but probably spread from there, most likely along these sea routes to a receptive secondary center in Mexico. The Mexicans developed their own style in copper and gold goods in the Late Classic period, and at the same time similar goods appeared in the Maya Area, some of which were certainly locally made. Thus the art of metallurgy was introduced to a broad area of southern Mesoamerica, and in the Postclassic period a distinctive Maya style began to emerge, with evidence of the mastery of such complex techniques as lost-wax casting, which im-

8.6. Obsidian core from the Ixtepeque source found on the islet of Wild Cane Cay. The core has been used for the production of thin parallel-sided blades, but still weighs some 500 grams (1.1 pounds) and could be further utilized.

plies the existence of specialist metalsmiths. Since no native copper ores exist in the Maya lowlands, the metal must have been imported, either as ingots or scrap, and it has been suggested that northern Honduras around the Ulua valley was the source. The Ulua area came under strong Maya cultural influence from the Late Classic period on, and by the time of the conquest Yucatecan nobles owned estates there; copper and cacao may have been the resources that prompted the takeover. Metal ingots could also have been traded down from the highlands, where there are plentiful references to metallurgy and smiths in Postclassic literature. The Maya metalwork is on the whole undistinguished, including copper bells, finger rings, and masks; the greatest achievement, in the early Postclassic period, was the *repoussé* working of thin gold discs, perhaps imported as blanks or ingots from Central America, but quite possibly locally made, with complex scenes of human sacrifice in a Toltec-Maya style (Figure 8.7).

The substance of greatest value to the ancient Maya was jade, "the first infinite grace." The green stone reflected

8.7. Repoussé gold disc from the Cenote of Sacrifice at Chichén Itzá, with a scene in Toltec-Maya style depicting the defeat of Maya by Toltecs. Although the workmanship is probably local, the metal disc (or an ingot) was imported as a blank from lower Central America: there are no gold sources in the Maya lowlands.

the color of growing corn and of flowing water, and hence became a synonym for "precious" and for life itself. Jade objects and jade symbolism are found throughout the Maya Area, but the stone itself is not found naturally in the limestone lowlands: it is an ultrabasic, metamorphic rock, formed at great pressure and high temperature far below the surface of the earth; it rarely outcrops, and within the Maya Area potential sources lie only within the twisted and fractured rocks of the ancient highlands. For many years no source of jade was known, but in the past three decades several outcrops and stream-bed occurrences of boulders eroded from the mountains have been located north of the Motagua Valley, from Zacapa west into El Quiché. It has proved possible, though difficult, to characterize some of these sources in terms of their mineral constitution and trace-element composition; but jade is a much more complex and inhomogeneous mineral than obsidian, so that although the attribution of artifacts to mineral sources may prove feasible, it is likely to be less frequently accomplished and less certain. The archaeological distribution of jades is as wide geographically as that of obsidian, if socially more restricted, and the same routes for its transportation may well have been used—perhaps even the same merchants, traveling with an assortment of low-bulk, high-value goods for ruler and peasant alike to purchase, or bringing supplies to the local ruler for local distribution in exchange for the collected produce of his realm.

All of the materials discussed, perishable and imperishable, demonstrate a wide range of contacts between the highland and lowland zones, using both inland and coastal trade networks; they also indicate external contact with areas as far away as Costa Rica in one direction and central Mexico in the other. The latter connection was due, during the period from A.D. 400 to 700, to the influence of Teotihuacan, but the nature of the link is debatable. Was it exchange between equals, the Teotihuacanos shipping green obsidian for salt and cacao, or was it a colonial tributary relationship, the raw material of the Maya lowlands receiving some recompense in small quantities of high-status Teotihuacan manufactured goods? The offerings from Becan and Altun Ha (see Chapter 4) show that ritually knowledgeable and presumably high-ranking Teotihuacanos (or their Kaminaljuyu surrogates) reached these two sites, and their presence at Tikal is highly probable. Earlier links with the Olmec world, and later with Tula and Tenochtitlan, have less concrete evidence to support them, but there seems little doubt that the Maya Area was from the Pre-classic period onward firmly embedded in the economic matrix of Mesoamerica.

During the Classic period, Jeremy Sabloff considers that "long-distance trade was principally in exotic or elite goods . . . [that] trade was controlled by the theocracy and was used to support its position as the ruling class. Merchants did not exist as a separable sociopolitical entity," unlike the *pochteca* of the Mexican empire. Although many scholars would dispute that the Maya elite was a theocracy rather than a secular ruling group with some priestly functions, it is true that most of the goods proved to have been traded over long distances in the earlier part of the Classic period were functional in a social sense rather than useful in an economic one: jade, marine shells, fine pottery vessels, and even obsidian contributed more to the status of their pos-sessors than to their survival. The skill shown in working some of these materials, however, and the local styles in which exotic goods were sometimes worked from the Late Preclassic stage on, does suggest the existence of mer-chant artisans, carrying their own materials and producing work on commission and demand, comparable with the bronzesmiths of prehistoric Europe. A good example is the set of four jade head-pendants (Figure 4.12) found in a Late Preclassic cache at Nohmul, in northern Belize. The style is characteristic of the northern half of the lowlands, although the raw material comes from far to the south, and all of the heads were probably made from a single block of jade, with a bead being worked from a leftover scrap. A very similar set, with an additional large head made from the outside of a spherical boulder, was found by David Freidel less than 50 kilometers (30 miles) away at the site of Cerros, and it is not impossible that the same craftsman made both sets. Since jade was not a common material in Late Preclassic times, however, it seems more likely that a traveling specialist was responsible for the delicate working of the stone (which has several natural flaws), rather than that a local man was experienced enough to undertake the rare commission. Thus merchants may have existed as a class of craftsmen in the Preclassic and Early Classic periods, but not as a distinct stratum in society.

During the Late Classic and increasingly through the Postclassic periods, Sabloff sees a broadening of the trade base, with mass-produced goods such as plain pottery vessels (like the dishes imported to Lubaantun), and bulk produce such as salt and cotton, being distributed far beyond their area of manufacture as economic and not status goods. He attributes much of the change to the rise of the Putun as merchant navigators, and suggests that they organized dispersed centers of production and then channeled all of the produce into the circumpeninsular trade route which they monopolized, and which was more cost-efficient than the old network of trails and river routes used by small canoes.

Whether these explicit interpretations will survive the impact of further research data is uncertain, but what will remain firm are the increasing numbers of analyses of traded goods, which tell us with ever-increasing accuracy and detail the origins, destinations, and probable routes used by the ancient Maya. From the Early Preclassic period on, when the people of Cuello began to acquire jade and obsidian from the highlands and *metates* from the Maya Mountains, the pattern was set for the exchange of goods —both practical and ornamental—between areas of complementary resources often many days' journey apart, which marks the contact between Maya and Maya and the Maya and their neighbors for the succeeding three millennia.

9.1. Architecture in art: a Maya
thatched hut depicted in low-
relief sculpture in the Monjas
quadrangle at Uxmal. The
snake on the roof has been
identified by Sir Eric Thompson as an *Itzam* saurian, forming with the house, *na*, a visual
pun on the name of the great
god Itzam Na (see Chapter 10
and Figure 10.1).

Architecture and Art

THERE was great variety in the buildings in the ceremonial precincts of the ancient Maya, in form and in function alike, and both the buildings and the layout of the precinct differed from site to site, within a series of broad regional traditions. Even the simplest form of architecture, the dwelling house, had its variant forms dependent on local materials and tastes, if modern Maya houses are any guide to the practices of the past.

As we noted in Chapter 5, their houses were of perishable materials but admirably adapted to the tropical environment—cool, waterproof, and well ventilated. All of the materials were acquired from the local forest: timbers of termite-resistant wood for the frame and roof, palm leaves for thatch, thin straight poles for the walls, and lianas to tie the elements together, or perhaps strips of bark. In the lowlands the floor of the single, open room was of trodden earth or of white *sascab*, the marl dug from beneath the limestone crust of bedrock; in the highlands different materials were used, but the plan with the single, open room was the same. In this single room stood the hearth; food and furniture could be stacked on the rafters or hung from the walls and brought down as needed. The interior of a modern Maya home is a logical clutter that an advanced interior designer would find appealing. Although the superstructures of the ancient houses have long since disappeared, leaving only postholes or low foundations on the basal platform, several depictions of them in stone sculpture have survived, including one on the facade of the Monjas quadrangle at Uxmal (Figure 9.1) and another on the archway at Labna.

The superstructures of some public buildings, even in large centers, were also of perishable materials, so that at Lubaantun only the pyramidal substructures of the temples remain; and there is a large area in southern Petén and Belize in which such buildings were the style. For the most part, however, a superstructure in stone was preferred in the lowlands, so that both pyramid and temple, platform and palace have survived, as at Tikal. The range of public buildings represented in any one large center is wide, although consistent combinations of structures recur from site to site.

It is debatable how far the Maya ceremonial precincts were deliberately planned, rather than just growing by accretion. Horst Hartung, an engineer, has argued that many sites were laid out with great precision and deliberation on alignments derived from astronomical observations, while Jorge Guillemin has detected a cosmological plan in the layout of the central part of Tikal. At Lubaantun the excavations showed that as the site grew in size the builders preferred to invest vast amounts of labor and materials to maintain a centralized plan, rather than have an elongated precinct along the ridge at much less cost. Clearly the overall design of the ceremonial precinct was important there.

In many sites there is a clear distinction between plazas surrounded by public buildings, easy of access from several directions, and private residential buildings set around plazas with restricted entry; the contrast between the Great Plaza of Tikal and the Central Acropolis immediately south of it is a good example (Figure 5.13). In calling these buildings religious, ceremonial, or residential we are obviously making certain assumptions, although the evidence on which we make them is fairly good. Tall pyramids with small-roomed structures on top are known to be temples all over Mesoamerica, as they were seen to be in several areas by the Spanish conquerors. Similarly, the two parallel structures with sloping benches flanking an alley between them are known, from ethnohistoric documents as well as sculptured portrayals of the game in action, to be a court for playing the sacred ball game *pok-ta-pok* (presumably named from the sound of the ball bouncing, as in ping-pong). In the same way the *temescal* or sweatbath has been identified at a number of sites, including Tikal and Chichén Itzá in the lowlands and several highland sites.

The long buildings with multiple doors and two or three ranks of rooms, long known to Mayanists as "palaces" (Figure 9.2), are the most disputed in function. They have been seen as dwellings of the ruling elite, and Richard Adams has even calculated the size of the elite group at Uaxactun by counting sleeping spaces in the palaces there; but uses as administrative buildings, men's houses, storehouses for tribute, and theological colleges similar to the Islamic *madrasah* have also been canvassed. In that a typical palace is in fact a series of houses, perhaps with a raised inner section, translated into stone and set end to end, a residential interpretation seems plausible. A multiple function is also feasible, as Peter Harrison has suggested for the buildings in the single palace complex of the Central Acropolis at Tikal (Figure 6.7).

We might also argue that, given the function of the major ceremonial centers as regional capitals exercising political, religious, and economic control over their dependent realms, the buildings in them must have accommodated these functions of management, in the same way as an English county town may hold the offices of the county council, a cathedral and bishop's palace, and a marketplace; Hereford, in whose cathedral Alfred Maudslay is buried, is a good example.

Although temples, palaces, ball courts, sweathouses, and other structures occur in many sites, there are distinct regional differences in their architecture, and these traditions also vary in date. At present the earliest buildings

9.2. The Palace of the Governors at Uxmal, built ca. A.D. 900. Such buildings are usually interpreted as elite residences, but administrative and religious functions have also been suggested.

known that are arguably nondomestic are those excavated in 1976–1980 at Cuello in northern Belize (Figures 4.7, 4.8); below a massive Late Preclassic platform was buried a small courtyard with buildings on its north, south, and west sides (and perhaps on the unexcavated east side also). The courtyard was first laid out around 900 B.C. over two pre-existing low plaster platforms, the larger of which had an area of some 75 square meters (797 square feet). Only the build-ings on the west and south sides were well preserved, that on the north having been razed when the courtyard was extend-ed northward at a later date. The western building was an ovoid platform, carefully built of small limestone boulders with earth fill, the whole being covered with plaster. The floor had evidence of two phases of perishable superstruc-tures, the second of a curious exedral plan. This platform was replaced by a larger one of similar ovoid plan which remained in use for many years—the internal floor was re-surfaced six times, each time over a heavily worn predeces-sor. The building on the south side of the courtyard, exca-vated in 1980, was an oval structure 8 by 4 meters (26 by 13 feet), with evidence of at least two phases of superstruc-ture associated with the earliest of several plaster floors. It had a central entrance step, which in a later phase opened on to a strange T-shaped ramp leading down into the in-terior of the building. As with the western building, the southern was progressively enlarged and refloored over a period of centuries, until, at about 600 B.C., its frontage was cut back, the courtyard extended south across the foundations, and the remainder of the building used as the core for a new construction. A series of burials of the Early Middle Preclassic, one of which was truncated by the demolition, are accompanied by pottery vessels that enable the successive phases of the building they penetrate to be firmly dated. Remodeling of the western and southern buildings seems to have occurred in more or less the same way through time.

There is little incontrovertible evidence that these early buildings were public rather than residential (apart from the exedral superstructure and the T-shaped ramp, which are not domestic features), but they were substantially built and lay on a site that in later centuries was definitely a sacred place. Some time after 500 B.C. the north and south sides of the courtyard were demolished, the courtyard area extended, and a masonry-walled superstructure erected on a substantial basal platform built with large boulders on the new northern margin of the courtyard. A dedicatory burial beneath the threshold of this building, its advanced architecture with freestanding walls of laid limestone cobbles covered in plaster, and most convincingly its ceremonial demolition and burial around 400 B.C., all argue for a public rather than a residential function. It is of course possible that the courtyard group combined ceremonial structures with elite residences—a formative stage in the evolution of the Maya ceremonial precinct, antedating the separation of these two functions into separate plazas.

From the Late Preclassic period on, we have a number of well-preserved structures at several sites, most of which still had perishable superstructures on top of increasingly elaborate platforms, with multiple levels and in some cases (as at Cerros, El Mirador, and Lamanai) attaining the elevation of profile characteristic of temple pyramids of the Classic period. Structure E-VII-sub at Uaxactun has been famous as an example of Preclassic architecture since it was discovered in the 1930s (Figure 9.3). A similar struc-

9.3. Structure E-VII-Sub at Uaxactun, the best known example of Late Preclassic architecture in the Maya lowlands. The four stairways are flanked by tiers of god masks in stucco, a common feature on pyramids of this period. The superstructure was of timber and thatch.

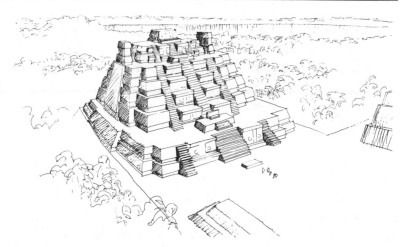

9.4. A colossal Late Preclassic pyramid: Structure N10-43 at Lamanai, Belize, which stands 33 meters (100 feet) high; even larger structures have recently been identified from this period in the site of El Mirador, and the scale and complexity of Late Preclassic architecture have clearly been seriously underestimated (drawing by H. Stanley Loten).

ture has recently been excavated at Cerros; although one of the smaller temples at the site, it is adorned with fantastic god masks in polychrome stucco, two to each side of the central stairway. This site, together with recent discoveries at El Mirador in northern Petén and Lamanai in Belize (Figure 9.4), has shown that Late Preclassic buildings were as large as, and in some cases larger than, those of the Classic period. Tikal, in spite of massive Late Classic construction, still has one major Preclassic pyramid standing exposed, Structure 5C-54, which was simply incorporated into the later site layout.

Standing masonry superstructures were not uncommon by the end of the Preclassic period. A notable example that requires further study is the building at Holmul in northeastern Petén, where in 1910 R. E. Merwin excavated two tombs filled with Protoclassic pottery vessels, and established the first stratified ceramic sequence in the Maya lowlands. Another Terminal Preclassic building of similar complexity existed at Nohmul in northern Belize: a 1974 study showed that Structure 277 had fifteen phases of architectural modification in four major construction periods, but the bulldozing of the building for road fill in 1977 prevented the planned excavation. The Nohmul building was also associated with Protoclassic pottery, but the large collection of vessels found in 1944 is not firmly tied to any one of the architectural phases.

Architecture of the Early Classic period is surprisingly little known, mainly because much of it is buried under

Opposite:
9.5. Successive modifications and overbuildings of Structure A-V at Uaxactun led to the transformation of a small Early Classic temple group into a complex Late Classic palace. This famous series of reconstruction drawings by Tatiana Proskouriakoff is based on the excavations of Ledyard Smith in the late 1930s.

Late Classic rebuilding; at Uaxactun the earlier structures of the A-V palace complex were greatly modified by Late Classic expansion (Figure 9.5). The largest sample of Early Classic architecture presently available is from the North Acropolis at Tikal, where the large-scale excavations by William Coe revealed a sequence of temples demonstrating the evolution, over a period of more than five hundred years, of the characteristic northeastern Petén architectural style (Figure 9.6).

9.6. The North Acropolis at Tikal was a focus of architectural activity in the Early and Middle Classic periods from the third century A.D. for at least half a millennium. The successive temples built there document the evolution of a characteristic northeast Petén style of architecture.

The bulk of our knowledge of Classic Maya architecture therefore comes from the Late Classic period, not only because of superposition of structures but also because many sites expanded during Late Classic times, increasing the stock of buildings. Hundreds of major public buildings are known in varying degrees of architectural detail, ranging from the sketch-plans and photographs of many C.I.W. ex-

9.7. The broad north stairway of Structure 14 at Lubaantun, a major piece of construction dating to the Terminal Classic period of the ninth century A.D. The steps are built of local sandy limestone over rubble fill, and any original plaster coating has long since eroded away.

ploratory missions to the precise recording, excavation, and reconstruction carried out at Tikal, Seibal, Dzibilchaltun, and other sites in the past two decades. As a result of this work a series of regional architectural styles has been isolated and described, which cover almost all of the Maya lowlands, and which in some instances overlap in space or time or both. All the styles share the use of local stone masonry—usually limestone, but including trachyte at Copan, rhyolite and sandstone at Quirigua, green sandstone at Lubaantun and Nim li punit, and reddish sandstone at Altar de Sacrificios, as well as fired clay brick at Comalcalco. The stone was used both for trimmed facing blocks and for rubble fill. All of the styles shared an attitude toward surveying accuracy that regarded anything between 80° and 100° as a right angle and a slope of up to 3° as perfectly flat, and all of the buildings were raised with the use of only human muscle power and stone tools; the lever, roller, plumb bob, and water level are the most complex equipment that we can reliably suggest the Maya possessed.

Also common to the regional styles were certain generalized architectural features that received varying emphasis. Almost all Maya buildings, whatever their function, stood on a substructure, whether it was a single-course foundation for a house, a massive terrace ironing out uneven terrain for a palace complex, or a towering pyramid for a temple. Except in the case of low house platforms some means of access to the superstructure was required, and the single axial stairway of one or more steps was the usual provision. Some stairs, such as the Hieroglyphic Stairway at Copan or the broad, late ceremonial stairs of Lubaantun, were major architectural constructions in their own right (Figure 9.7). On top of the substructure, usually on a low plinth, stood the masonry or timber superstructure. This might be entirely of perishable materials, or with stone walls roofed with timber and thatch, or with a flat, beamed ceiling covered with plaster, but the commonest form of roofing for public buildings (and for some elite residences) was a stone vault (Figure 9.8), built by stepping successive courses of stones inward until the narrow gap remaining at the top could be spanned with a capstone. The inner faces of the stones were usually cut on a bevel to give a smooth slope to the interior of the vault. This technique, the closest the Maya got to the Old World concept of the stressed arch, began to be used in the Late Preclassic period, and as experience and confidence increased, taller walls and wider vaults were used. Even so, rooms could remain very narrow, and the cramped space inside

9.8. Stone vault construction in one of the side chambers of the main structure at Rio Bec B in the center of the lowlands.

9.9. Veneer masonry technique with thin slabs of finely worked limestone attached to a rubble-concrete hearting used on a Puuc-style building at Kabah. The stairway (left) rises over the lowest floor of the building to which access was maintained through a half-vaulted passage (center). The doorway on the right is spanned by a stone lintel. The plain lower wall is characteristic of Puuc architecture, and the ornamented upper portion has collapsed.

Maya temples is an argument against any sort of participatory ritual involving more than one or two celebrants.

The technique of construction consisted of retaining a rubble core with dressed stone walls. Early buildings used the facing stones as an integral part of the load-bearing structure, but in some areas, notably in northern Yucatan in the Late Classic period with the Puuc style, this facing became only a veneer of finely dressed stone over a solid concrete hearting of limestone rubble and mortar (Figure 9.9). (The same technique was used, to even greater effect, in the buildings of Imperial Rome.)

Openings such as doorways were often buttressed with larger stones to take the extra stress. Lintels in many buildings were of wood, usually the rot-resistant sapodilla, and these provided yet another surface for the sculptor to use to celebrate elite activities (Figure 9.31). In some Late Classic styles the doorways multiplied and widened until the wall became a colonnade, as at Sayil (Figure 9.10); such colonnades could also be used to open up and expand interior space, although the major use of this technique is in the Toltec phase at Chichén Itzá and is not part of the Classic Maya repertory.

Some openings led to stairways: many buildings at Tikal, for instance, were multistoried and internal stairs can be found twisting up from secluded corners. Two of the most notable internal stairways are at Palenque: one ascends the

9.10. The Palace at Sayil: the second story has doorways widened with columns to lighten the interior space and vary the effect of the otherwise rather solid architecture.

four-story tower of the Palace, while the other descends through the Pyramid of the Inscriptions to the tomb of Pacal.

The walls and roofs of buildings in the ceremonial precincts were adorned with architectonic embellishments. A substantial part of the impressive height of some temples was provided by roof combs, which could be apparently solid (though in reality chambered and hollow) as at Tikal, or open lattices obtaining their effect with a graceful interplay of stone and sky, as in the Cross Group temples at Palenque and some early Puuc-style buildings. In general the solid roof comb is restricted to the southern part of the lowlands, the perforated-screen type to the northern, with Palenque being, as in so many other characteristics, idiosyncratic.

Walls were often interrupted with horizontal moldings, with from one to six members and placed anywhere from the base of the wall to the cornice. Sometimes the molding almost overwhelms the wall it is meant to adorn, as with the massive fivefold molding on the Caracol at Chichén Itzá (Figure 9.11), a building that Eric Thompson scorned as "a wedding cake sitting on top of its square box." Often the molding divided the wall into registers, and in the Puuc area, where moldings as decorative embellishments were used in greatest variety, the upper register of the walls was itself the vehicle for complex architectural sculpture in repeating patterns of startling verve and imagination, such as the enormous frieze of the Palace of the Governors at

9.11. The Caracol at Chichén Itzá, a Puuc-style cylindrical tower with a dominant quintuple molding, modified in the Toltec period by the addition of an enveloping rectangular terrace and stairways.

Uxmal (Figure 9.2) or the mind-dazzling mask wall of the Codz Pop at Kabah (Figure 9.12). The latter shows very well the production-line methods used in this formal and geometric development of Maya art—each eye, eyebrow, and jaw is made to a standardized pattern and a single mask is assembled from a standard set of parts.

9.12. The front wall of the Codz Pop at Kabah is covered with interdependent masks of the rain god Chaac, each eye being used in two overlapping visages. The eyeballs, hooked noses, eyesockets, and fangs are standardized and interchangeable—sparepart sculpture.

Some of the most conservative architecture, in its relative plainness and its long retention of early features, is that characteristic of northeastern Petén, western Belize, and southern Campeche and Quintana Roo—the area often called the Maya heartland. The massive public architecture of the Classic period developed first in this region, as the Tikal excavations showed, and the use of heavy apron moldings and inset corners on buildings persists from the Early Classic period well into the Late. Ledyard Smith's excavation of the A-V complex at Uaxactun, and its reconstruction in Tatiana Proskouriakoff's superb drawings, showed how the architectural style remained static throughout the Classic period, even while the original courtyard group of three small temples was being gradually transformed into a massive palace complex (Figure 9.5). Recent work has shown that this style extends down the Rio Hondo corridor northward through Belize and Quintana Roo as far as Coba.

To the north of this central zone, in Campeche and western Quintana Roo, is the area characterized by the twin styles of Chenes and Rio Bec; David Potter has proposed that the two styles should be amalgamated into a Central Yucatan style. This style overlaps the Petén style in time, persisting roughly from A.D. 550 to 830, and precedes the most highly ornamented buildings in the Puuc style, which sometimes occur in sites with essentially Central Yucatan architecture. The style features facades divided into three horizontal units, with sculptural decoration on any or all of them in semimosaic relief technique. The most elaborate facades, such as that at Chiccanna (Figure 9.13), are those in which the whole building is worked in a single design of a colossal serpent mouth, with the doorway forming the maw of a monster, fringed with great stone fangs.

In the Rio Bec area, the southern portion of the region, some buildings have twin towers rising from the ends of the facade, solid stone features with impossibly steep stairs and topped by solid, false, miniature temples in a style copied from that of Petén to the south. One of the most notable examples of this style is Rio Bec B, found by Merwin in 1910 and then lost until 1974 (Figure 9.14).

The Puuc style, found throughout most of modern Yucatan and a short way farther south into Campeche, is

9.13. The facade of this building in Chicanna, a small site close to Becan in the central lowlands, is in the form of a monster mask, with the doorway forming its maw, so that entering the building, one is swallowed by the monster. This notion of the building as sculpture is characteristic of the Chenes variant of the Central Yucatan architectural style, found from Uxmal southward to Rio Bec.

9.14. The site of Rio Bec B, discovered by R. E. Merwin in 1910 and then lost until 1974, has a main structure decorated with two towers, each in the form of a miniature false temple approached by an almost vertical stair. The temples copy the architecture of the major pyramids at Tikal, 120 kilometers (75 miles) to the south (compare Figure 6.8). This Rio Bec variant of the Central Yucatan style is found in the central lowlands; the best known and most accessible buildings are at Becan and Xpuhil.

thought to have emerged in the seventh century, partly from the Central Yucatan style, and to have lasted until the eleventh century. The earliest buildings in the style occur at sites around the Puuc Hills, the low range that crosses western Yucatan, and the most notable Puuc sites also lie in this region, among them Uxmal (Figures 1.8, 9.1, 9.2), Labna (Figure 1.9), Sayil (Figure 9.10), and Kabah (Figures 9.9, 9.12). Chichén Itzá lies close to the northeastern limit of the region where this style is found. Puuc buildings characteristically have a plain lower facade and an ornamented upper one with long-nosed masks and geometric designs; the masonry is a veneer over the concrete core

9.15. The Temple of the Warriors at Chichén Itzá, one of the major structures in the northern extension of the ceremonial precinct constructed in Toltec-Maya style after A.D. 900. The temple uses Puuc techniques in an unfamiliar style, with colossal serpent piers (Figure 9.16) in the doorway and a pillared hall in front of the stair at ground level. To the south of the building (right), the pillared halls continue, enclosing the plaza of the Mercado. Note the recumbent Chac-Mool figure visible in front of the doorway of the temple (see p. 287).

and the finest masonry is used on the exterior rather than the interior of the buildings.

At Chichén Itzá a hybrid Puuc-Toltec style developed (often called by scholars working in the northern lowlands Modified Florescent, with Puuc as the preceding Florescent); the techniques and materials are still Puuc in character, but the basic design of the buildings is Toltec. Good examples of this are the forest of square piers supporting a roofed gallery in front of the Temple of the Warriors and around the adjacent plaza (Figure 9.15), the serpents forming a doorway (Figure 9.16) or slithering down the stairways of the Castillo, and the detached platforms with their decorative panels of eagles or severed heads (Figures 9.17, 9.18). Toltec Chichén is a northward extension of the Puuc site, and some buildings such as the Caracol started as Puuc structures and became adapted to Toltec ideas (Figure 9.11).

The northern part of the Yucatan Peninsula is the only area of the Maya lowlands to maintain a tradition of public architecture after A.D. 1200, but it was a tradition in which

9.16. Twin serpents form the entrance to the temple of the Warriors, their tails supporting the lintel over the triple doorway.

9.17. The Platform of the Eagles and Jaguars, a four-stairwayed detached platform in the plaza of the Toltec-Maya precinct at Chichén Itzá. Low-relief panels show eagles and jaguars eating human hearts; panels are thought to be related to Toltec warrior orders.

9.18. The *tzompantli*, "skull platform," beside the great ball court at Chichén Itzá is covered with hundreds of grinning skulls in low relief. It is thought to have been used in the same manner as the later Aztec *tzompantli* in central Mexico, for the display of heads of captured enemies, sacrificed victims, or both.

9.19. Late Postclassic buildings at Tulum, on the east coast of Quintana Roo, at the time of its discovery in 1842 by Stephens and Catherwood. The derivation from Puuc and Toltec styles is apparent in this smaller-scale and cruder edifice, which lies in a tightly planned ceremonial precinct surrounded by a protective wall.

design and craftsmanship had lost much of their originality and quality. At Mayapan, the last capital of a Maya confederacy, the main pyramid was a small copy of the Castillo at Chichén (Figure 4.21), and at the major East Coast sites of Tulum and Cozumel the buildings are again miniaturized derivatives of earlier Yucatecan styles (Figure 9.19), some of the little coastal shrines being almost too small to enter.

Other Classic period styles of more limited distribution existed in various parts of the lowlands, their characteristics often governed by the available building material as much as anything. In southern Belize the easily split limestones and sandstones around the Maya Mountains inspired the terraced architecture of Lubaantun, while on the far side of the lowlands, in the alluvial plain of Tabasco, the absence of building stone resulted in the brick architecture of Comalcalco in a style related to that of Palenque. The architecture of Palenque forms a style all its own, with

9.20. The unique architecture of Palenque is characterized by heavy mansard roofs with fretted roof combs and ornate decoration in painted stucco. The Temple of the Sun, built in the late seventh century, had a roof decorated with the figure of a ruler flanked by gods and, in its final phase, was painted red. The photograph is by Alfred Maudslay.

heavy mansard roofs and an abundance of polychrome stucco sculpture on the exteriors of buildings (Figures 9.20, 9.21); in the final phase at the site most of the buildings were colored red. The temples in the Cross Group have interior, roofed shrines, miniature temples themselves, each containing a large sculptured tablet with dynastic iconography and inscriptions (Figure 1.7) that tell us that the buildings were erected at the end of the seventh century A.D. The tracery roof combs of Palenque are as unique as the four-story tower of the Palace.

In the southeastern corner of the Maya Area, lowland in culture but lying in an upland valley, is Copan, which like Palenque is unique in the range and innovation of its architecture. The Great Plaza, studded with stelae carved in the round, is probably the most impressive public space at any Maya site (Figure 9.22). At one corner the Hieroglyphic Stairway, with a dynastic inscription covering more than twenty-five hundred glyphic blocks, runs from bottom to

9.21. One of the stucco panels on the front of the Palace at Palenque photographed by Maudslay. The figures were built up over a stone core as nude bodies and were then clothed with garments separately modeled in fine plaster. The whole composition, an exercise in dynastic propaganda, was then painted in several colors (compare this photograph with Catherwood's drawing in Figure 1.5).

9.22. The Great Plaza at Copan, studded with statuelike stelae of the rulers XVIII-Jog and New-Sun-at-Horizon, lies west of the massive acropolis. This reconstruction by Tatiana Proskouriakoff shows Copan at its apogee in the eighth century A.D.

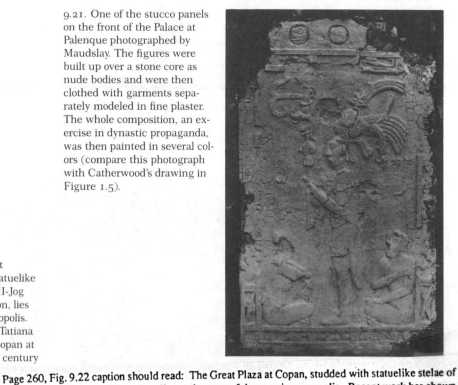

Page 260, Fig. 9.22 caption should read: The Great Plaza at Copan, studded with statuelike stelae of the rulers XVIII-Jog and Yax Pac, lies at the west of the massive acropolis. Recent work has shown that dense settlement lay around the center, including elaborate dwellings of the elite (see Figure 6.6).This reconstruction by Tatiana Proskouriakoff shows Copan at its apogee in the eighth century A.D.

top of a major pyramid with a series of rulers' statues set at intervals down the center of the stair. Similar life-sized human figures are found elsewhere on the Copan acropolis, including two snarling gods shaking rattles and others diving around a doorway, and these figures and the stelae together give the site, even when deserted, the feeling of being populated. The buildings of Copan lack the towering outlines of those in Petén, perhaps because the hills would dwarf them anyway, and the spaciousness of the site derives from its builders' use of long horizontal lines.

The highland zone has been little studied from the point of view of architecture except for a succession of partly uncovered buildings at Kaminaljuyu that reflect the influence of Teotihuacan in the Middle Classic period, and also a number of Late Postclassic sites that have been excavated and restored. The two most impressive are Iximche (Figure 4.22), the Cakchiquel capital, and Zaculeu, capital of the Mam, restored as they stood in 1524 and 1525, respectively; the influence of Mexican highland architecture is apparent, as it had been in the highlands since the Teotihuacan penetration in the Early Classic period. Only in Preclassic times does there seem to have been a truly Maya architectural tradition in the highlands, and this is known only from deeply buried buildings at sites such as Kaminaljuyu.

Most of the lowland Maya standing architecture that survives is that of public buildings, so that its decoration must be seen as public art designed to impress or instruct, rather than just to give pleasure. The Maya decorated their buildings in several media, which included colossal carvings forming part of the building itself, as on the roof combs of Tikal, stuccos or murals using the wall as a convenient surface, and carved wooden or stone lintels. Freestanding stelae and altars might also be brought into the architectural ensemble, as they were in the twin-pyramid groups of Tikal.

Architectural sculpture was often on a massive scale: even in Late Preclassic times huge god masks were used to embellish the temples of Uaxactun, Tikal, and Cerros, and in the Classic period entire buildings form the background to a single design, as at Chiccanna and Uxmal (Figures 9.13, 9.2, 1.8). Stuccoworking reached its apogee at Palen-

9.23. A scene from the Bonampak murals showing a band of musicians playing for a festival celebrating the designation of an heir to the ruler Chaan-Muan. The left-hand figure carries a small drum and rattle (compare Figure 6.3), and in front of him are two trumpeters and a group of five figures dressing in grotesque masks for a drama or dance. The stationary man playing the *pax*, an upright drum, is passed by four men beating turtle shells with deer antlers (which produce three resonant notes) and by five men each shaking a pair of rattles made from gourds. The overall effect must have been strongly rhythmic, but not necessarily melodious.

que, where the life-sized figures were modeled naked and then "dressed" in stucco clothes so that the drapery would look correct, before being painted in brilliant colors (like Classical Greek sculpture). Inside the Palace polychrome stucco reliefs and murals were used together.

Relatively few Maya murals are known, because of the ease with which they can be destroyed by the climate or by the collapse of the buildings they adorn. The earliest murals known are from a Late Preclassic burial chamber at Tikal, but neither they nor the fragmentary Early Classic scene found in Structure A-XVIII at Uaxactun are of outstanding quality. The most famous Maya murals are those at Bonampak, discovered by Giles Healey in 1946, and they are truly masterpieces. They cover the upper walls and vaulted ceilings of three rooms of a modest building at this small site not far from Yaxchilan, and range from the ordered and static to well-designed chaos in their planning. Several interpretations have been placed on the paintings, including a raid for captives and a celebration of its success, the punishment of a failed peasant revolt, and the punishment of captive raiders from another center. One of the rooms portrays a battle in progress, with the figures falling across each other, in a composition of enormous energy; many of the figures wear crested helmets, with animal or other devices that presumably identified them.

Page 262, fifth line from bottom, add sentence: . . . center. The most recent interpretation is of the designation of a royal heir, accompanied by captive-taking for sacrifice common in Mesoamerica. One of . . .

Whether the helmet was actually worn pushed back from the face, or whether the artist has used this as a convention to show the participants' faces we do not know, but it seems clear that the mural commemorates an actual event, and that the people in it are intended to be recognized. Another scene shows the robing of Maya lords for some ceremony, in towering headdresses of quetzal plumes, with a band of musicians below playing trumpets, drums, rattles, and turtle shells (Figure 9.23), and a group of men attiring themselves in grotesque deity costumes for a ritual or masque. Yet a third depicts what has been interpreted as a judgment: the principal figure, richly attired, stands glowering at naked captives who have had their fingernails torn out; beside them a human head lies on a bed of leaves.

Maya mural painters seem also to have been responsible for the decoration of two buildings far from the Maya lands: at Cacaxtla in the central highlands of Mexico, not far from Puebla, recent excavations have revealed well-preserved murals. One, facing onto a courtyard, is a battle scene in a single horizontal register with scenes more gruesome than those at Bonampak, including corpses cut in half and others with their entrails hanging out or receiving a spear in the eye. The second building has murals flanking a doorway, with a figure in the guise of a great bird but with clearly Maya features, like many of the figures in the battle scene. The portrayal of the figures is so similar to both the Bonampak murals and to Late Classic Maya relief sculpture that it seems probable that Maya artists were responsible; but how they came to this highland place, what struggle was portrayed, and why the figures should be Maya remain a mystery. It does, however, seem likely that the range and impact of Maya art and artists beyond their own land has until now been underestimated.

In the Postclassic period of the lowlands several murals have survived at East Coast sites, notably Tancah and Tulum, and others are known to have existed at Santa Rita in northern Belize. The style of these murals (Figure 9.24) recalls the folding codex books—they were presumably painted by the same craftsmen—and especially those of the Mixteca-Puebla region of central Mexico. Donald Robertson has called this the "International Style of the Late Postclassic," and its presence along the Maya coast attests to the cosmopolitan contacts of the Putun merchants.

Apart from architectural adornment, probably the most important Maya art form was the stela, a stone slab or pillar

9.24. The Santa Rita murals were found by Thomas Gann in 1896 at a site in northern Belize that was probably the ancient capital of Chetumal, one of the small Late Postclassic polities into which the northern lowlands had split by the time of the Spanish conquest. Only one small fragment of the murals survives today, but Gann's drawings show them to have been in a style derived from southern central Mexico. The delicate pastel colors were also used on small pottery sculptures from the site and on the two late Maya codices, the Paris and Madrid, which were made in the northern lowlands during this period.

set in the ceremonial precinct in front of a building (or occasionally inside it), but essentially freestanding and often with a flat circular "altar" set in front of it. Many stelae are plain (although they could have once had painted decoration) but some hundreds are carved. Most of these have only the front face decorated in low relief, usually with a single, standing figure or a scene involving two or more figures, but on some monuments (notably at Copan and Quirigua) the carving is taken around the sides to the back to give a statue rather than a picture. Hieroglyphic inscriptions may be found on the sides and back of a stela also, and they are now known to refer to events in the life of the ruler depicted on the monument. The ruler is shown in a formal pose (Figures 4.16, 7.5), elaborately accoutred and carrying symbols of his power and office, which may include a ceremonial bar with twin serpent heads, or a manikin scepter, a small humanoid figure with one serpent leg which may be an ornamented *atlatl* or spear thrower. The ruler may stand on a bound captive or face a smaller subordinate figure. On the stelae at Nim li punit in southern Belize, discovered in 1976, the ruler scatters copal incense (a product of this part of the lowlands) into a flaming brazier, flanked by his wife and a young man, perhaps his son and successor; on one of the Piedras Negras stelae he communicates with a deified ancestor by casting copal. Several of the Piedras Negras monuments and one at Quirigua have the ascension motif (see Chapter 7) of an enthroned figure at the top of a ladder.

Stelae at various sites treat the human figure in different ways, from the framed pictorial panel to the statue in the round; the treatment changes also through time in a general way, which Proskouriakoff has demonstrated can be used to give an approximate date to an uninscribed carving. The factors that alter are the pose of the figure and the degree of elaboration and realism in depiction. Some monuments are not in stela form—at Quirigua there are the zoomorphs on which the design is adapted to the rounded shape of a huge boulder and the shape itself suggests an animal form—while some altars, as for instance Altar V at Tikal (Figure 9.25), compress a stela-type scene into a circular panel with a circumferential inscription. Sometimes the monument may become simply a large sculpture with-

Above left:

9.25. Altar V at Tikal, carved A.D. 711 and placed in front of a stela in the enclosure of a twin-pyramid group. The elaborately dressed figures confer over a stack of human long bones surmounted by a skull; the inscription is around the edge of the scene.

Above right:

9.26. One of the ball-court markers from Lubaantun, excavated in 1915 by R. E. Merwin. It shows two players in action against an apparently stepped wall. Further excavation in 1970 showed that the Lubaantun court had stepped sides and was eighth century A.D. in date.

out inscription, as at Copan where two altars in the Great Plaza are in the form of a turtle (with detachable head) and a massive ball.

The ball game and its courts are the focus of some elaborate sculpture also: the markers that divided the court into halves are often carved with scenes of the game in progress (Figure 9.26). In the Toltec period at Chichén Itzá there are panels depicting what may be the aftermath of the game when one player, winner or loser, is decapitated (Figure 9.27).

Many of the motifs in this public art recur in the private patronage art created for individuals by master craftsmen in ceramics, painting, and lapidary work. The ball game was a favorite subject with vase painters, some of whom were skilled enough to stand comparison with the Dipylon workshop masters of ancient Athens. In the Late Classic period figure painting on cylindrical vases became a major means of artistic expression; the majority of such vases were deposited in burials, and unfortunately most of those known are from looted sites so that they have lost most of their archaeological importance. Michael Coe has studied a large corpus of these vases, and argues persuasively that not only were they made specifically for funerary deposition but the scenes they portray are in fact of events in the underworld to which the deceased is journeying. He believes that many of the scenes are not genre, but specific episodes in a lost epic literature of which the *Popol Vuh* of the Quiché is a surviving fragment. Thus the famous

9.27. The great ball court at Chichén Itzá (see Figure 1.10), part of the Toltec-Maya ceremonial precinct, is decorated with relief panels showing two teams of players: the leader of one has just cut off the head of the other leader, and blood in the form of vegetation and serpents spouts from the stump of the neck. The head and a chert or obsidian knife are held by the winning (?) leader; the knife is similar to that used in the self-decapitation scene on the Altar Vase (Figure 7.14) and to many excavated examples.

Page 267, Fig. 9.27 caption, add: It has been suggested that the game shown is the mythical one of the Hero Twins against the Lords of Xibalaba, as described in the *Popul Vuh.*

from a conch shell, or a humanoid bat with crossed bones on its wings, or a ball game in progress, all reflect parts of this story (Figure 9.28).

Some vases do, however, depict real people and events, as Richard Adams demonstrated for an elaborate vessel excavated at Altar de Sacrificios (see Chapter 7, Figure 7.14), and as seems to be the case on the Bonampak murals, in another medium; the boundaries between myth and history, as between public and private art, were flexible. The work of Jacinto Quirarte and others has shown that some vases depict rituals, real or mythical, that involve the administration of hallucinogenic enemas and the killing of a

9.28 Polychrome vase in Chamá style depicting a scene from Classic Maya myth. *possibly* -Probably- the *Popol Vuh*.

victim, with a celebratory dance; these scenes sometimes include both gods and people.

The vase painters were probably the same craftsmen who painted the folding codex books (and the murals described earlier in this chapter), and occasionally a vase has a vertical line ending a scene as though a page had just been wrapped around the vase; or the codex technique of painting on a thin layer of lime plaster applied to the vessel is used, as on the famous Uaxactun vase of Early Classic date. Since no Classic period codices survive, these vessels are a valuable indication of their appearance, as is the codex style of fine-line painting used on some vases. A great deal of our recent knowledge about the underworld and afterlife in Maya thought has come from vase paintings, but the information is frustratingly incomplete because the vessels lack both site identification and cultural associations as the result of being looted; and, as with other stolen goods, the less the information available on these, the better from the dealers' and collectors' point of view. The vases and their paintings survive, but their relevance to ancient Maya society is irrevocably lost.

In the same way as the painter of temple murals could turn his hand to codices and vases, so the sculptor of stelae could miniaturize his art in lapidary work. Maya jades are among the finest artistic achievements of the civilization, the stone being very hard and difficult to carve. The same techniques of low-relief and occasional in-the-round carving were used as in large sculpture, producing plaques such as the "Gann Jade" (Figure 6.10), now in the British Museum, or boulder sculptures such as the head of the sun god from Altun Ha (Figure 9.29) or the crouching jaguar from Tikal. Jade, as noted in Chapter 8, is not native to the Maya lowlands, but was traded there from about 600 B.C. on; the earliest carvings are a small, duck-billed figure and effigy jaguar claw, both dating to about 450 B.C., from Cuello, Belize (Figure 9.30).

Recent research suggests that rough blocks of jade were exported from the sources in the Motagua Valley and the highlands to the west, and worked in the lowlands in local style. Even the chips left over were not wasted: at Tikal a superb mosaic of the Early Classic period was found, 37 centimeters (15 inches) high, made from fragments of jade

9.29. Jade head of the sun god, Kinich Ahau, from a Classic period tomb of ca. A.D. 600 at Altun Ha, Belize. The head is carved in the round on a small boulder and weighs more than 4.5 kilograms (9.75 pounds); it is about 15 centimeters (6 inches) in diameter.

and shell. Another figure only 11 centimeters high, a standing effigy of a man in wood and stucco, had miniature jewelry including a double necklace, ear ornaments, and a high headdress, made from tiny flakes of jade.

Other materials were worked into mosaics as well as jade and shell (the latter usually being the red lip of the *Spondylus* oyster), including obsidian and metallic iron ores such as hematite. One of the finest Maya mosaics comes from the Toltec period at Chichén Itzá, a geometrically decorated disc found on the back of a carved red stone jaguar throne in the inner earlier temple of the Castillo; the jaguar itself was inlaid with large green jade spots.

One aspect of Maya art of which we know relatively little is woodcarving; we have the lintels of Tikal and Tzibanche made from hard sapodilla wood (Figure 9.31), but other woods survive only under exceptional circumstances. At Tikal a set of stuccoed figures of the rain god was recovered (Figure 10.5), but only because the plaster coating had survived in the tomb, leaving a hollow space that could be filled with plaster. Dry caves are the source of most of the wooden objects known, including a seated figure from an unknown site reputedly in Tabasco, and an elegant, simple box from Actun Polbilche in central Belize.

Of Maya metalwork we have a large sample, but few pieces are earlier than Terminal Classic in date. Most of the early metalwork is Maya in context only, having been imported from lower Central America, and many of the later objects are simple pieces of types common from Oaxaca eastward, and not demonstrably Maya in manufacture. Most of the metalwork with distinctively Maya characteristics dates from the Early Postclassic period, such as the Maya-Toltec, hybrid-style gold discs from the Cenote of Sacrifice at Chichén Itzá (Figure 8.7). Although the discs themselves were possibly brought in as blanks, the presence in the lowlands of Maya-style objects cast in the lost-wax technique, as well as the quality of decoration on the discs, indicates the operation of highly skilled metalsmiths in the Maya Area. The large quantity of copperwork found at some eastern lowland sites, such as Lamanai, suggests that local manufacture from ingots may have occurred.

The art of the stelae depicts the rulers of the Maya realms in official acts; that of the vases seems to reflect a

9.30. Among the earliest Maya jade carvings so far discovered are this claw pendant, 2 centimeters long, this "duck billed" pendant, broken from a larger piece, and two tiny disc beads of very fine jade. All were found in late Early Preclassic burials of 600 – 400 B.C. at Cuello, Belize. (See pp. 115, 268.)

9.31. One of the carved sapodilla-wood lintels of Tikal, with an elaborate figure and hieroglyphic inscription similar to those on the stelae. This lintel is from Temple IV, dating to ca. A.D. 750 (photographed by Alfred Maudslay).

lost literature; for portrayals of daily life and the common people we have few sources. One that does exist, however, surprising in its detail and variety, is the large number of pottery figurines. They are too common and widespread to be elite art, and although some of the people they portray are clearly rulers and other high-ranking persons, many are equally obviously nonelite individuals engaged in their normal occupations.

In the Preclassic period the figurines are usually hand-made, with clothes and other details added in strips and tic—having, for instance, double-punched eyeslits in some cases—those of the highlands give some indication of tattooing and hairstyles as well as clothing.

The most naturalistic and detailed figures were made in the Late Classic period; they were usually mold-made, and often had a three-note whistle chamber incorporated in the body or attached to the back—whether they were toys, or whether the whistle had some practical or ritual function for adults is unknown. The design was probably made in clay or beeswax and a mold taken from it; the fired mold was then lined with fine clay in several layers to make a cast, which was hollowed out or had the whistle chamber attached. As the cast shrank and dried it would pull free of the mold, and it could then be fired in an open bonfire in a batch with other figurines or with pottery vessels.

The degree of detail shown varies from site to site. The figurines of Jaina Island, off the Campeche coast, were both hand- and mold-made and are among the most delicate and accomplished, but the recent discoveries by Susanna Ekholm at Lagartero in Chiapas have shown that the highlands also had gifted folk artists (Figure 8.3). Another remarkable collection comes from Lubaantun in southern Belize, where a large group of the figurines depict masked men in heavy visored helmets (Figure 9.32) and others show activities such as the killing of a deer (Figure 5.3), a woman grinding corn on a *metate* (Figure 6.2), and a musician with drum and rattle wearing a cacao-pod pendant (Figure 6.3). At all three of these sites the detail extends to the pattern woven or embroidered on a woman's *huipil* and the precise elaboration of coiffure and headdress.

In the Postclassic period the figurine tradition continues, and a series of hand-made effigies, delicately tinted in pastel colors like those of contemporary murals and codices, is known from Santa Rita, Belize; the forms include warriors clutching spears and strange saurians with human heads appearing in their mouths. On a larger scale, gods in human form adorn the *incensarios* of the Late Postclassic period, which by the seventeenth century have become mere faces attached to bowls; this final form of Maya representational art has continued among the Lacandon of the Chiapas rain forest to the present day.

9.32. Classic Maya folk art: pottery figurine ca. 5 centimeters (2 inches) high of a helmeted man from Lubaantun, eighth century A.D. The figure wears a loincloth, chest cloth, and heavy glove, and a polychrome vase from the same site shows such men engaged in combat. Although the helmeted figures have been identified as ball players, they lack the elbow, knee, and chest protectors usually employed, which are, however, found on other figurines, on the ball-court markers, and on a vase from the site showing the ball game being played.

The arts that we have considered so far—carving, painting, modeling, and drawing—are the substantial ones that can leave behind material traces for us to appreciate and analyze. Like our own society, however, that of the Maya possessed insubstantial arts, of performance rather than manufacture: drama, music, dance, epic tales, and poetry. We see hints of these in murals, vase paintings, and figurines: the stately movement of robed men on the Bonampak murals to a wind and percussion band, the graceful dance of Bird-Jaguar of Yaxchilan on the Altar de Sacrificios vase, and the grotesque cavortings accompanying the act of sacrifice on many other vessels. There are many depictions of musicians, and some of their instruments survive; we can play the same notes that were heard more than a thousand years ago, and reconstruct the personnel and hence the sound of a Maya band, but the melody, the rhythm, and the counterpoint have gone forever.

Of poetry, drama, and epic tales we have fragments, preserved among the conservative highland Maya and recorded by scholars such as Brasseur de Bourbourg; these fragments may well be, as Michael Coe argues, related to the lost literature of the lowland Maya. The *Popol Vuh*, with its tale of the hero twins and their battle against the lords of the underworld, the *Annals of the Cakchiquels*, and the Quiché drama of the *Rabinal-Achí*, in which a warrior is captured and sacrificed after feasting and dancing, are enticing reminders of the world we have lost.

Men and Gods

ONE of the prime subjects of Maya art was their pantheon of gods, who were comparable in range and function to the historically known gods of Aztec Mexico. In some cases the comparison is so close as to suggest the existence of an overall Mesoamerican religious *oikumene* within which the Maya, Aztec, and even Olmec gods and cults were regional variants.

The identification of the Maya deities began early in this century with the work of Paul Schellhas, who isolated a series of gods from the Madrid, Paris, and Dresden codices and assigned to each one of them a letter as identification, rather than presuming to give him or her a name. Most of Schellhas's identifications have stood up to more than seventy years of subsequent scholarship, although some have been split into several gods and others conflated into aspects of a single deity.

The principal god in the Maya pantheon was, as Eric Thompson demonstrated, *Itzam Na* ("iguana house"), the creator and framer of the universe. He was a god with a protean diversity of forms and aspects embracing many parts of Maya life, and Thompson has argued that toward the end of the Late Classic period the worship of Itzam Na approached monotheism, as more and more deities were arrogated as facets of the all-powerful creator god.

In the contact period Itzam Na was regarded as the god "from whom all things proceeded, and who was incorporeal," and he was worshipped as the god of bountiful harvest, of the sun, of the earth, and of rain (this last because *itz* means "teardrops" or "raindrops," and the Maya made of this homophone one of their frequent puns). The Itzam is basically an iguana, a large terrestrial lizard common in the Maya lowlands and perhaps remarkable to the Maya because of its fierce and primitive appearance, but the god also has aspects of the freshwater crocodile or cayman, and the hooves and antlers of deer may appear on occasion as well. Itzam Na was clearly not a simple lizard, nor for that matter a single lizard: as in many other facets of Maya life, their great god was fourfold, each part assigned to one of the four world directions and colors, so that there was a red Itzam Na of the east, a white of the north, a black of the west, and a yellow of the south. This fourfold monster is often portrayed with planetary symbols along its body, and Thompson suggested that the Maya saw it as the framework of a house, *na*, "the roof and walls of which were formed by four giant Itzams, upright but with their heads downwards," each forming "a side of the sky from zenith to horizon" and even below that to form the floor of man's terrestrial environment. "The Itzam," says Thompson, "take on fresh functions when they exchange their celestial locations for the floor of the world house." As celestial creatures they send rain to earth, as terrestrial ones "they are the soil in which all vegetation has its being, and now they receive that rain which formerly they dispensed from on high." There is some evidence that the Maya believed that the earth rested on the back of a great cayman floating in a pond, and Dennis Puleston suggested that the patterns of raised fields, which produced essential crops, bore a recognized resemblance to the scaly back of such a creature, an interpretation that fits well with Thompson's.

One of the best-known portrayals of Itzam Cab Ain, this earth aspect of the god, is in the frontal mask on the carved panel in the Temple of the Foliated Cross at Palenque (Figure 10.1), where his head is decorated with vegetation and attached to a conventionalized iguana body with planetary symbols. Other portrayals, emphasizing the god as the world house, can be seen in the frames of stelae such as Piedras Negras 25, where the enthroned ruler has set himself within the circuit of a celestial and terrestrial Itzam Na, proclaiming hyperbolically the notional extent of his power. The rear head of the Itzam is inverted with the fleshless jawbone symbolic of death and the underworld, but also with the symbol of the sun, *kin*, on its forehead; this is a reference to the Maya belief that the sun passed below the horizon and through the realm of death during the night, and emphasizes the essential unity of the celestial and terrestrial aspects of Itzam Na.

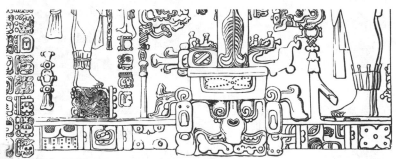

Page 275, Fig. 10.1 caption, add: Recent studies suggest that Itzam Na may have been less important in the Maya pantheon than previously thought.

10.1. Itzam Cab Ain, an earth-god avatar of the Maya creator deity Itzam Na. The body has planetary symbols showing how Itzam Na frames the universe, while life-giving plants sprout from the head. This depiction is found at the base of the tablet in the Temple of the Foliated Cross at Palenque, dating to the late seventh century A.D.

Thompson identified Itzam Na with Schellhas's God K in the codices, and suggested that his harvest-god aspect, Itzam Na Kauil, was the being recorded in the sixteenth century as *Bolon Dz-acab*—"Nine (or many) Generations" —who was described to the Spanish clergy in Yucatan as an eternal being. A second god from the codices, God D, is another aspect of Itzam Na and is shown as an aged man; there is evidence for yet a further function for this old man, as a fire god comparable with the Mexican *Xiuhtecutli*. With creation, fire, rain, crops, and earth as his provinces, Itzam Na permeated Maya life as well as framing it within the protection of the great Iguana House.

Standing apart from Itzam Na were the deities of the sun and moon, called in Yucatan *Kinich Ahau* and *Ix Chel*. *Kin* means "sun" or "day," *ahau*, "lord." Other Maya groups use names that mean "bright" or "fiery," and this aspect is notable in the codices, where the sun god is malignant, scorching the crops; in the Classic period, however, he was a popular and respected deity, if the number and magnificence of his portraits are anything to go by. He has distinctive characteristics, including a square eye with inward-squinting pupils, front teeth filed to a T-shape, and a curly barbel, like those on catfish, emerging from the corners of his mouth. He may also wear the glyph sign *kin* on his forehead, or the water lily, indicative of his night aspect when he passes through the underworld. In recent years a number of impressive portrayals of Kinich Ahau have been discovered, including the jade boulder carving from Altun Ha (Figure 9.29) and the huge stucco masks on the front of a pyramid at Kohunlich in Quintana Roo (Figure 10.2).

The moon goddess, Ix Chel (Figure 10.3), was usually seen as the wife of the sun god, and there are numerous

10.3. The moon goddess, Ix
Chel, from the Dresden Codex.
This Postclassic codex probably
derives from a Late Classic
original and is much more sophisticated in style than the
Madrid and Paris codices (compare Figure 5.2).

10.2. Stucco portrait of the sun
god, Kinich Ahau, on a Late
Classic pyramid at Kohunlich
in southern Quintana Roo. The
mask, some 2 meters (6.5 feet)
high, is painted red.

tales of her inconstancy. One example is the story in which
she eloped with the king vulture; the sun god dressed himself in a deerskin and lay pretending to be dead, sending
a blowfly to tell the vultures where the carrion was. He
grabbed the first vulture to arrive and forced it to take him
to the king vulture's palace, where he repossessed his errant wife. This was both a popular tale and an early one: it
is illustrated on a number of Late Classic polychrome and
carved vessels, of which the best known is the Yalloch vase
on which Thompson first recognized the myth in the 1930s.
On it the sun god/deer, the blowfly, the vulture, and the
hummingbird (a symbol of the sun god) all appear, but on
other vases it was thought sufficient to show only the sun/
deer and a vulture or hummingbird to allude to the myth.
The earliest portrayal of the story is on an Early Classic
bowl from Nohmul, where the sun god, obviously human
under a skimpy deerskin, appears with his hummingbird
avatar and two vultures (Figure 10.4). Thompson collected

the story from living Maya, and his identification of it in the Classic period is a good example of the uses of ethnographic data in illuminating the Maya past. One irony in the modern period, given the moon goddess's imperfect reputation, is her conflation with the Virgin Mary, because Spanish colonial depictions of the Assumption show the Virgin standing on the crescent moon (itself derived from another pagan civilization as an emblem of the virgin goddess Diana). Ix Chel was patron of curing and medicine, and of childbirth; she was also associated with lakes, and Thompson felt that she had once been "goddess of the earth and its products, but lost ground to rival cults of the maize god" and of Itzam Na.

The most popular present-day Maya deities are the *Chaacs*, the rain gods (Figure 10.5); they are fourfold, one Chaac being assigned to each world direction with an appropriate color; they send the life-giving rains and are thus the maintainers of life. The Yucatec think of them as old men, and in the codices they are represented by God B, a long-nosed deity with a curl above the nose and the long tip

10.4. A Classic Maya myth: the sun god, dressed in a deer skin, waits for a vulture to carry him off so that he can recover his errant wife, the moon goddess, who has eloped with the king vulture to his sky palace. This bowl from Nohmul, Belize, probably dates to the fourth or fifth century A.D. and is the earliest known representation of this well-known myth, which still survives today among the Maya. The use of only the sun god, vulture, and hummingbird to evoke the myth suggests that it was already widespread when the bowl was made.

10.5. Chaac, the rain god, seen here in two of his four aspects in stuccoed wooden figures from a Classic-period tomb at Tikal of ca. A.D. 600.

of that organ hanging down. The Chaacs are also, logically enough, gods of thunder, and ancient axes found in *milpas* are thought of as their thunderbolts (a belief also common about prehistoric stone axes in Renaissance Europe). The role of the Chaacs as water givers is shown in the codices, where they are depicted pouring water from vessels. Their favors are secured by burning *pom*, copal resin incense, which makes clouds of black smoke, simulating the black rain-clouds that are desired and informing the Chaacs what is requested of them.

An animal associated with the Chaacs is the small *uo* frog that appears noisily at the beginning of the rains and thus symbolizes the end of drought; in the ceremony of *ch'achac* ("summoning the Chaacs"), which takes place at this time of year, four small boys are tied to the corners of the altar and imitate the croaking of the frogs. The deposition of offerings, of jade, copal, and sacrificed humans, often children, in the Sacred Cenote at Chichén Itzá is seen by Thompson as the official equivalent of the domestic *ch'achac* ceremony.

Official art also has many representations of the Mexican rain god, *Tlaloc*, with his characteristic goggles; some are from the period of Teotihuacan contact, as on highly decorated ceramics at Tikal, while in later examples Tlaloc is conflated with the Chaacs. On the north range of the Monjas quadrangle at Uxmal a pile of Chaac masks is surmounted by a Tlaloc. At the cave of Balankanche at Chichén Itzá a Tlaloc shrine was found, dating to the ninth or tenth century and reflecting the same Mexicanization seen in the Castillo and the Temple of the Warriors.

Rain gods are often conflated with the deities of the earth they nourish, in both the lowlands and the highlands; the Tzotzil in Chiapas believe that their gods live in the mountains around the villages, and make offerings and hold ceremonies at caves on the slopes. Rain cults survive in most parts of the Maya Area under a veneer of Christianity, and may be among the most ancient parts of Maya religion; Thompson's judgment was that the uniformity of the rain cult over a wide area of Mesoamerica "with world color and directional features and with quadripartite deities deriving from or fused with snakes, had developed in all essentials in the Formative [Preclassic] period, probably as an Olmec creation."

Other deities of the earth exist, notably the *Tzultacah* ("mountain valley"), gods of the earth's surface who live in mountain caves and protect crops and game. Karl Sapper, a German geologist who did much valuable work in the highlands around the turn of the century, recorded the following prayer to them:

> The offering I have brought thee is in truth not much and of little good for thy eating, for thy drinking. Whether it be so or not, what I say and what I think, O God, is that thou art my mother, thou art my father. Now I shall thus sleep beneath thy feet, beneath thy hands, thou lord of the mountains and valleys, thou lord of the trees, thou lord of the liana vines. Tomorrow is again day, tomorrow is again light of the sun. I do not know where I shall then be. Who is my mother? Who is my father? Only thou, O God, thou seest me, thou protectest me on every path, in every time of darkness, from every obstacle which thou mayest hide, which thou mayest remove, thou, O God, thou my lord, thou lord of the mountains and valleys.

The eloquence of this hunter's prayer, translated by Eric Thompson, makes us wonder about, and mourn, the lost glories of Maya literature.

A group of rather curious gods were called *Bacabs*; they were four in number, but instead of being aspects of one deity they were distinctive. They sit in two pairs above the door of the Iglesia at Chichén Itzá, facing each other (Figure 10.6): one has a conch shell on his back, the second a spider's web, the third wears a turtle carapace, and the fourth a spiral shell. They wear loincloths with a design that Thompson identifies as a bee's wing and were patrons of apiculture. They appear also at Chichén as Atlas figures supporting architectural members, reflecting their function as supporters of the sky (according to Landa), and in the Dresden Codex they appear disguised as opossums, bearing the god of the incoming year.

10.6. The four figures of Bacabs (or perhaps the related Pauahtuns): a detail from the Iglesia at Chichén Itzá, an elaborate Puuc-style building of the eighth or ninth century. (Detail from a photograph by Alfred Maudslay.)

All of these deities, together with the wind god and others, reflect the features and forces of the natural environment—heavens, earth, sun, moon, wind, and rain. In the firmament the planet Venus was both feared and worshipped as morning and evening star, *Xux Ek* ("wasp star"), which could with its chill rays endanger life and crops.

To protect it against Venus and other perils, the maize had its own god, or rather it *was* a god, usually shown as a handsome young man whose head may appear in place of the ear of corn, or who may have corn leaves rising from his head as though it were the seed. One of the finest portrayals of the god, from Copan (and taken from there to the British Museum by Maudslay), shows him with one hand raised palm outward, the other lowered in a similar gesture, and lips parted in a serene expression (Figure 10.7). From behind his swept-back hair rises maize vegetation, and he wears magnificent jewelry—ear-flares, bracelets, and a mask-pendant—all presumably representative of jade. Thus the Maya ideas of jade meaning "precious" and its association with growing corn all come together in a harmonious piece of symbolic sculpture that may have yet further significance if the image portrays, as some think, one of the rulers of Copan in maize-god guise. That men dressed like the god and impersonated him we know from the Bonampak murals, and from a scene in the Dresden Codex where the head (or mask) of an impersonator lies on a stepped altar surrounded by musicians playing the drum, rattle, and flute.

The importance of maize is reflected also in the comments of an eighteenth-century Franciscan missionary: "Everything they did and said so concerned maize that they almost regarded it as a god. The enchantment and rapture with which they look upon their *milpas* is such that on their account they forget children, wife, and any other pleasures, as though the *milpas* were their final purpose in life and source of their felicity."

Another god who was often impersonated by men was the jaguar god, a patron of the number 7 and the calendar day *Akbal* ("night"); the sun in his nightly passage through the underworld was thought of as a jaguar, the night-prowling cat, and the starry heavens were sometimes described metaphorically as the jaguar's spotted skin. The skin was also a symbol of power and rank, used for throne coverings or for the tailored trousers of lordly figures (Figure 7.14), while on the great shield that forms the center of the carved tablet in the Temple of the Sun at Palenque the visage of the jaguar god of the night appears, grinning (Figure 1.7).

10.7. The young maize god: a human-size figure from Copan, collected by Alfred Maudslay and now in the British Museum, eighth century A.D. Perhaps an idealized ruler portrait.

The underworld through which the sun god passed at night was the abode of the death gods; Thompson has identified the most common of these in the codices, the walking skeleton who often has a macabre grin and who was called God A by Schellhas, as *Cizin* ("stench")—a deity worshipped across the Maya Area from Chiapas to Yucatan. The underworld had a large and varied population, according to recent work by Michael Coe, including two old gods who ruled Xibalba (the infernal region), deadly bats, and other unpleasant fauna. A Death Stag may also be a denizen of Xibalba; it appears on a number of polychrome vases, but its function is not understood. The old gods, Schellhas's M and N, are seen in various episodes on vase paintings that coincide with events in the *Popol Vuh* (see p. 267) involving their challenge by the Hero Twins.

The actual practices of Maya religion are not often portrayed, but we know that they were not entirely the calm worship of the gods by the offering of *pom* and produce that has been suggested by some scholars. Even before the introduction of heart sacrifice by the Toltec at Chichén Itzá the Maya had engaged for centuries in the decapitation of victims for sacrifice; in both Late Preclassic and Early Classic structures at the small site of Cuello, for instance, were found the detached heads of slaughtered children and adolescents, in some cases with the body, in others without. Several of the Classic figurines of Lubaantun have trophy heads hanging from their waists, suggesting the killing or sacrifice of enemies in battle, and in the Terminal Classic site at Seibal the remains of what seems to be an entire ball team—nine young men—were buried in the ball court. Decapitation is a favorite method of dispatch for victims portrayed in vase paintings; on a looted vase now in Princeton, reputedly found near Uaxactun, a figure interpreted as one of the first set of Hero Twins in the *Popol Vuh* is having his neck severed by two masked figures, and on the Altar vase the young woman found in the burial is shown cutting her own neck with a knife, with the marks of death already on her cheek (Figure 7.14).

Self-sacrifice was not always fatal: a common practice was blood-letting, from the tongue, lips, or penis. One of the finest lintels from Yaxchilan (Figure 10.8) shows a woman pulling a cord set with thorns through her tongue,

10.8. Blood sacrifice: on this lintel from Yaxchilan of A.D. 709 a woman in richly decorated garments (compare Figure 3.12) kneels in front of the ruler Shield-Jaguar, pulling a cord set with thorns through her tongue. The dish of bark paper in front of her is to collect the drops of blood as an offering.

the blood dripping on to bark paper in a dish beside her; the blood-spattered paper would then be offered to the gods. A vase now in the University Museum of the University of Pennsylvania in Philadelphia shows a line of squatting men, each with a decorated perforator which he is thrusting into his penis, and another vase recently excavated at Cahal Pech in the Belize Valley has a sun-god impersonator doing the same thing, with blood spraying out from the pierced member.

Some forms of religious activity were more pleasurable. A series of vases has recently been identified as showing the administration of enemas, and it has been suggested

10.9. Time as a burden: the Initial Series date 9.15.5.0.0. 10 Ahau 8 Chuen (A.D. 736) on the back of Stela D at Copan has the time periods personified as the bearers of burdens, using the pre-Columbian tumpline to carry the load. The period glyph can be seen in the headdress of the personified *katun* and *tun* (second row down), and the fleshless jawbone of the *katun* signifies that his number is greater than ten. The Ahau glyph is shown as a full figure, sitting inside the normal glyph cartouche.

that these were of a hallucinogenic liquid such as the Maya *balche*, a fermented honey drink into which a *Bufo marinus* toad had been placed; the skin of the animal contains a powerful drug. Both gods and men are shown partaking of these enemas, which are inserted with a characteristic squeezer (perhaps a rubber bladder) with a spout at the end; the squeezer is shown lying on a necked jar which apparently contains the enema liquid, or is in the hands of a young woman who is about to administer the enema. The exact function of the enema ritual in Classic Maya society is unknown, but from its portrayals it would seem to have been restricted to the elite: this activity does not appear on the pottery figurines illustrating workaday activities in the artisan and peasant classes.

Another aspect of Maya religious activity lies far from the severed heads, enemas, and blood letting: the worship of time, which pervaded Maya life. Each day and number had its patron deity—the sun god was the patron of the calendar day Ahau and the number 4, and the maize god of the day Kan and the number 8. These associations were part of a grand concept in which, in Thompson's words, "the Maya conceived of the divisions of time as burdens carried through all eternity by relays of divine bearers. The burdens were carried on the back, the weight supported by túmplines across the forehead. In the most elaborate hieroglyphic inscriptions one god raises his hand to the tumpline to slip it off his forehead, and others have slipped off their load. The night god, who takes over when day is done, is in the act of rising with his load: with his left hand he eases the weight on the tumpline; with his right hand on the ground he steadies himself as he starts to rise; it is the typical scene of the Indian carrier resuming his journey." A superb example of time borne as a burden exists in the Initial Series date on the back of Stela D at Copan (Figure 10.9), where the *baktun*, *katun*, *tun*, *uinal*, and *kin* are personified and their burdens depicted in various forms, including a giant toad and a jaguar-skin bundle.

Each number from *1* to *13* was associated with a god and a day, beginning with the day Caban, the number *1* and the moon goddess Ix Chel; the number *13* was also associated with the number of layers in the heavens, which rose in six steps from the eastern horizon to the zenith, following the sun god as he moved across the sky, and then descended in six more steps in the western horizon. Below the horizon, on into the underworld, there were four more steps down to the nadir, then four back up to the eastern horizon, a total of nine infernal strata before the sun could step back into the new day. The thirteen gods of the heavens, the *Oxlahun ti Ku*, were in constant struggle with the *Bolon ti Ku*, the nine lords of the underworld. Several sets of nine black obsidians, which may portray these infernal deities, have been found in offerings beneath stelae at Uaxactun and Tikal, and the design of the twin-pyramid groups at Tikal may epitomize the solar cycle through day and night.

Another aspect of Maya religion involved the veneration of ancestors, although it is not certain whether they were worshipped as gods or whether they were, perhaps, seen as intermediaries with the divine. Early stelae at Tikal such as Stela 31 (Figure 4.16) show the ruler's predecessor, in this case Curl Nose, father of Stormy Sky, hovering above, while, on the domestic level, some burials in shrines attached to courtyard groups have been interpreted as founding fathers of lineages. The whole center of Tikal was dominated by great pyramids raised over the burials of rulers, and the temple building on top of the pyramid of Temple 1 (Figure 6.8) probably housed a cult connected with the veneration of the deceased Ruler A, buried in splendor below the pyramid. At Palenque, the great ruler Pacal seems to have been regarded as semidivine after his death, and he figures prominently on inscriptions of his son and successor Chan-Bahlum. The ancient Maya do not seem to have regarded death so much as a final break as a change of status, which left ancestors still connected to their living descendants.

Caves were also regarded as links with the underworld, "pathways to Xibalba," as Barbara McLeod and Dennis Puleston have called them, and evidence has come to light of activities in parts of caves that would not normally be penetrated for shelter or collection of water. Cave use goes back to at least the Middle Preclassic period in the Maya Mountains, and the western foothills near Poptun yielded in 1980 a spectacular find in the form of murals deep within a cave, with hieroglyphic inscriptions, musicians playing a drum and conch trumpet, seated figures making offerings, and a ball-game player. They appear to be Late Classic in date.

Both in the Classic period, when there was influence from Teotihuacan, and in the Postclassic with Toltec incursions and Aztec influence, alien gods were imported into the Maya lands. The presence of the Mexican rain god Tlaloc has already been noted, and another important introduction was the cult of the feathered serpent—*Kukulcan* to the Maya, *Quetzalcoatl* to the Mexicans; both names combine the name of the quetzal bird with the word for snake, *can* or *coatl*. Although Kukulcan/Quetzalcoatl was a prominent deity, conflated with the planet Venus, he may also have had a historical origin as a ruler of Tula who fled to Yucatan in the late tenth century. The feathered-serpent iconography is older than this, however, so the man would have had to arrogate to himself a mythic persona already familiar. It has been posited that he was the leader of the Toltec incursion at Chichén Itzá, but some doubt the truly Toltec origin of that phase and attribute it to the Putun Maya from Tabasco. Whatever the standing of Kukulcan as a man, as a god he was certainly important at Chichén Itzá, where in Thompson's words "plumed serpents writhe in low-relief sculpture, descend on balustrades which flank steep staircases, and rise behind warriors or priests performing human sacrifices."

A second and rather curious introduction from highland Mexico was the semirecumbent figure popularly called a "Chac-Mool" (the name has nothing to do with the Chaacs, and was in fact invented by one of the more eccentric Maya explorers, Augustus Le Plongeon, in the late nineteenth century). The figure lies on its back with knees and head raised, supporting a shallow dish on the belly which may have been to receive offerings. The location of a notable example at the entrance to the Temple of the Warriors at Chichén Itzá supports such an interpretation (Figure 9.15), although not the popular notion that freshly removed human hearts were the gift expected.

Several other Mexican deities of the Postclassic period are explicitly depicted in sculpture, mainly at Chichén Itzá and Mayapan; they include *Tezcatlipoca* ("smoking mirror")—the legendary vanquisher of Quetzalcoatl—*Tlalchitonahtiuh*, the rising sun, and *Xipe Totec*, the flayed god of

human sacrifice with his covering of a victim's skin. Together these deities document a substantial ideological intrusion into the Maya lowlands, which means that we cannot project colonial documentary evidence back to the
Classic period without a great deal of care. Since the bulk
of our interpretive evidence for Maya religion comes from
such survivals and from more recent ethnographic records,
we can be certain about the general Mesoamerican nature
of the gods, but less so about their specific presence in a
peculiarly Maya avatar in the Classic or Preclassic period.
The sculptures and vase paintings of the Classic period
give us a great deal of evidence, but we cannot interpret it
as an unbroken tradition.

The Maya Mind

MAYA art and religion, as we have seen in the two preceding chapters, are complex developments with their roots in the Preclassic period, with a Classic florescence, and with additional stimuli from contact with other parts of Mesoamerica, in particular highland Mexico—an area where the political development of an organized society in urban concentrations was carried much further than it ever was in the Maya lands. In some areas, however, the civilization of the Maya was preeminent in pre-Hispanic America. This is true especially of the realms of the mind: in mathematics, in astronomy, and in the development of writing as a vehicle for the expression of abstract ideas as well as cold facts, the Classic Maya were the equals of any of the early civilizations of the Old World.

We have already gained some idea of the use of mathematics by the Maya in their rather complicated calendar (see Chapter 4, Figures 4.2–4.4), with the vigesimal system of counting (to base 20) and the utilization of a vertical positional notation to differentiate orders of magnitude (Figure 4.5). A large number could of course be expressed positionally in other ways, as, for instance, in the successive period glyphs of a Long Count date, where the size of the unit involved in each glyph block was indicated by the appropriate sign (Figure 10.9). There has been much argument over whether the Maya did, like the Hindus of India, truly invent the concept of *zero*; the present consensus is that they did. It has been demonstrated that the bar-and-dot system with vigesimal notation could easily be used for addition and subtraction, but George Sanchez has argued that division and multiplication were equally possible. Multiplication was certainly used in working out the permutations of the 260-day, the 365-day, and the Long Count cumulative calendars, and in assessing the omens for any given future date, and the Dresden Codex has a number of tables of multiples. Some of the numbers the Maya reached in their fascination with time were very large—on one inscription at Quirigua a date 90 million years ago is recorded, and on another a period of 400 million years. In a sense the Maya were just playing with numbers, since even the inauguration of the Long Count in 3114 B.C. lay beyond their memory and perhaps beyond their history, but some concept of eternity consonant with the everlasting nature of Bolon Dz'acab may also be indicated.

One reason for this fascination with the distant and less distant past was a notion that history was cyclical. We see this most clearly in the historical-prophetic Books of Chilam Balam, where two *katunob* with the same number, both for instance ending in the day 2 Ahau, will have the same portents, and in a posthumous paper Dennis Puleston argued for a similar awareness in the Classic period. Migration, drought, privation, and occasionally good fortune are seen to recur. The *katunob* always ended with a calendar day Ahau from which the Maya took their names and luck, with the day number decreasing by 2 each time (7 Ahau, 5 Ahau, 3 Ahau, 1 Ahau, 12 Ahau, 10 Ahau . . .) in the endless circle of thirteen, until after 260 *tunob*, about 257 years, the first number was repeated and the past and the future came together. The *katun* 8 Ahau had a history and a prophecy of strife, and Thompson points out that the last Maya stronghold to fall to the Spanish, the Itzá settlement of Tayasal in the Petén in 1697, did so without a struggle as such a *katun* was about to begin, after the Franciscan monk Avendaño had persuaded the Itzá rulers that the time was ripe for change. Time was "an endless relay march to eternity."

Numbers and calculation were used by the Maya both for the maintenance of their complex calendar and for more mundane purposes such as economics and business transactions; in the latter a number of cacao beans laid out on the ground were manipulated rather like an abacus; the beans themselves were also the unit of currency. The field in which the mathematical ability of the Maya is best displayed is that of astronomy, however—not the simple cycles of sun and moon, although those were observed and lunar information recorded in great detail as part of each Long Count date on the stelae, but the longer cycle of Venus. Venus was observed mainly because of its dire aspect: the Maya liked to keep an eye on the Wasp Star.

Our best evidence for the observation of Venus comes from the Dresden Codex, where six pages of tables cover 65 synodical revolutions of the planet averaging 584 days in length (Figure 11.1). The Maya measured the cycle of Venus from heliacal rising after inferior conjunction, when the star emerged from the underworld, and divided it into four parts: 230 days from rising to disappearance before superior conjunction, 90 days after reappearance, then 250 days as Evening Star and finally 8 days of invisibility at the inferior conjunction before the new heliacal rising. The ac-

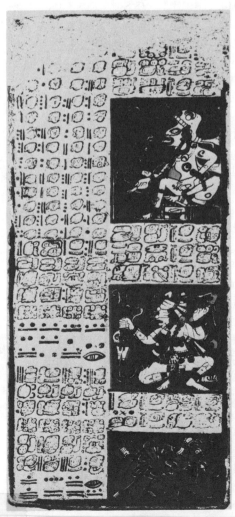

11.1. Astronomy and mathematics: the Venus tables in the Dresden Codex document 65 revolutions of the planet, and with interpolated corrections, the Maya were able to reduce their observational error on the length of the cycle to 14 seconds per year. Calculations of the moon's cycle, also found in the Dresden Codex, are equally accurate. The small polychrome pictures that accompany the calculations are distantly related in style and use of color to Classic Maya murals.

Page 291, Fig. 11.1 caption, add: The screenfold codex dates to about A.D. 1450. It was painted somewhere on the east coast of the Yucatan Peninsula. At least eight scribes worked on it, and it contains almanacs, New Year ceremonies, *katun* prophecies, and eclipse tables in addition to the Venus and lunar data. Some of the information in the codex was already several centuries old when it was painted.

tual conjunctions, which cannot be observed, were paid no attention.

The Dresden Codex contains 65 such cycles because this total of days—37,960—equals 146 of the 260-day cycles of the Sacred Round, the lowest common multiple of the two, and also 104 years of 365 days. The Maya were aware that the actual length of the Venus cycle varied, and also that their approximation of 584 days was slightly too long, so that a correction would have to be made; but since the Maya had no concept of fractions, the correction would have to be of a whole day, and most importantly, in such a way as not to disrupt the correlation between the cycle of Venus and the 260-day Sacred Round. What they did was to wait for 61 revolutions of Venus, by which time the error had accumulated to 4 days, and then subtract this to recover the vital day 1 Ahau to begin the new cycle. This still left an error of 0.88 days in a century, so the Maya again waited until 4 further days had accumulated, making the total error 8 days, and then subtracted this in a Venus cycle that terminated that period after the day 1 Ahau. So the first correction of 4 days was used four times, and then the larger correction of 8 days, once only. This still left an error of 0.08 of a day in 481 years, but given the Mayas' total lack of mechanical or optical observatories the overall accuracy is not bad—some 14 seconds of error per year. (Credit for discovering this set of corrections must be given to an American chemical engineer, John Teeple, who undertook the study of Maya applied mathematics to keep his brain in trim during long railroad journeys; his publication of this in 1930 came in the middle of a most productive period of research on Maya glyphs which included Eric Thompson's refinement of a correlation of the Maya and Christian calendars, the discovery of *Baktun* 8 stelae at Uaxactun, and the compiling of Morley's massive *Inscriptions of Petén*.)

The main function of the study of Venus seems to have been to be able to predict the time of the feared heliacal rising after inferior conjunction. In the Dresden Codex the Venus god is shown hurling down a spear, representing the "cause of sickness, something evil when it came to emerge." In other words, the purpose of the observations was less astronomical than astrological.

Following the Venus tables in the Dresden Codex is a set of tables for predicting eclipses of the moon. The pattern of use is similar to that of the Venus tables; a most important feature again is a series of corrections applied during the currency of the table, running for a total of 11,960 days, which serve to recover the day 12 Lamat as a base in the same way that 1 Ahau was recovered for the Venus cycle. The lunar table includes 405 months, equal to 46 rounds of the 260-day cycle, with an error over this period of 0.11 day.

The tables also include the figures necessary for calculating solar eclipses, but the Maya would not have seen all of these and could not have predicted whether any particular eclipse would be visible in the Maya Area. The important thing was to know of the likely approach of an eclipse, since these also were times of peril in which the world might come to an end.

John Teeple not only worked out how lunar information was recorded in the hieroglyphic inscriptions, where the age of the moon in its current cycle and the position of that cycle in a group of five or six were specified in a whole series of glyphs following the Long Count date, but was also able to elucidate the way in which the Maya had put together their astronomical tables. They used a double 260-day period, 520 days, in which eclipses clustered in three almost equal groups of days—173, 173, and 174; eclipses of the sun occurred within 19 days of these central divisions.

It has been claimed that the Dresden Codex, which remains our major source of information on Maya astronomy, contains tables for the synodical revolutions of other planets, including Jupiter, Mars, Saturn, and Mercury, but since various students have assigned different pages to particular planets, and the subject matter of the predictions is not obviously related to planetary matters, it seems likely that the sun, moon, and Venus are the only heavenly bodies referred to in the book.

That there was some interest in other planets or stars seems clear from a second codex, that in Paris, where a zodiac with thirteen animal signs is found. The animals include two species of bird, a turtle, a bat, a scorpion, and a rattlesnake, together with several imaginary beasts, each

carrying in its beak or teeth a sun glyph. The 28-day intervals between the signs give a 364-day approximation of the
solar year, and five such zodiacs equal seven rounds of the
sacred 260-day cycle.

In other parts of Mesoamerica constellations such as the
Pleiades were considered important, as in the Aztec "New
Fire" ceremony, and the Aztec also recognized the constellations we call the Great Bear or Dipper, and the Little
Bear with the Pole Star, calling them Scorpion and *Xone-
cuilli*, respectively; two groups of modern Maya also make
the Great Bear–Scorpion equation.

It has been suggested that the layout of Maya buildings
and ceremonial precincts was governed by the use of astronomical alignments, and that some buildings were themselves used as observatories. One such group of buildings
for which this function was suggested many years ago is
that of Group E at Uaxactun, where an observer at the base
of the west temple could sight eastward to three small
temples across the plaza; the doorway of the northern
temple lies close to the line of the summer solstice, that of
the southern temple to the winter solstice, and that of the
central temple to close on due east. Karl Ruppert noted that
similar building clusters occur at several other sites in the
central part of the Maya lowlands.

A more famous example of a possible observatory is the
Caracol at Chichén Itzá (Figure 9.11), where it has been
suggested that sight lines diagonally across the windows,
from jamb to jamb, were astronomically significant. A recent reexamination of the building by professional astrono-
mers has not convincingly confirmed the proposition.

What does seem likely is that the Maya, even if they
lacked formal observatories, or had no structures more
sophisticated than the Uaxactun grouping, nevertheless
used some kind of hand-held instrument for noting the
precise positions and movements of heavenly bodies. In
Mexican codices a pair of crossed sticks is used to denote
observation, but Adrian Digby has suggested that a rather
more sophisticated apparatus was used. Digby noted a design found in sculpture and elsewhere with two unequal
trapezes attached to a circle; he argued that this represented a three-dimensional object with a circular base and
two vertical trapeziform bars crossing at right angles, and

that the shadows cast by such an object would trace the path of the sun. Practical experiment with a wooden reconstruction indicated that the device gave surprisingly accurate results, but its use, if it *was* used by either the Mexicans or the Maya, would seem to have been confined to solar observation.

The orientation of certain Maya buildings indicates a possible astronomical consciousness, less from actual direction than from otherwise inexplicable changes in direction of successive buildings through time. At Chichén Itzá the buildings in the northern part of the site, built in the ninth and tenth centuries under Toltec or Putun influence, lie on a markedly different general orientation from the earlier Puuc-style buildings to the south. On a smaller scale, a house platform at Nohmul in northern Belize proved to have two periods of construction. The later building, a rectangular walled structure, lay on top of a two-level podium; the later phase dated to the ninth to eleventh centuries, the earlier to sometime in the Classic period. The later building lay on an axis 5° off that of the earlier, even though this meant additional difficulty in construction. A second building across the small courtyard had precisely the same sequence of structures and changed orientation.

From an earlier period, at the site of Cuello, again in northern Belize, there is a small pyramid with two phases. The first dates to about A.D. 200, the second to about A.D. 300–400; the stair and sidewalls of the second phase were constructed over the earlier and smaller pyramid, but on an alignment 10° further to the east; again, the effort in so doing must have been greater than that involved in simply adding to the extant building on the same alignment, and hence the movement of the axis must have been of some importance to the Maya of the Early Classic period.

Two possible phenomena could account for the change: one is an alteration in the position of some heavenly body; the other is the secular variation in the earth's magnetic field. The second solution would mean that the Maya had some way of detecting this change, by the use of a device essentially the same as the magnetic compass. A piece of evidence has recently come to light that renders this plausible, even though no Maya compass has yet been found: a piece of magnetic iron ore was found in the excavation of the Olmec site of San Lorenzo, on the Gulf Coast of Mexico, with a groove cut in it. It was found that when the object was floated in a water bath, with a pointer laid in the groove, it functioned as a magnetic compass.

In their combination of astronomical and mathematical expertise the Maya were far in advance of their neighbors in Mesoamerica, even the urbanites of Teotihuacan and the imperialists of Aztec Tenochtitlan; when Classic civilization collapsed, much—but not all—of the skill died also. The Dresden Codex in particular, and also the Madrid and Paris codices, show that a substantial body of astronomical/astrological information and the mathematical concepts necessary for utilizing it survived until the coming of the Spaniards. The 260-day calendar still survives in the Maya highlands, correct to the day after more than four centuries of use *sub rosa*, and only a few years ago Gary Gossen found a calendar board in use in the village of Chamula, on which the owner had marked off each day with charcoal until the board was filled, then wiped it clean and begun again (Figure 3.14). Such ephemeral means of recording time and its divisions must have existed in the Classic period and perhaps the Preclassic also, alongside the almanacs in the codices and the majestic count of *katunob* graven in stone on the stelae.

From Landa's account, both the 260-day and the 365-day cycles with their named days and months were still known in the sixteenth century—the beginning of *Baktun* 12 was celebrated as recently as 1618—and it is clear that epigonal Maya culture still preserved much of the intellectual apparatus of the lost Classic civilization; had a scholar such as Sahagún come to Yucatan at the time when Landa was making bonfires of codices, much of this knowledge might have been an open book to us, instead of being wrung painfully from the remnants, and in particular we might have a better idea of the nature and content of Maya hieroglyphic writing.

The Maya script, the most complex in the ancient Americas and the only true writing to evolve in the New World, is one of the most astonishing features of their culture, and the one that above all else entitles the Maya to the sobriquet of "civilized." That the strange hieroglyphs inscribed on stelae were a form of writing was recognized from the

beginning of Maya studies (see Chapter 1), and their decipherment began as long ago as 1864, when Brasseur de
Bourbourg published Diego de Landa's "alphabet." This
contained only some three dozen signs; Eric Thompson's
Catalog of Maya Hieroglyphs showed that there were more
than 800, of which nearly 300 appeared in the codices and
the remainder on monumental inscriptions. Some of these
are alternatives with the same meaning: thus the day Ahau
has a *symbolic* form, a surprised-looking round face (Figure 4.3), and also a *head variant*, a profile of a young man
with an almond-shaped eye. The head variant may have a
body attached to it in some elaborate inscriptions, such as
Stela D at Copan, to give a *full-figure* glyph (Figure 10.9).

Certain conventions are also used: since glyphs are normally arranged in columns, the position of any one glyph is
referred to by coordinates; the columns from left to right
are labelled A, B, C, and so on, and the rows from top to
bottom 1, 2, 3, . . . The coordinate B7 will then refer to a
discrete block in the inscription, the *glyph block*, which
may contain one or several separate signs brought together
to form a compound expressing a single idea or statement.
One sign, the *main sign*, usually occupies most of the
space, with *affixes* attached (e.g., Figures 7.1, 7.13); these
may be *prefixes*, above or to the left of the main sign, or
postfixes below or to the right. Occasionally an *infix* is
placed within the main sign. David Kelley has recently proposed an extended terminology, in which a sign is called a
grapheme, made up of *elements*; two or more graphemes
may occur in regular juxtaposition to form a *glyger* (from
"glyph group"), the rough equivalent of a "word." Two or
more graphemes and/or glygers may combine to form a
clause, with a grammatical structure.

Many features of Maya hieroglyphic writing are now
generally agreed on among scholars; others are still the
subject of acrimonious dispute. Areas of agreement include the existence of variant forms of the same glyph
(symbolic and head forms), the reading order (which may
vary in detail within the left-to-right and top-to-bottom
structure), the use of pairs of glyphs/graphemes to express
a single idea, the existence of grammatical affixes, and the
presence of a grammatical structure. It is also common
ground that the nature of the script is mixed—it is neither

wholly ideographic, nor alphabetic, nor syllabic: there are
far too many signs for either of the latter possibilities (our
alphabet has, after all, only 26 signs) and far too few for the
former—an average literate Chinese must memorize some
7,000 ideographic characters. Neither is the script pictographic—a depiction of an object standing for that object
—although there are some pictographic elements in it. The
script is instead a blend of all of these features except the
alphabetic, although the existence of a phonetic element
has recently begun to be accepted by many workers. For
many years the view of Eric Thompson held sway, that the
script was a combination of ideographic signs, some of pictographic origin, and rebus writing; rebus, or punning on
similar sounds, is familiar to all of us from such childhood
games as drawing an eye, a saw and a yew tree (or a sheep)
to denote the sentence "I saw you." The Maya used this
same homophony to employ, for example, the head of the
fish called *xoc* as the verb *xoc* ("to count").

The notion that there was a phonetic element in Maya
writing goes back to Brasseur de Bourbourg's original publication of Landa's *Relacion de las cosas de Yucatan* in
1864 (see Chapter 2), with its "alphabet," and to the work
shortly thereafter by Leon de Rosny and Cyrus Thomas;
excessive claims by Thomas and by Benjamin Whorf, demolished by Thompson, made phoneticism unfashionable
for several decades, until in the early 1950s the Russian
linguist Yurii Knorosov again raised the question. His suggestion was that many signs represented single syllables,
and could be combined to build up words; exactly the same
idea was being applied simultaneously to Minoan Linear B
script by Michael Ventris. Knorosov suggested that the
term for "turkey," *cutz*, was made up of two signs with the
values *cu-tz(u)*, and that the same sign for *tzu* was then
used in the word *tzu-l(u)* for "dog"; in each case the final
vowel is redundant, and the meanings of the component
signs are irrelevant to the meaning of the compound "word."

There are still too many signs for a completely phonetic
system to be the answer, and Michael Coe suggested that
"phonetic complements were often attached to ideograms
to help in their reading, either prefixed as a representation
of the initial sound of the sign, or postfixed as the final
consonant."

An impressive demonstration of phoneticism in the
Maya script was produced by Floyd Lounsbury. A prefix
long known colloquially to scholars as the "ben-ich" prefix
appears as part of emblem glyphs (Figure 7.1) and also
with *katun* numbers indicating the length of a ruler's
reign. Lounsbury showed that the two parts of the prefix
could be read separately as *ah* and *po*, with consistent
meaning in different contexts (*po*, for instance, being part
of the term for copal incense, *pom*, a cake of which formed
the pictographic origin of the sign); and that when brought
together they formed *ahpo* ("lord"), again in contexts
where this meaning made complete sense. In a further
study Lounsbury has shown that another word for "lord,"
ma-kin-a, uses in its glyph Landa's signs for *ma* and *kin*.
Makina is used as a title at Palenque, where Lounsbury, together with Linda Schele and Peter Mathews, has translated major portions of the monumental inscriptions using
a phonetic model. One striking translation there is that of
the name of the first great ruler of Palenque—*Pacal*—as
"shield," from three separate elements read as *pa-ca-l(a)*, a
reading reinforced by the emblem of the ruler, a round
shield (see Chapter 7, Figure 7.13). Phonetic readings for
other Palenque rulers have also been established, including
a woman ruler called *Zac Kuk* ("white quetzal-bird"). A recent and detailed summary of the position by David Kelley,
an established protagonist of the phoneticist school, in *Deciphering the Maya Script* (1976) concludes that "despite
the reluctance of many competent Mayanists to accept the
evidence of the existence of purely phonetic glyphs in the
Maya script, the data which support this conclusion seems
to me overwhelming," although "the relative rarity of phonetic glyphs in the deciphered material means that they do
not automatically lead us to a cumulative series of new
decipherments."

Such decipherments are, however, appearing at frequent
intervals, mostly elucidations of dynastic sequences in
which such relationships as those between mother and son
can now be detected. In addition to our understanding the
meaning of more and more specific glyphs, the grammar of
Maya writing is also becoming clearer, with the existence
of possessives, locatives, numerical classifiers, and deter-
minatives being accepted to a greater or lesser degree.

What was it that the Maya were saying and recording that required, and justified, this complex writing system? Eric Thompson wrote in 1954, in the first edition of *The Rise and Fall of Maya Civilization*, that "so far as is known, the hieroglyphic texts of the Classic Period deal entirely with the passage of time and astronomical matters . . . they do not appear to treat of individuals at all. Apparently no individual of that period is identified by his name glyph. . . ." Since then, there has been a revolution in our understanding of the content of the Maya texts, many of which on the Classic stelae can now be seen to deal with dynastic succession, political marriage, alliance, and acts of war (see Chapter 7).

We have lost a great deal of presumed philosophy and glorification of the endless cycles of time, but we have gained a great deal of history, some of it trivial, as in the monuments that announce the capture of some rival chieftain, and we are in some cases now able to give names to the haughty lords who pose in their regalia on the stelae and altars of the Classic period. An incidental development has been an appreciation of the importance of women in the higher strata of Maya life, as wives, mothers, sometimes perhaps rulers in their own right, sometimes as the links through which dynasties were maintained, and occasionally as pawns in the establishment of a diplomatic marriage with a far-distant center. The importance of this new picture for understanding Maya society is outlined in Chapter 7; in David Kelley's words, "the framework of a history which is somewhat more than a mere list of dates is beginning to emerge. There is still a great deal which is obscure to us, but now we see human beings rather than astronomical abstractions. For the first time we know something of the history of an American Indian group . . . based on contemporary records and directly correlated with archaeological information . . . which is comparable to what we know of many Eurasian groups."

Not all Maya texts, even on the monuments, deal with dynastic and historical matters: the regular erection of monuments at the end of each *katun* suggests that Thompson's majestic march of time may still form part of the subject matter. The Madrid, Paris, and Dresden codices contain no historical matter at all (unlike those of the Mixtec, which have extensive genealogies in pictographic form), but record instead the information needed to predict the movements of the heavenly bodies considered most important to man, together with almanacs of astrological information of use to the farmer and appropriate ceremonies and rituals. Historical codices existed, and are mentioned by Spanish colonial sources, but none are known to survive, although Thompson suggested that the *katun* prophecies in the Paris Codex might be history recycled into prediction, as with many of the events detailed in the Books of Chilam Balam.

The third major source of hieroglyphic texts apart from the monuments and the codices consists of pottery vessels, many of which have a band of glyphs around the rim, and some also panels on the sides. Michael Coe has argued that a Primary Standard Sequence exists, which is found in whole or in parts on vessels, and this records an incantation from something like a Maya "Book of the Dead." It is also clear, from vessels such as the Altar vase from Altar de Sacrificios (see Chapter 7 and Figure 7.14) that texts referring to actual places, events, and individuals may appear on vessels, and reflect the same historical preoccupation as do the monuments.

These three categories of written evidence give us insight into only certain areas of the Maya mind: a preoccupation with, and consummate ability to manipulate, numbers; a desire to record and commemorate the activities, both marital and military, of a ruling class; a developed understanding of some aspects of astronomy and its application to astrological prediction; and a way of life governed by complex rituals that extended into the grave. From colonial sources we have additional information on Maya literature that may, with caution, be projected back into the pre-Hispanic period to illuminate such works of art as the portrayals of the myth of the moon goddess's adultery (Figure 10.4). From these sources also we have some notion of Maya morals and laws in the Postclassic period. Authors such as Gaspar Antonio Chi, Lopez de Cogolludo, Bartolomé de las Casas, and Diego de Landa offer many items of incidental information that show that adultery and

sodomy were disapproved of, that rape and theft were punished by death or enslavement, and that slavery placed a
person in a different category of treatment under the law.
Maya penalties were notably less harsh than those of the
Aztec, with fines of quetzal feathers (a most precious commodity) and cacao beans (the standard unit of currency)
often replacing death. Occasional adultery (in Verapaz)
was punished by fine, habitual adultery by death; fornica-
tion with a widow or slave incurred a much lower fine. Two
slaves fornicating were both killed, however. Perjury was
punished by fine. A woman who left her husband was not
punished, and if she did not wish to return could marry
elsewhere; but for her accusation of rape to be acted on required a witness. These examples show a set of customary
laws similar in nature to those of other peoples: although
we are not justified in retrodicting them to the Classic period or earlier, there is nothing improbable in such rules
having operated then.

Another area of Maya thought on which we have very
little information is the use of, and motives for using, hallucinogenic drugs. That such drugs were available, ranging
from mushrooms to the exudate of toads, is certain; on the
evidence of vase paintings they may have been administered as enemas, as well as eaten. The work of Ralph Roys
established that the colonial Maya had a complex ethno-
botany, much of which clearly survived from pre-Hispanic
times, but in the absence of written sources from the earlier period retrodiction is again an uncertain benefit.

Many corners of the Maya mind thus remain, and probably ever will remain, obscure: we know less about the way
in which the thought and intellect of the Classic Maya
functioned than we do about some of the other early civilizations of the world. Both Mesopotamia and China have
yielded far more information in this field, although the
Indus and Minoan civilizations remain equally or more
unilluminated. Nevertheless, nearly a century and a half of
serious study has left us with a large amount of archaeological, aesthetic, and epigraphic data that tell us far more
about the Maya and their culture than we know about most
other peoples of pre-Hispanic America. An early preoccupation with texts, works of art, and monumental architecture has broadened in recent years to embrace subsis-

tence economics, settlement pattern and planning, social
structure, and dynastic politics. We may still see the ancient Maya through a glass darkly; but we see them more
clearly than we have done heretofore.

Further Reading

Preface

~~General books on the ancient M...~~

Page 305, para 1 should read:

General books on the ancient Maya are: George E. Stuart and Gene S. Stuart, *The Mysterious Maya* (Washington, D.C.: National Geographic Society, 1977); Michael D. Coe, *The Maya* , rev. ed. (London and New York: Thames and Hudson, 1987); T. Patrick Culbert, *The Lost Civilization: The Story of the Classic Maya* (New York: Harper and Row, 1974); Sylvanus G. Morley, *The Ancient Maya*, 4th ed., rev. Robert J. Sharer (Stanford: Stanford University Press, 1983); J. Eric S. Thompson, *The Rise and Fall of Maya Civilization* , 2nd ed. (Norman: University of Oklahoma Press, 1967).

~~Oklahoma Press, 1967). A third edition is planned.~~

Of these books, *The Mysterious Maya* is avowedly popular, but very accurate ~~and up-to-date~~; *The Ancient Maya* is an unrivaled compendium of information and illustrations; *The Maya* and *Rise and Fall* both present lively, sometimes idiosyncratic points of view and are both stylishly written; *The Lost Civilization* is a short, sparsely illustrated study leaning toward culture process rather than culture history. Finally, a work worth reading for its prescience and good sense, although it is now somewhat outdated and unfortunately out of print, is George W. Brainerd, *The Maya Civilization* (Los Angeles: Southwest Museum, 1954).

The literature on Maya civilization is extensive, and much recent work is still in *samizdat* form as conference papers or preliminary reports. The selection here concentrates as far as possible on sources in English since these are more likely to be accessible to the reader. The advanced student or specialist will need the extensive Spanish literature published in Mexico and Guatemala, and the major French and German journals: the general works in English cited here contain references to much of this.

Two recent books give broad coverage of Maya highland archaeology in the Quiché zone and some idea of topics neglected in this present volume: Robert M. Carmack, *Quichéan Civilization* (Berkeley and Los Angeles: University of California Press, 1973), and John W. Fox, *Quiché Conquest* (Albuquerque: University of New Mexico Press, 1978); recent site reports are listed under Chapter 4 readings.

1. Discovery of the Maya

The travels of Stephens and Catherwood cannot be appreciated better than by reading John L. Stephens, *Incidents of Travel in Central America, Chiapas, and Yucatan* (1841) and *Incidents of Travel in Yucatan* (1843), which have been extensively quoted in this chapter. The original editions are, in spite of their many reprintings, rare and expensive, but there are recent, tolerably reproduced, paperback editions by Dover Publications (New York, 1969, 1973), both as two-volume sets. There is also a hardback edition of *Yucatan*, ed. Victor W. Von Hagen (Norman: University of Oklahoma Press, 1963).

Von Hagen has produced several other books about the two explorers, including *Search for the Maya* (Farnborough, England: Saxon House, 1973), *Maya Explorer: J. L. Stephens and the Lost Cities of Central America and Yucatan* (Norman: University of Oklahoma Press, 1947), and *Frederick Catherwood, Architect.* (New York: Oxford University Press, 1950). *Maya Explorer* is useful. None of these secondary sources has the verve or charm of the originals. One chapter of Robert L. Brunhouse, *In Search of the Maya* (Albuquerque: University of New Mexico Press, 1973) deals with the travels of Stephens and Catherwood.

2. *Precursors and Successors*

The history of Maya studies has been dealt with in a number of books and articles. Its place in the general development of American archaeology can be appreciated to some extent from Gordon R. Willey and J. A. Sabloff, *A History of American Archaeology* (London: Thames & Hudson and San Franciso: W. A. Freeman, 2d ed., 1980) and in Mesoamerica in particular from I. Bernal, *A History of Mexican Archaeology* (London and New York: Thames and Hudson, 1980). Bernal has also published a paper on the early Spanish antiquaries in the Maya area in Norman Hammond, ed., *Social Process in Maya Prehistory* (New York: Academic Press, 1977), a paper to which this chapter owes much; the same book has a paper by Gordon R. Willey comparing attitudes to the ancient Mayas' neighbors in 1940 and 1975 and also a biographical sketch of J. Eric S. Thompson.

J. Eric S. Thompson's autobiography *Maya Archaeologist* (Norman: University of Oklahoma Press, 1963) gives the best flavor of what Maya fieldwork is like; there are biographies of Morley—*Sylvanus G. Morley and the World of the Ancient Maya* (Norman: University of Oklahoma Press, 1971)—and of Frans Blom—*Frans Blom, Maya Explorer* (Albuquerque: University of New Mexico Press, 1976)—both by Robert L. Brunhouse. Both Morley and Blom are also dealt with at essay length in Brunhouse's anecdotal *Pursuit of the Ancient Maya* (Albuquerque: University of New Mexico Press, 1975), which also has brief chapters on Maler, Maudslay, Frederick Mitchell-Hedges, Spinden, and Thomas Gates. Brunhouse has also produced, in the same vein, *In Search of the Maya* (Albuquerque: University of New Mexico Press, 1973) dealing with Del Rio, Dupaix, Galindo, Waldeck, Stephens, Brasseur de Bourbourg, Augustus Le Plongeon, and Edward H. Thompson. In both books, minor eccentrics and major scholars receive equally uncritical attention, and there are errors, but no similar or better books exist. A short essay and exhibition catalog, *The Art of Maya Hieroglyphic Writing* (Cambridge, Mass.: Peabody Museum, 1971) by Ian Graham is excellent and well-illustrated and covers the major figures in the study of the Maya script. (It has been used freely as a source for this chapter.)

William Gates's edition of Diego de Landa's *Relación de las cosas de Yucatán* has recently been reprinted (New York: Dover Publications, 1978), but the scholarly edition by A. M. Tozzer in the *Papers of the Peabody Museum*, vol. 18 (Cambridge, Mass: Peabody Museum 1941) is still preferable, though rare in the original and costly as a reprint (Kraus Reprints).

Recent developments in Maya archaeology (1958–1968) are covered in a summary review by R. E. W. Adams in the *Latin American Re-*

search Review, 4 (1969): 3–45, and trends between 1975 and 1980 are discussed by R. E. W. Adams and Norman Hammond, *Journal of Field Archaeology* (forthcoming).

3. The Maya Lands and Their People

The major compendium of information on the natural environment of the Maya Area is R. Wauchope, ed., *Handbook of Middle American Indians*, vol. I, ed. R. C. West (Austin: University of Texas Press, 1964), and much of the information in the text and maps in this chapter is derived from it. The vegetation of the lowlands is described by Cyrus L. Lundell in two monographs, *Preliminary Sketch of the Phytogeography of the Yucatan Peninsula* (Washington, D.C.: *Carnegie Institution of Washington Pub.* 436, Contribution 12, 1934) and *The Vegetation of the Petén* (Washington, D.C.: *Carnegie Institution of Washington Pub.* 478, 1937).

Several excellent regional studies of physical and human geography exist: A. C. S. Wright et al., *Land in British Honduras* (London: Her Majesty's Stationery Office, 1959) deals with the relationship of ancient Maya settlement to the observed soil and vegetation patterns and is a model study. A soil study with less explicit anthropological reference is C. S. Simmons, J. M. Tárano, and J. H. Pinto, *Clasificación de reconocimiento de los suelos de la República de Guatemala* (Guatemala: Ministerio de Agricultura, Instituto Agropecuario Nacional, 1959). F. W. McBryde, *Cultural and Historical Geography of Southwestern Guatemala* (Washington, D.C.: *Smithsonian Institution, Institute of Social Anthropology Pub.* 4, 1947) places emphasis on the relationship between man and his environment.

Numerous ethnographic studies of Maya communities exist: the two most relevant to the highland and lowland groups cited as examples in this chapter are: Evon Z. Vogt, *Zinacantan* (Cambridge, Mass.: Harvard University Press, 1969) and Robert Redfield and Alfonso Villa Rojas, *Chan Kom: A Maya Village* (Washington, D.C.: *Carnegie Institution of Washington Pub.* 448, 1934). Redfield, *The Folk Culture of Yucatan* (Chicago: University of Chicago Press, 1941) is also useful. The range of information encoded in perishable artifacts can be appreciated from Walter F. Morris, Jr., *A Catalog of Textiles and Folkart of Chiapas, Mexico* (San Cristobal de Las Casas, Mexico: Publicaciones Pokok, 1979). Little work has been done on the Maya of the rain-forest zone, although A. M. Tozzer, *A Comparison of the Mayas and the Lacandones* (New York: Macmillan, 1907) was a pioneering work. The most recent comprehensive survey of ethnography is in R. Wauchope and Evon Z. Vogt, eds., *Handbook of Middle American Indians*, vol. 7 (Austin: University of Texas Press, 1969), pp. 1–311.

4. The Flowering and Fall of the Maya

Brief outlines of the development of Maya culture are presented in four extant general works: Sylvanus G. Morley, *The Ancient Maya*, 2d ed. rev. George W. Brainerd (Stanford, Calif.: Stanford University Press, 1956); J. Eric S. Thompson, *The Rise and Fall of Maya Civilization*, 2d ed. (Norman: University of Oklahoma Press, 1967); Michael D. Coe, *The Maya*, 2d ed. (London and New York: Thames and Hudson, 1980); T. Patrick Culbert, *The Lost Civilization* (New York: Harper & Row,

1974). Further revisions of the Morley and Thompson volumes are in preparation.

The many articles in volumes 2 and 3 of R. Wauchope and Gordon R. Willey, eds., *Handbook of Middle American Indians* (Austin: University of Texas Press, 1965) are the most accessible summary of the factual material up to the early 1960s, subsuming the vast output of the Carnegie Institution of Washington's Maya projects (many of the HMAI authors being Carnegie staff); a supplement to the Handbook edited by V. R. Bricker and J. A. Sabloff is in press, where the sites of Tikal and Dzibilchaltun are taken as exemplars of the last two decades' work in the rain-forest and scrubland zones of the lowlands, respectively.

The workings of the Maya calendar are explained in J. Eric S. Thompson, *Maya Hieroglyphs Without Tears* (London: Trustees of the British Museum, 1972) and at greater length in Thompson's *Maya Hieroglyphic Writing: Introduction*, 3d ed. (Norman: University of Oklahoma Press, 1971). Radiocarbon chronology and its calibration using the bristlecone-pine tree-ring sequence are clearly explained in Colin Renfrew, *Before Civilization* (London: Jonathan Cape and New York: Cambridge University Press, 1974); the logical and statistical merits of various calibrations have been discussed in various articles in the journal *Antiquity* through the 1970s.

The evidence for preagricultural occupation of the Maya Area includes in the highlands the excavated site of Los Tapiales: R. Gruhn and A. Bryan *Los Tapiales, Transactions of the American Philosophical Society*, 121 (1977) 235–273, and a survey of the Quiché basin just to the north (Kenneth L. Brown, *American Antiquity*, 45 [1980]: 313–324). In the lowlands, the archaic sequence proposed by Richard S. MacNeish, S. Jeffrey K. Wilkerson and Antoinette Nelken-Terner is outlined in the *First Annual Report of Belize Archaic Archaeological Reconnaissance* (Andover, Mass.: Robert S. Peabody Foundation for Archaeology, 1980); and that for Loltun cave, only in *Mexikon*, vol. 2, no. 4 (1980): 53–55. The claimed early site at Richmond Hill, Belize, is described by Dennis E. Puleston in *Actas del XLI Congreso Internacional de Americanistas, Mexico*, 1 (1974): 522–533. The best known archaic sequence in Mesoamerica is from Tehuacan in central Mexico, described in detail in the five extant volumes of the final report, *The Prehistory of the Tehuacan Valley*, ed. D. S. Byers (vols. 1–2) and Richard S. MacNeish (vols. 3–5) (Austin: University of Texas Press, 1967). A sixth summary volume is in preparation by MacNeish. A complementary sequence from the Valley of Oaxaca is gradually being published in the *Memoirs of the Museum of Anthropology (University of Michigan)* edited by Kent V. Flannery.

An early lowland Maya settlement with maize agriculture and a distinctive ceramic tradition at Cuello, Belize, is described in *American Antiquity*, 44 (1979): 92–110 and *Nature*, 289 (1981): 56–59. The transition from a coastal gathering economy to an inland agricultural one on the Chiapas coast has been documented in two monographs of the New World Archaeological Foundation: Barbara Voorhies, *The Chantuto People* (Provo, Utah: NWAF Pub. 41, NWAF/Brigham Young University, 1976) and Gareth W. Lowe, *The Early Preclassic Barra Phase of Altamira, Chiapas: a Review with New Data* (Provo, Utah: NWAF Pub. 39, NWAF/BYU, 1975). Abaj Takalik, a site on the Pacific slope with early Maya monuments deriving partly from an Olmec tradition, is described in a preliminary report of the 1976 season in *Contributions of the Uni-*

versity of California Archaeological Research Facility, 36 (1976): 85–114, and briefly in *Archaeology*, 30 (1977): 196–197. The Olmec, western neighbors of the Preclassic lowland Maya, had major centers at La Venta, Tabasco, excavated a generation ago (P. Drucker, R. F. Heizer and R. J. Squier, Washington, D.C.: Smithsonian Institution, *Bureau of American Ethnology Bulletin* 170, 1959), and San Lorenzo, Veracruz, investigated in the 1960s (Michael D. Coe and Richard H. Diehl, *San Lorenzo and the Olmec Civilization* [Austin: University of Texas Press, 1980]). Ignacio Bernal, *The Olmec World*, trans. D. Heyden and F. Horcasitas (Berkeley and Los Angeles: University of California Press, 1969) gives an overview of Olmec culture that can be supplemented by the papers in Elizabeth S. Benson, ed., *Dumbarton Oaks Conference on the Olmec* (Washington, D.C.: Dumbarton Oaks, 1968). The exchange model advanced in Flannery's paper in this volume is notable for its methodology as well as its content.

The nature of the spread of Preclassic Maya populations in the lowlands, although now rendered somewhat outdated by the widespread discoveries of archaic preceramic and preagricultural people (who may or may not have been biologically ancestral to the Maya, although it is more likely that they were) is discussed by Dennis E. Puleston and Olga S. Puleston in *Archaeology*, 24 (1971): 330–337; by Joseph W. Ball in terms of a social fission model in R. E. W. Adams, ed., *The Origins of Maya Civilization* (Albuquerque: University of New Mexico Press, 1977), pp. 101–132; and in varying terms by the other contributors to the volume also. The widespread nature of Middle Preclassic settlement in the lowlands was recognized as the result of a number of major projects in the 1960s: the initial Preclassic sequence established at Uaxactun (A. Ledyard Smith, *Uaxactun, Guatemala, 1931–1937* [Washington, D.C.: *Carnegie Institution of Washington Pub.* 588]; R. E. Smith, *Ceramic Sequence at Uaxactun, Guatemala* [New Orleans: Tulane University, *Middle American Research Institute Pub.* 20, 1955]) was confirmed and augmented at Tikal (William R. Coe, *Tikal: Handbook to the Ancient Maya Ruins* [Philadelphia: University of Pennsylvania Museum 1967], William R. Coe, *Expedition*, vol. 8, no. 1 [1965]: 5–56, *Science*, 147 [1965]: 1401–1419); in northeastern Petén, Altar de Sacrificios, and Seibal on the Pasión (Gordon R. Willey et al., *Papers of the Peabody Museum*, vols. 62–64 [Cambridge, Mass.: Peabody Museum, 1969–1973], *Memoirs of the Peabody Museum*, vols. 13–14 [Cambridge, Mass.: Peabody Museum, 1975–1978]; volumes 15–17 in preparation); and Dzibilchaltun in northwestern Yucatan (New Orleans: Tulane University, *Middle American Research Institute Pubs.* 31, 47, 48) further volumes in preparation under the editorship of E. Wyllys Andrews V.

The Becan project, including the notable Terminal Preclassic fortifications, is reported in several volumes of *Middle American Research Institute Publications*, including the important ceramic sequence (Joseph W. Ball, *Pub.* 43) and architecture (David F. Potter, *Pub.* 44) and the fortifications (David L. Webster, *Pub.* 41); miscellaneous papers including preliminary reports are also in *Publication* 31.

The important Late Preclassic site at Cerros, Belize, is reported in a preliminary volume, *Archaeology at Cerros, Belize*, edited by Robin Robertson and David A. Friedel (Dallas: Southern Methodist University Press, 1986); and fuller publication is in preparation. The massive site of El Mirador has been reported briefly in *National Geographic Research* 2 (1986): 332–353.

The Protoclassic manifestation at the end of the Late Preclassic has of late received renewed attention: the original Holmul discoveries published by R. E. Merwin and G. C. Vaillant in *Memoirs of the Peabody Museum*, vol. 3, no. 2 (Cambridge, Mass.: Peabody Museum, 1932) were supplemented by an important collection from Nohmul (A. H. Anderson and H. J. Cook, *Carnegie Institution of Washington Notes on Middle American Archaeology and Ethnology*, No. 40 [Cambridge, Mass., 1944]; reconsidered by D. C. Pring in Norman Hammond, ed., *Social Process in Maya Prehistory* [London: Academic Press, 1977], pp. 135–165). An interpretation of Protoclassic pottery as evidence of population intrusion into the Maya lowlands from the Guatemala-Salvador highlands was advanced by Gordon R. Willey and James C. Gifford in S. K. Lothrop et al., eds., *Essays in Pre-Columbian Art and Archaeology* (Cambridge: Harvard University Press, 1961), pp. 152–170, and maintained by Gifford (*Memoirs of the Peabody Museum*, vol. 18 [Cambridge, Mass.: Peabody Museum, 1976]) and also in Norman Hammond, ed., *Mesoamerican Archaeology: New Approaches* (Austin: University of Texas Press, 1974), pp. 77–98. A similar view was taken by R. E. W. Adams on the basis of the Altar de Sacrificios pottery (*Papers of the Peabody Museum*, vol. 63, no. 1 [Cambridge, Mass.: Peabody Museum, 1971]), and at the highland end by Robert J. Sharer in *The Prehistory of Chalchuapa, El Salvador* (Philadelphia: University of Pennsylvania Press, 1977) and Payson D. Sheets in *Ilopango Volcano and the Maya Protoclassic* (Carbondale: University of Southern Illinois Museum of Anthropology, 1976). An evolutionist view of lowland continuity embracing the Protoclassic as part of the Preclassic-Classic continuum has been advanced by Norman Hammond (*Antiquity*, 48 [1974]: 177–189; and R. E. W. Adams, ed., *The Origins of Maya Civilization* [Albuquerque: University of New Mexico Press, 1977], pp. 45–79). Gordon R. Willey (*Papers of the Peabody Museum*, vol. 64, no. 3 [Cambridge, Mass.: Peabody Museum, 1973]) has changed from an invasionist viewpoint to one where local development is predominant; Willey also summarizes the Protoclassic problem neatly in R. E. W. Adams, ed., *The Origins of Maya Civilization* (Albuquerque: University of New Mexico Press, 1977), pp. 391–394. A provocative model for the rise of Classic civilization by William L. Rathje is in *American Antiquity*, 36 (1971): 275–285.

The problem of Teotihuacan contact with the Maya Area (one which may also be relevant to the Protoclassic phenomenon—see D. M. Pendergast, *American Antiquity*, 36 [1971]: 455–460, but also D. C. Pring, *American Antiquity*, 42 [1977]: 626–628) has been the subject of much recent, and largely unpublished, research. The Teotihuacan sequence and the nature of Teotihuacan urbanism are outlined in volume 1 of *Urbanization at Teotihuacan, Mexico*, ed. Rene F. Millon (Austin: University of Texas Press, 1974), and the detailed ceramic sequence with which comparisons with the Maya Area may be made is in volume 4 (in press) by Evelyn C. Rattray. The Carnegie Institute of Washington's *Excavations at Kaminaljuyu, Guatemala*, are examined in the monograph by A. V. Kidder, J. D. Jennings, and E. M. Shook (Washington, D.C.: *Carnegie Institute of Washington Pub.* 561, 1946), which was reprinted (1977) in the current series of Kaminaljuyu reports published by the Pennsylvania State University Press (University Park). The volumes so far available are: W. Sanders and J. Michels, eds., *Teotihuacan and Kaminaljuyu* (1977); R. Wetherington, ed., *The Ceramics of Kaminaljuyu*

(1978); J. Michels, ed., *Settlement Pattern Excavations at Kaminaljuyu, Guatemala*(1979); and J. Michels, ed., *The Kaminaljuyu Chiefdom* (1979). The whole question of a Middle Classic dominated by Teotihuacan is discussed by the contributors to *Middle Classic Mesoamerica*, ed. E. Pasztory (New York: Columbia University Press, 1976). Some of the best evidence in the Maya lowlands for Teotihuacan contact is at Tikal, discussed by Clemency Coggins in Norman Hammond and Gordon R. Willey, eds., *Maya Archaeology and Ethnohistory* (Austin: University of Texas Press, 1979), pp. 35–50, and in *Actes du XLIIme Congrès International des Américanistes Paris 1976*, 8 (1979): 251–269, with an earlier useful summary by William R. Coe in *Teotihuacan: XI Mesa Redonda* (Mexico: Sociedad Mexicana de Antropologia, 1972), pp. 257–271.

The hiatus in stela erection in the sixth century is considered by Gordon R. Willey as presaging the final collapse of Classic civilization; see his paper in Norman Hammond, ed., *Mesoamerican Archaeology: New Approaches* (Austin: University of Texas Press, 1974), pp. 417–430. The collapse itself, a subject of perennial discussion, is the subject of a symposium volume, *The Classic Maya Collapse*, ed. T. Patrick Culbert (Albuquerque: University of New Mexico Press, 1973), and of several later papers in Norman Hammond, ed., *Social Process in Maya Prehistory* ([New York: Academic Press, 1977], papers by Culbert, Robert J. Sharer, Hosler, et al; the last of these uses an interesting computer simulation to recreate the collapse process). A recent study by Robert L. Hamblin and Brian L. Pitcher, *American Antiquity*, 45 (1980): 246–267, revives the peasant-revolt model advanced by J. Eric S. Thompson to explain the collapse; the history of that model is examined by Marshall J. Becker in Norman Hammond and Gordon R. Willey, eds., *Maya Archaeology and Ethnohistory* (Austin: University of Texas Press, 1979), pp. 3–20.

The nature of the Mexican intrusion in Yucatan is considered by J. Eric S. Thompson in Chapter 1 of his *Maya History and Religion* (Norman: University of Oklahoma Press, 1970); a changing view of the Postclassic period from the old notion of decadence to one of vigorous mercantilism is outlined by J. A. Sabloff et al. in Norman Hammond, ed., *Mesoamerican Archaeology: New Approaches* (Austin: University of Texas Press, 1974), pp. 397–416 and in *Monographs of the Peabody Museum*, no. 3 (Cambridge, Mass.: Peabody Museum, 1975). A recent view of the highland Postclassic is in Dwight T. Wallace and Robert M. Carmack, eds., *Archaeology and Ethnohistory of the Central Quiché* (Albany: Institute of Mesoamerican Studies, 1977) and another in John W. Fox, *Quiché Conquest* (Albuquerque: University of New Mexico Press, 1978). Since the Carnegie Institution's final project at Mayapan (*Carnegie Institution of Washington Pub.* 619, ed. H. E. D. Pollock, 1962), there has been little recent concentration on the Postclassic apart from J. A. Sabloff's and William L. Rathje's work on Cozumel and unpublished field projects in central Petén and northern Belize. Postclassic occupations continuing into the period of Spanish conquest are documented by Peter D. Harrison in Norman Hammond and Gordon R. Willey, eds., *Maya Archaeology and Ethnohistory* (Austin: University of Texas Press, 1979), pp. 189–207, for southern Quintana Roo; and by D. M. Pendergast, *Archaeology*, 30, 129–131, and *Journal of Field Archaeology*, 8, (1981) 29–53, for Lamanai in northern Belize. A historical view of the Spanish takeover in the north is in Robert S. Chamberlain,

The Conquest and Colonization of Yucatan 1517–1550 (Washington, D.C.: *Carnegie Institution of Washington Pub.* 582, 1948). The final Maya resurgence in the nineteenth century, when they all but drove the hated *dzul* (whites) from Yucatan, is enthrallingly described by Nelson Reed in *The Caste War of Yucatan* (Stanford: Stanford University Press, 1964).

5. Subsistence and Settlement

The traditional swidden-based model of ancient Maya farming is described in Sylvanus G. Morley, *The Ancient Maya*, 2d ed. rev. George W. Brainerd (Stanford: Stanford University Press, 1956), and in J. Eric S. Thompson, *The Rise and Fall of Maya Civilization*, 2d ed. (Norman: University of Oklahoma Press, 1967). The new orthodoxy is summarized by the papers in Peter D. Harrison and B. L. Turner II, eds., *Pre-Hispanic Maya Agriculture* (Albuquerque: University of New Mexico Press, 1978), which also has a very full bibliography; it is attacked in the review of the book by W. Sanders, *Reviews in Anthropology* (1979) and defended by Harrison and Turner in the reply that follows Sanders's review. Several aspects of raised-field agriculture and its implications are discussed in the papers by Dennis E. Puleston and Harrison in Norman Hammond, ed., *Social Process in Maya Prehistory* (New York: Academic Press, 1977), and Turner's work on terracing is summarized in his paper in Norman Hammond and Gordon R. Willey, eds., *Maya Archaeology and Ethnohistory* (Austin: University of Texas Press, 1979), pp. 103–115. Aspects of the Rio Hondo Project's examination of ancient raised fields and experiments and reconstruction are covered in A. H. Siemens, ed., *The Rio Hondo Project* (Belize City, Mexico: Belize Institute for Social Research and Action, 1977).

Articles on aspects of subsistence include Dennis E. Puleston's study of *ramón* as a resource (unpublished M.A. thesis, University of Pennsylvania, 1968) and his following experimental work on *chultun* construction and storage use, *American Antiquity*, 36 (1971): 322–335. The question of *chultun* storage has been raised again by Ruben Reina and James Hill in *American Antiquity*, 45 (1980): 74–79. The evidence for the use of root crops is summarized by Bennet Bronson, *Southwestern Journal of Anthropology*, 22 (1966): 251–279. The question of marine protein and its availability are discussed by Frederick Lange in *American Anthropologist*, 73 (1971): 619–639, and the case for inland fish-farming in the canals between raised fields is made by J. Eric S. Thompson in Norman Hammond, ed., *Mesoamerican Archaeology: New Approaches* (Austin: University of Texas Press, 1974), pp. 297–302.

The exploitation of animal resources is a subject not yet sufficiently studied, although the unpublished work of Elizabeth Wing, Mary Pohl, and Stanley Olsen on the animal remains from recent major projects in the lowlands promises to yield much information on both the economic and the ritual uses of mammals, birds, and fish. Site monographs apart, *American Antiquity* and the *Journal of Field Archaeology* are the most likely publication media for articles on ancient Maya subsistence.

Summaries of settlement pattern work in the highlands and lowlands, respectively, until the early 1960s are in R. Wauchope and Gordon R. Willey, eds., *Handbook of Middle American Indians*, vol. 2 (Austin: University of Texas Press, 1965), pp. 59–75 (by Stephen de Borhegyi) and pp. 360–377 (by William R. Bullard, Jr.). Bullard also wrote one of the pioneering analyses of Maya settlement patterns (*American Antiquity*, 25: (1910) 355–372) and was a senior member of Gordon R. Willey's team in the project at Barton Ramie in 1953–1956, which laid the foundations of Maya settlement studies (*Papers of the Peabody Museum*, vol. 54 [Cambridge, Mass.: Peabody Museum, 1965]). The development of the field up to 1977 is summarized in the papers in Wendy Ashmore, ed., *Lowland Maya Settlement Patterns* (Albuquerque: University of New Mexico Press, 1981), which includes regional studies, theoretical discussions, and an extensive bibliography.

Sites for which settlement maps are available include Barton Ramie, Tikal (Tikal Report 11 [Philadelphia: University of Pennsylvania Museum, 1961]), Altar de Sacrificios (*Papers of the Peabody Museum*, vol. 62, no. 1 [Cambridge, Mass.: Peabody Museum, 1969]), Seibal (*Memoirs of the Peabody Museum*, vol. 13 [Cambridge, Mass.: Peabody Museum, 1975]), Lubaantun (*Monographs of the Peabody Museum*, no. 2 [Cambridge, Mass.: Peabody Museum, 1975]), and Dzibilchaltun (*Middle American Research Institute Pub.* 47 [New Orleans: Tulane University, 1979]). Other site surveys are available in preliminary form and small scale only; for instance, those of Nohmul, San Estevan, Santa Rita, and Colha in northern Belize in *Archaeology in Northern Belize* (Cambridge, England: Cambridge University, Centre of Latin American Studies, 1975). The largest compilation of ceremonial-center plans is in Sylvanus G. Morley's *Inscriptions of Petén*, vol. 5 (Washington, D.C.: *Carnegie Institute of Washington Pub.* 437, 1937–1938), but later work on some sites has shown variable reliability. The *Archaeological Atlas of Yucatan*, now being prepared by the Instituto Nacional de Antropología e Historía in Mérida, will bring a vast increase in the quality and quantity of information available on the northern part of the lowlands; a settlement map of Coba is also in preparation under the Instituto's auspices. The Copan settlement survey, to be published in final form by the Peabody Museum in the *Memoirs* has been described in preliminary articles by Gordon R. Willey and Richard M. Leventhal in Norman Hammond and Gordon R. Willey, eds., *Maya Archaeology and Ethnohistory* (Austin: University of Texas Press, 1979), pp. 75–102; and Willey, Leventhal, and W. Fash in *Archaeology* 31, No. 4 (1978): 32–43. The settlement study of the neighboring major center of Quirigua will be published as part of the Quirigua monograph series by the University of Pennsylvania Museum; the first volume of the series, with a section on the settlement survey by Wendy Ashmore, was published in 1979. The most important recent settlement-pattern work in the highlands has been at Kaminaljuyu, presented in the final report, J. Michels, ed., *Settlement-pattern Excavations at Kaminaljuyu, Guatemala* (University Park: Pennsylvania State University Press, 1979).

A useful introduction to some of the methods of settlement study, with examples drawn mainly from the arid central Mexican highlands, is ed. Kent V. Flannery, *The Early Mesoamerican Village* (New York: Academic Press, 1976).

6. The Structure of Society

Little has been written on the class structure of ancient Maya society, although Marshall J. Becker in Norman Hammond and Gordon R. Willey, eds., *Maya Archaeology and Ethnohistory* (Austin: University of Texas Press, 1979), pp. 3–20, does consider how the now-discarded two-class model, of a peasant society ruled by theocrats, came into being. References to the new notion of secular ruling dynasties can be found in Further Reading, Chapter 7. Several studies of occupational specialization that implicitly accept a multiclass model of Classic society include R. E. W. Adams, *Papers of the Peabody Museum* vol. 61 (Cambridge, Mass.: Peabody Museum, 1970), pp. 489–502; Marshall J. Becker in *American Antiquity*, 38 (1973): 396–406; E. Wyllys Andrews IV and I. Rovner in *Middle American Research Institute Publication* 31 (New Orleans: Tulane University, 1973), pp. 81–102, and Olga S. Puleston, "Functional Analysis of a Workshop Tool Kit from Tikal" (M.A. thesis, University of Pennsylvania, 1969).

Much of the information we have on social structure is derived directly from the concrete evidence of settlement patterns, and the differential access to materials and skilled manpower evident in the range of dwellings found around Classic sites (see Further Reading, Chapter 5), especially Wendy Ashmore, ed., *Lowland Maya Settlement Patterns* (Albuquerque: University of New Mexico Press, 1981). Several works by William A. Haviland are worth consulting: *The Ancient Maya and the Evolution of Urban Society* (Greeley, Colo.: University of Northern Colorado Museum of Anthropology, 1975); *Middle American Research Institute Publication* 26 (New Orleans: Tulane University), pp. 21–47 and 93–117; *American Antiquity*, 32 (1967): 316–325, and 42 (1977): 61–67; and Haviland's paper in the Ashmore volume just cited. Haviland's data derive from Tikal, the largest sample of settlement pattern, domestic-structure excavations, and nonelite human remains currently available. Evidence of social stratification in the form of better nourished and taller individuals in more elaborate tombs and a higher incidence of malnutrition in simple burials, is brought out by Frank P. Saul's report on the human remains from Altar de Sacrificios (*Papers of the Peabody Museum*, vol. 63, no. 2 [Cambridge, Mass.: Peabody Museum, 1972]).

7. Politics and Kingship

There is no single publication that covers the current material on ancient Maya kingship, and much of the most important discussion is in articles of a technical nature. Some important recent work, such as that of Linton Satterthwaite, Jr., and Carl Beetz on the Caracol inscriptions and Peter Mathews on the Bonampak dynastic succession, is not yet published.

Heinrich Berlin's important article in Spanish, demonstrating the existence and importance of emblem glyphs is in the *Journal de la Société des Américanistes*, 47 (1958): 111–119. Tatiana Proskouriakoff's Piedras Negras paper can be found in *American Antiquity*, 25 (1960): 454–475, and her two-part article on Yaxchilan is in *Estudios de Cultura Maya*, 3 (1963): 149–168, and 4 (1964): 177–202, published in Mexico City; the articles are in English. David H. Kelley's paper on the Quirigua rulers is in *American Antiquity* 29 (1962) 323–335, and the recent reassessment by Christopher Jones is in press in the *Quirigua Reports* of the University of Pennsylvania Museum. The Copan monuments were first published by Sylvanus G. Morley in 1920 in *The Inscriptions at Copan* (Washington, D.C.: Carnegie Institution), and many of the Petén monuments are in his massive five-volume *The Inscriptions of Petén* (Washington, D.C.: Carnegie Institution, 1937–1938) and have been reassessed by Gary Pahl in a Ph.D. thesis available through University Microfilms.

The Tikal dynasties have been studied by Clemency Coggins in a Harvard University Ph.D. thesis, and a short extract is published as "A New Order and the Role of the Calendar: Some Characteristics of the Middle-Classic Period at Tikal" in Norman Hammond and Gordon R. Willey, eds., *Maya Archaeology and Ethnohistory* (Austin: University of Texas Press, 1979), pp. 38–50. The Late Classic rulers of Tikal are discussed by Christopher Jones in *American Antiquity*, 42 (1977): 28–60, and the revitalization movement of Ruler A in a Temple University Ph.D. thesis by Bruce Dahlin and in an unpublished paper by Wendy Ashmore and Robert J. Sharer (on file in the American Section of the University of Pennsylvania Museum).

Most of the Palenque work by Peter Matthews and Linda Schele is published in the privately printed volumes of the *Mesas Redondas de Palenque*, all edited by Merle Greene Robertson and reissued by the University of Texas Press in 1980. The idea of marriage-alliances was put forward by John Molloy and William L. Rathje in a paper "Sexploitation among the Late Classic Maya" in Norman Hammond, ed., *Mesoamerican Archaeology: New Approaches* (Austin: University of Texas Press, 1974), pp. 431–444 and is also discussed by Joyce Marcus, *Emblem and State in the Classic Maya Lowlands* (Washington, D.C.: Dumbarton Oaks, 1976). The Altar de Sacrificios burial is discussed by R. E. W. Adams in "The Glyphic Inscriptions of the 'Altar Vase'," Norman Hammond, ed., *Social Process in Maya Prehistory* (New York: Academic Press, 1977), pp. 409–420.

The 1976 book by Marcus has a useful bibliography; Gordon R. Willey's introduction has a supplementary bibliography of recent work.

8. Trade and External Contacts

A general consideration of Classic and Postclassic trade within the Maya area by J. Eric S. Thompson was first published in *Estudios de Cultura Maya*, 4 (1964) and reprinted in Thompson's *Maya History and Religion* (Norman: University of Oklahoma Press, 1970). A later general study by Brian Dillon is in *Contributions of the University of California Archaeological Research Facility*, 24 (1975): 80–135. A distinction between trade in useful goods and socially functional objects was made by J. A. Sabloff and Gair Tourtellot in *American Antiquity*, 37 (1972): 126–135 (see also the comment by Marshall J. Becker in 38, 222–223). Sabloff has followed up this article with two others, one (with David A. Freidel) in, J. A. Sabloff and C. C. Lamberg-Karlovsky, eds., *Ancient Civilization and Trade* (Albuquerque: University of New Mexico Press, 1975), pp. 369–408 (the articles by Colin Renfrew and Malcolm Webb in this volume are also well worth reading); the other, in Elizabeth P. Benson, ed., *The Sea in the Pre-Columbian World* (Washington, D.C.: Dumbarton Oaks, 1977), pp. 67–88. The Cozumel Project, of which Sabloff and William L. Rathje were codirectors (see Chapter 2), was an explicit study of trading mechanisms (*Monographs of the Peabody Museum*, no. 3 [Cambridge, Mass.: Peabody Museum, 1975]). A recent work that combines theoretical and practical studies of trade under the currently fashionable, and perhaps more neutral sobriquet of exchange, is T. Earle and J. Ericson, eds., *Exchange Systems in Prehistory* (New York: Academic Press, 1977), which includes an attempt to characterize Maya jade sources as a first step toward tracing the movement of this important material into the lowlands. (A major program of jade-source and artifact analysis is currently in progress at Brookhaven National

Laboratory, but Ronald Bishop and his collaborators have so far not published any reports.)

Studies of particular commodities include considerations of obsidian trade in Mesoamerican perspective; for example, Jane W. Pires-Ferreira, *Memoirs of the Museum of Anthropology* (Ann Arbor: University of Michigan, 1975); Thomas R. Hester, ed., *Studies in Mesoamerican Obsidian* (Socorro: Ballena Press, 1973), a collection of reprinted papers. An outline of Maya Area obsidian trade routes was suggested by Norman Hammond in *Science*, 178 (1972): 1092–1093, and modified in articles by the same author and J. Johnson in a volume that contains other obsidian studies: Thomas R. Hester and Norman Hammond, eds., *Maya Lithic Studies: Papers from the 1976 Belize Field Symposium* (San Antonio: University of Texas, 1972). Obsidian trade is also considered by R. Sidrys in *American Antiquity*, 41 (1976): 449–464 and in *Current Anthropology*, vol. 20, no. 3, (1979): 594–597.

Pottery trade in the Palenque region is analyzed in a series of papers by Robert L. Rands and his collaborators; one, in C. L. Riley and W. W. Taylor, eds., *American Historical Anthropology* (Carbondale: University of Southern Illinois Press, 1967), pp. 137–151, outlines the problem, and another, in *Actas, XLI Congreso Internacional de Americanistas, Mexico*, 1 (1975): 534–541, correlates petrographic and trace-element analyses. A small-scale study of the Lubaantun ceramics and clays is in *Archaeometry*, 18 (1976): 147–168 and involves only a single site with a few external comparisons; the use of iterative clustering and multidimensional scaling to evaluate the results of neutron-activation analysis may be of interest. In contrast is the multisite study of Late and Terminal Classic fine paste wares, mainly from the Usumacinta basin, in press in the *Memoirs of the Peabody Museum* 15 (Cambridge, Mass.: Peabody Museum) when this book was being written.

Maya metalwork has not been analyzed systematically as evidence of trade: the absence of ores in the limestone lowlands resulted in the assumption that all metal goods were traded, although the working of ingots or blanks into artifacts within the Maya lands was recognized early; the general assumption was that copper came from central Mexico or Honduras, gold and its alloys from lower Central America. A useful recent survey of Maya metalwork by Warwick Bray in Norman Hammond, ed., *Social Process in Maya Prehistory* (New York: Academic Press, 1977), pp. 365–403 is the prerequisite to compositional and technical studies of the objects to determine the sources of their ore and regions of manufacture; several decades of such investigations in European prehistoric studies have indicated the problems involved, and it may well be that stylistic analysis will remain the prime means of attributing sources to Maya metal objects.

Studies of trade in perishable goods are, understandably, rare, although the existence of these commodities is recognized and frequently invoked *ex silentio* as an explanatory device (the function of Kaminaljuyu to control cacao trade is suggested by Lee A. Parsons and Barbara Price in *Contributions of the University of California Archaeological Research Facility*, 11 (1971): 169–195, for example). One of the few serious studies of perishable trade is in recent work by Anthony P. Andrews on the Maya salt industry in which, as in J. Eric S. Thompson's work, ethnohistoric data are used to illuminate the fragmentary evidence of archaeology; a summary article in *Archaeology*, 33 (1980):

24–33, derives from his *Salt-making, Merchants, and Markets: The Role of a Critical Resource in the Development of Maya Civilization* (Ann Arbor: University Microfilms, 1980).

9. Architecture and Art

Much of the basic work on Maya architecture was done by the Carnegie Institution between the two World Wars and is to be found in the Institution's various publications. The work is summarized, with references to work published up to the early 1960s, in volume 2 of the *Handbook of Middle American Indians* (series editor R. Wauchope, volume coeditor Gordon R. Willey) in which the architecture of the highlands is described by A. Ledyard Smith (pp. 76–94) and that of the lowlands by H. E. D. Pollock (pp. 378–440); the disparity in length between these two articles is a fair reflection of the relative knowledge of the two areas at the time. A superb book of reconstructions of both highland and lowland architecture, illustrations from which were used in the *Handbook of Middle American Indians* articles, is Tatiana Proskouriakoff's *An Album of Maya Architecture* (Washington, D.C.: *Carnegie Institution of Washington Pub.* 448, 1946; reissued in 1963 at Norman: University of Oklahoma Press). This little book does more to make the Maya buildings interesting and comprehensible than any other publication I know, although a good second is R. Wauchope's *Modern Maya Houses: A Study of Their Archaeological Significance* (Washington, D.C.: *Carnegie Institution Pub.* 502, 1938), which uses the perishable buildings of the present Maya to recreate the dwellings of the Classic period. Wauchope had been launched on his study by his excavation of five Classic period house platforms at Uaxactun (Washington, D.C.: *Carnegie Institution Pub.* 436, 1934); large-scale programs of domestic architectural excavation were later carried out at Barton Ramie (*Papers of the Peabody Museum* 54 [Cambridge, Mass.: Peabody Museum, 1965]), Seibal, and Tikal (the latter sites still to be published in final form).

The contrast between sites where public buildings were also of perishable materials and those where they were of stone was first noted by A. Ledyard Smith in C. L. Hay et al., eds., *The Maya and Their Neighbors* (New York: Appleton-Century, [1940]: 200–221). The question of deliberate planning of ceremonial centers has been discussed by Horst Hartung in *Die Zeremonialzentren der Maya* (Graz, Austria: Akademische Druck- und Verlagsanstalt, 1971) using Piedras Negras, Yaxchilan, Uxmal, and Chichén Itzá as major examples, while contrasting cosmological and practical models explaining site layout have been advanced for Tikal by Jorge Guillemin in *Ethnos*, 33 (1968): 1–35, and for Lubaantun by Norman Hammond in *Scientific American*, 226 (1972): 82–91. The use of a magnetic or astronomical datum for aligning buildings in a center is indicated by R. H. Fuson's analysis of Chichén Itzá in *Annals of the Association of American Geographers*, 59 (1969): 494–511. Analysis of the functions of individual buildings has rarely been carried out, since functions are usually described on the basis of appearance—"temple," "palace," and so on—but Peter D. Harrison's Ph.D. dissertation on the Central Acropolis at Tikal (*The Central Acropolis, Tikal, Guatemala: A Preliminary Study of the Functions of its Structural Components during the Late Classic Period* [Ann Arbor: University Microfilms, 1970]) is a good example of the possibilities of this underused source of information. (Figure 6.7 of this book is taken from Harrison.)

Regional styles in architecture have been discussed in a variety of publications ranging from short papers to massive monographs; a general survey, still useful, is Ignacio Marquina's *Architectura prehispanica* (Mexico: Instituto Nacional de Antropologia e Historia, 1951), which includes a section on the Maya; another, considering a selection of Maya sites mainly in Yucatan, is George Andrews's *Maya Cities: Placemaking and Urbanization* (Norman: University of Oklahoma Press, 1975). The most recent and most impressive of the regional studies is H. E. D. Pollock's *The Puuc* (*Memoirs of the Peabody Museum*, vol. 19 [Cambridge, Mass.: Peabody Museum, 1980]) and David F. Potter's definition of the central Yucatan style embracing the old Rio Bec and Chenes styles (*Middle American Research Institute Pub.* 44 [New Orleans: Tulane University]) is also very useful. Studies of the Petén style based on the Tikal data have not yet been published; the same is currently the case for one of the fastest growing areas of knowledge in Maya architecture, the Preclassic, where the site reports for Cerros, Lamanai, and Cuello will present a wide range of structures from the domestic to the monumental, spanning the period from the later third millennium B.C. down to the third century A.D. Postclassic architecture is best documented in the reports on Chichén Itzá and Mayapan.

The architecture of Tikal, Palenque, Copan, and Quirigua can to some extent be studied in the superb photographs by Maudslay in the *Biologia Centrali-Americana: Archaeology* (London: Dulau, 1889–1902) and the style of Palenque has been further examined in several papers in the volumes of the *Mesa Redonda de Palenque* from 1974 onwards (now reissued by University of Texas Press). *Copan* by Francis Robicsek (New York: Museum of the American Indian, 1972) has wide photographic coverage of the site in a more publicly accessible form than the scarce Carnegie and Maudslay publications, but is not so good. The architecture of Quirigua has been reexcavated by a University of Pennsylvania museum project directed by Robert J. Sharer and William R. Coe, and a series of reports is currently beginning to be published by the museum. In the Pasión valley, the architecture of Altar de Sacrificios has been described by A. Ledyard Smith (*Papers of the Peabody Museum*, vol. 62, no. 1 [Cambridge, Mass.: Peabody Museum, 1972]) and Smith's publication on the architecture of Seibal is in press in the Peabody Museum *Memoirs* series. The buildings of a small ceremonial precinct are described in the first volume of D. M. Pendergast's Altun Ha report (Toronto: Royal Ontario Museum, 1979). Work at other sites including Coba, Dzibilchaltun, and Cozumel is being prepared for publication; but the emphasis on architectural recording by the Carnegie Institution up to, and including, the Mayapan project led to criticism and to a reaction against such purely data-based work, and this aspect of Maya culture has been underinvestigated and underdiscussed in the past two decades.

Architectural sculpture is in some styles, such as the Puuc, inseparable from the architecture itself, but in others, it forms an embellishment to the basic form of the building, as in the stucco reliefs of Palenque. The architectural sculpture of Tikal is being prepared for publication by Arthur G. Miller in the monograph series issued by the University of Pennsylvania museum, and that of Palenque is being published by Merle Greene Robertson in a series of volumes currently in press at Princeton University Press. Preliminary studies by Robertson on the stucco sculptors and painters of Palenque are in *Actas del XLI Con-*

greso Internacional de Americanistas, Mexico 1974, 1, 449–472; Norman Hammond, ed., *Social Process in Maya Prehistory* (New York: Academic Press, 1977), pp. 297–326; Norman Hammond and Gordon R. Willey, eds., *Maya Archaeology and Ethnohistory* (Austin: University of Texas Press, 1979), pp. 149–171.

Mural painting has not been considered in detail over the whole Maya Area, although its position among the other arts is considered by Tatiana Proskouriakoff in *Handbook of Middle American Indians*, 2 (1965): 469–497. The Bonampak murals were first published by K. Ruppert, J. Eric S. Thompson, and Tatiana Proskouriakoff in *Carnegie Institution of Washington Publication* 602 (Washington, D.C., 1955) with color reproductions of the murals by A. Tejeda. Their narrative content and structure have been studied by R. E. W. Adams and others, who have traced specific individuals from room to room and scene to scene, and M. E. Miller. (Another form of publication is the two full-sized replicas of

Page 319, para. 2, line 10, add: . . . M. E. Miller, *The Murals of Bonampak* (Princeton: Princeton University Press, 1987).

Museum). Photographs of the murals when they were first discovered by Giles G. Healey are published for the first time in volume 5 of the *Mesa Redonda de Palenque*, edited by Merle Greene Robertson (Austin: University of Texas Press, 1980).

The Postclassic murals of Tancah and Tulum are considered in the most recent general discussion of Maya wall paintings, by Arthur G. Miller (*On the Edge of the Sea: Mural Painting at Tancah-Tulum* [Washington, D.C.: Dumbarton Oaks, 1982]). The destroyed murals at Santa Rita, Belize, were published by Thomas Gann in *Proceedings of the Society of Antiquaries of London*, 16 (1895–1897): 308–317 and in more detail, in *Smithsonian Institution, Bureau of American Ethnology, 19th Annual Report* (Washington, D.C., 1900), pp. 655–692. Donald Robertson's paper on the "International Style of the Late Postclassic" is in *Verhandlungen der XXXVIII Amerikanistenkongresse*, (Stuttgart-München, Germany) 2 (1968): 77–88.

A style sequence for Maya stelae was established by Tatiana Proskouriakoff in *Classic Maya Sculpture* (Washington, D.C.: *Carnegie Institution of Washington Pub.* 593, 1950); their historical content is discussed in Chapter 7 of this book. More recently discovered stelae have been reported from numerous sites including Tikal, Altar de Sacrificios, Seibal (and included in the monograph series on those sites), and Nim li punit; the latter site is in southern Belize and is so far reported only in a preliminary article (*Illustrated London News*, 264 [1976], archaeology section no. 2919), but the great size of Stela 14, 9.5m (31 feet) and the variety of sculptural styles in this small site make it of great interest.

Classic Maya vase painting, long considered to depict merely genre scenes, has been interpreted by Michael D. Coe in three important publications as reflecting lost and surviving myths. His theories are set forth in *The Maya Scribe and His World* (New York: Grolier Club, 1973), *Classic Maya Pottery at Dumbarton Oaks* (Washington, D.C.: Dumbarton Oaks, 1975), and *Lords of the Underworld* (Princeton, N.J.: Princeton University Press, 1978). The vessels in these books are almost all looted and, thus, have lost most of their archaeological utility, but Coe does as complete a job as possible on the remaining iconographic data. Mythic interpretation of a Maya vase painting was carried out as early as 1939 by J. Eric S. Thompson in *The Moon Goddess in Middle America* (Washington, D.C.: *Carnegie Institution of Washington Pub.* 509, contribution 79). A contrasting historical interpretation of the "Altar Vase" by R. E. W. Adams is in Norman Hammond, ed., *Social Process in Maya Prehistory* (New York: Academic Press, 1977), pp. 409–420.

The art of jade working in the Maya lands has been summarized by Robert L. Rands in *Handbook of Middle American Indians*, 3 (1965): 561–580 with a short bibliography, and Adrian Digby, *Maya Jades* (London: Trustees of the British Museum, 1964) includes a technical discussion of jade carving; a typology of jade types forms part of A. V. Kidder's discussion of the artifacts of Uaxactun in *Carnegie Institution of Washington Publication 576* (Washington, D.C., 1947). The major recent work on Maya jades is Tatiana Proskouriakoff's monograph on those from the Cenote of Sacrifice at Chichén Itzá (*Memoirs of the Peabody Museum*, vol. 10, no. 1 [Cambridge, Mass.: Peabody Museum, 1974]). The small site of Altun Ha produced a large number of fine jades during D. M. Pendergast's excavations in the 1960s, including the head of the sun god made from a small boulder and weighing over 4 kilograms (9 pounds), and Pendergast has issued a preliminary report on this in *Royal Ontario Museum Art and Archaeology Occasional Papers*, 19 (1969).

Maya woodcarving has not been treated as an art in itself, but either as architectural sculpture, as in Tatiana Proskouriakoff, *Handbook of Middle American Indians*, 2 (1965): 469–497, or simply as the vehicle for dynastic inscriptions and art, as xylic stelae. This is mainly because only a few wooden objects have survived, among them the carved lintels of Tikal and Tzibanche, which are architectural members bearing official inscriptions and art. The most striking freestanding object is a seated wooden figure, looted allegedly from a cave in Tabasco, illustrated in Michael D. Coe's *The Maya*, 2d ed. (London and New York: Thames and Hudson, 1980), Figure 45. The simple box and spear from Actun Polbilche, Belize, are published by D. M. Pendergast in *Royal Ontario Museum Art and Archaeology Monograph*, 1 (1974).

Two catalogs of Maya metalwork have been compiled, one by D. M. Pendergast in *American Antiquity*, 27 (1962): 520–545, and another by Warwick Bray in Norman Hammond, ed., *Social Process in Maya Prehistory* (New York: Academic Press, 1977), pp. 365–401; an important collection from the Sacred Cenote at Chichén Itzá is published by S. K. Lothrop in *Memoirs of the Peabody Museum*, vol. 10, no. 2 (Cambridge, Mass.: Peabody Museum, 1952).

Pottery figurines were made from the Early Preclassic onward; their development from the Middle Preclassic at Uaxactun and other lowland sites is described by Robert L. Rands and Barbara C. Rands in *Handbook of Middle American Indians*, 2 (1965): 535–560, and the parallel Preclassic sequence in the highlands, based almost entirely on Kaminaljuyu, is described by A. V. Kidder in the same volume, pp. 146–155; Robert L. Rands covers the Classic and Postclassic periods in the highlands on pages 156–162 of that volume. Since the publication of these articles, the Preclassic figurines of Chalchuapa, El Salvador, have been published by Bruce Dahlin in Robert J. Sharer, ed., *The Prehistory of Chalchuapa, El Salvador*, vol. 2 (Philadelphia: University of Pennsylvania Press, 1977), pp. 134–211, and a preliminary article on the Classic figurines of Lagartero, Chiapas, by Susanna Ekholm has appeared in Norman Hammond and Gordon R. Willey, ed., *Maya Archaeology and Ethnohistory* (Austin: University of Texas Press, 1979), pp. 172–186.

No major studies of lowland figurines have appeared since 1965, although those of Palenque and Lubaantun (the latter first published by T. A. Joyce in the *Journal of the Royal Anthropological Institute*, 63 [1933]: xv–xxv) are being prepared for publication, and the site reports on Seibal, Altar de Sacrificios, and other recent projects have increased the data available for the lowlands somewhat.

Heavily illustrated and badly written books on Maya art are common; good ones are rare, and the recent reissue by Dover Publications of Herbert J. Spinden's 1913 *A Study of Maya Art: Its Subject Matter and Historical Development* (*Memoirs of the Peabody Museum*, 6 [Cambridge, Mass.: Peabody Museum]) is welcome. *The Art and Architecture of Ancient America* by George Kubler (Harmondsworth, England: Penguin Books, 1962) deals partly with the Maya, as does Pál Kelemen's *Medieval American Art*, 2d ed. (New York: Macmillan, 1956), which has also been reissued by Dover Publications. A revised edition of Kubler's book is in press. In general, however, the *Handbook of Middle American Indians* articles form the best and most recent survey of Maya art, though with the disadvantage of fragmented, rather than integrated coverage.

10. Men and Gods

The best guide to the literature on ancient Maya religion, as well as the best summary of what is known, is J. Eric S. Thompson's *Maya History and Religion* (Norman: University of Oklahoma Press, 1970), which includes a fundamental study of Itzam Na and another of the major and minor gods; I have used it extensively in preparing this chapter. Some aspects of Maya religion were not apparent a decade ago, however; the study of looted pottery vessels suggests bloody sacrifices and the use of drugs to an extent unimagined by Thompson; some aspects of this are dealt with by Michael D. Coe in *Lords of the Underworld* (Princeton, N.J.: Princeton University Press, 1978) and by Jacinto Quirarte in Norman Hammond and Gordon R. Willey, eds., *Maya Archaeology and Ethnohistory* (Austin: University of Texas Press, 1979), pp. 116–148. An article by Coe and Peter T. Furst in *Natural History*, 86 (1977): 88–91, discusses the use of hallucinogenic enemas.

The extent to which ancestor veneration played a part in Maya religion is only now beginning to be appreciated, to a large extent as a result of the work done on the iconography and inscriptions of Palenque by Linda Schele, Peter Mathews, Floyd Lounsbury, and Merle Greene Robertson (much of this work and the relevant bibliography are to be found in the volumes of the *Mesa Redonda de Palenque* edited by Merle Greene Robertson and reissued by the University of Texas Press). Important work has also been done at Tikal by Clemency Coggins, Christopher Jones, and others on the deification of ancestors into tutelary beings; the best guides at present to this are Jones's article in *American Antiquity*, 42 (1977): 28–60 and Coggins's in Norman Hammond and Gordon R. Willey, eds., *Maya Archaeology and Ethnohistory* (Austin: University of Texas Press, 1979), pp. 38–50.

A useful synoptic volume, not yet available in English, is F. Anders's *Das Pantheon der Maya* (Graz, Austria: Akademische Druck- und Kunstverlag, 1963).

11. The Maya Mind

Probably the best recent book dealing with the workings of the Maya mind is J. Eric S. Thompson's edition of the Dresden Codex (*Memoirs of the American Philosophical Society*, 92 [Philadelphia: American Philosophical Society, 1972]), which goes into astrology, astronomy, mathematics, and calendrics with the aid of information derived from ethnohistoric and archaeological sources. Thompson's *Maya Hieroglyphic Writing: Introduction*, 3d ed. rev. (Norman: University of Oklahoma Press, 1966) is also useful, as is David H. Kelley's *Deciphering the Maya Script* (Austin: University of Texas Press, 1976). Thompson's little guide to Maya writing, *Maya Hieroglyphs Without Tears*, has been reprinted (1980) by the British Museum in unrevised form; in using it, it is important to remember that Thompson's view of the basic nature of Maya writing has been challenged; Kelley's book is the best source at present for the generally accepted view. An early, but still useful and easily available book that deals with some aspects of Maya writing and mathematics is Sylvanus G. Morley's *An Introduction to the Study of the Maya Hieroglyphs*, originally issued in 1915 as *Bulletin* 57 of the Bureau of American Ethnology, Smithsonian Institution (Washington, D.C.) and reprinted by Dover Books (New York, 1975) in paperback with an introduction by Thompson. The basic source for all scholars working on glyphs is Thompson's *A Catalog of Maya Hieroglyphs* (Norman: University of Oklahoma Press, 1962), which tabulates occurrences of each glyph; such numbers as T568 used in papers on Maya epigraphy refer to Thompson's catalog. The pioneering work of Yurii Knorosov in recognizing the phonetic nature of Maya writing can be read in English (as opposed to Russian) in his paper in *American Antiquity* 23 (1958): 284–291, and in Sophie D. Coe's translation of selections from Knorosov's *The Writing of the Maya Indians*, (*Peabody Museum of Archaeology and Ethnology Russian Translation Series*, vol. 4 [Cambridge, Mass.: Peabody Museum, 1967]).

Maya astronomy has been discussed by J. Eric S. Thompson in *Philosophical Transactions of the Royal Society, A*, 276, 83–98, and a recent paper by Anthony Aveni on "Venus and the Maya" appeared in *American Scientist*, 67, 274–285. A later paper by Aveni is in *Science*, 213 (1981): 161–171. Maya arithmetic was discussed, again by Thompson, in *Carnegie Institute of Washington Contributions to American Anthropology and History*, 36 (Washington, D.C., 1942), while a more recent short book is George I. Sánchez' *Arithmetic in Maya* (Austin, Texas: private pub., Library of Congress ref. 61–42041). The mathematics of the calendar are analyzed by Linton Satterthwaite, Jr., in "Concepts and Structures of Maya Calendrical Arithmetics," *Museum of the University of Pennsylvania and the Philadelphia Anthropological Society Joint Publications*, no. 3 (1947). Sánchez' work has been subsumed in a more accessible popular article in *American Scientist*, 68 (May–June 1980): 249–255.

Gary Gossen's discovery of the Chamula calendar board still in use is described by him, together with a structural analysis of the board by Alexander Marshack, in Norman Hammond, ed., *Mesoamerican Archaeology: New Approaches* (Austin: University of Texas Press, 1974), pp. 217–270. A sensitive discussion of Maya mental attitudes is Miguel Leon-Portilla's *Time and Reality in the Thought of the Maya*, English ed., 1973, orig. 1968 (Boston: Beacon Press, 1973). The most recent summary of Maya civilization, including an assessment of recent work on ideology and religion, is Gordon R. Willey's 1979 Huxley Lecture, reprinted in *Man*, 15 (1980): 249–266.

List of Illustrations

Index